文物背后的
故事

Stories Behind Cultural Relics
compiled by Beijing Municipal
Administration of Cultural Heritage

北京市文物局／编

北京燕山出版社
BEIJING YANSHAN PRESS

图书在版编目（ＣＩＰ）数据

文物背后的故事 / 北京市文物局 编
. -- 北京：北京燕山出版社，2016.6
ISBN 978-7-5402-4166-7

Ⅰ. ①文… Ⅱ. ①北… Ⅲ. ①文物－中国－通俗读物
－汉语、英语 Ⅳ. ① K87-49

中国版本图书馆 CIP 数据核字 (2016) 第 147505 号

文物背后的故事
WENWU BEIHOU DE GUSHI

编　　者	北京市文物局
项目负责	李满意
责任编辑	王梦楠　陈雪　郭东梅　葛瑞娟
营销编辑	涂苏婷
责任校对	杜　睿　岳　欣　甄飞
责任质检	石英
封面设计	闻江文化
社　　址	北京市西城区陶然亭路 53 号（100054）
网　　址	http://www.bjyspress.com/
微　　博	http://weibo.com/u/2526206071
微　　信	yanshanreading
电　　话	01065240430；01063581036
印　　刷	小森印刷（北京）有限公司
开　　本	710mm×1000mm 1/16
字　　数	300 千字
印　　张	17.5
版　　次	2016 年 6 月第 1 版
印　　次	2016 年 9 月第 1 次印刷
定　　价	98.00 元
出版发行	北京燕山出版社 YSP BEIJING YANSHAN PRESS

编委会名单

主　　编：于　平

副 主 编：哈　骏　陈　果　薛　俭

编　　委：李学军　张振松　杨志国

　　　　　王　静　景　旭　程根源

　　　　　王姣芬　刘　鹏　李满意

　　　　　王梦楠

Editorial Committee

序言

第一次全国国有可移动文物普查工作，是根据国务院统一部署开展的一次国情国力调查。北京市第一次全国国有可移动文物普查工作，既是一次市情市力的调查，也是健全北京市可移动文物保护体系的重要基础工作，得到辖区内中央和北京市各级机关及企事业单位及十六个区普查工作办公室的大力支持与帮助，成果丰硕。

通过普查，北京市首次基本摸清了国有可移动文物家底，初步掌握了北京市文博系统和各级党政机关、国有企事业单位可移动文物的数量和分布情况，以及文物的本体状况、基本数据等；首次在北京市域范围内初步建立了一套比较全面、准确的国有可移动文物数据档案和大数据库，进一步健全了文物登录备案机制和文物保护体系；首次给申报文物颁发"文物身份证"，对国有可移动文物管理现代化打下基础，相关管理体系也初见成效；首次让非文博单位系统学习了解了可移动文物保护、管理知识，增强了对所收藏的文物管理与保护的责任意识，建立并培养了文物保护管理专业队伍；强化了藏品管理基础，利用普查成果进一步提升文物资源服务社会的能力，丰富了公众文化生活，为有效发挥文物在北京市经济、文化和社会发展总体布局中的积极作用打下坚实的基础。

特别重要的是，通过普查了解和发现了一批具有很高历史、艺术和科学研究价值的珍贵文物，以及文物背后的精彩故事。这些有代表性的、承载着中华优秀传统文化的珍贵文物及其背后的故事得以被深入挖掘，并纳入了国家文物保护管理体系中，使落实习近平总书记提出的"让文物活起来""讲好中国故事"更加具体化。

历时 5 年的北京市全国第一次可移动文物普查工作，对市域内 15463 家街道、乡镇以上级别的国有单位进行了调查。最终，确认有可移动文物的收藏单位共计 339 家。其中，中央单位 145 家，市属单位 59 家，区属单位 135 家。在此次普查中，新发现 208 家国有单位收藏有可移动文物，包括中央单位 99 家，市属单位 17 家，区属单位 92 家。截至 2016 年 8 月 31 日，北京市申报的普查可移动文物 6,924,809 件 / 套，其中珍贵文物 463,146 件 / 套。北京市申报的普查可移动文物数占全国的 18.93%，珍贵文物数占全国的 22.76%，可移动文物普查总数与珍贵文物数量均居全国前列。

北京是一座有着三千多年建城史的历史文化名城。众多不可移动文物，是一笔巨大的不可再生的珍贵资源，是弘扬优秀传统文化的重要载体和媒介。文物背后的故事不仅记述着文物本身的经历，还静静地向人们诉说着与其相关的历史。普查中发现的种类繁多、数量庞大、价值巨大的可移动文物，是北京先民文明智慧的结晶，也是城市历史发展的实物见证。这次普查工作中有许多新发现，许多文物背后的故事，不仅包含着古人的智慧，也将我们带回文物产生的年代，通过对这些文物身世的探究，更能够让人们直观、形象、真实地了解文物背后的文化价值。

本书收录的 39 篇文章，都是由普查工作一线员工，或亲身参与了宣传报道工作的媒体记者，现场调查了解并记述的第一手资料，从一个个侧面反映出北京市第一次全国可移动文物普查工作的收获。正是作者们的深入挖掘与研究，精心梳理与思考，才有了能呈现给读者的一个个生动、鲜活、精彩、有趣的历史故事。

值此该书出版时，谨向参与北京市第一次全国国有可移动文物普查工作的每一位同仁表示衷心的感谢！向积极支持、配合开展普查工作的 339 家文物收藏单位表示衷心的感谢！

The first national census on movable cultural relics is a survey over national preservation condition of cultural heritages based on the unified deployment of the State Council. The first national census on movable cultural relics in Beijing was not only a survey on the condition and capability of its preservation system, but also a basic work to improve it. The census was a complete success thanks to the great support from the governments and organizations at all levels, state-owned enterprises, as well as all census offices of 16 districts in Beijing.

During the census, Beijing has formulated a general picture about all the state-owned movable cultural relics in Beijing and the distribution, statistics, preservation condition of these relics in museums, cultural preservation sites, Party and government agencies at all levels, as well as in state-owned enterprises. Beijing has also established its first comprehensive and accurate database of these state-owned movable relics, further improved the registry system and preservation system; A "cultural identity" system was established during the census, laying a solid foundation for the modern management of state-owned movable relics, and it has already shown initial success; Those non-museum entities have learned more about the preservation and management of cultural relics, thus to enhance the the sense of preservation and responsibility on cultural relics, thus expanding the team of management professionals; The collection management basis has been strengthened. And we have employed the census results to serve the need of our society, enrich the cultural life of the public, thus to allow these cultural relics to play a positive role in Beijing's economic, cultural and social landscape.

More importantly, through the census, we have discovered a number of precious relics of high research value in terms of history, art and science. We have also unveiled many wonderful stories behind these relics. Through the census, we could better understand the traditional culture and the stories behind these representative cultural relics. All these relics have already been included in the National Cultural Relics Preservation Management System, in line with President Xi Jinping's guideline of

"Revitalize Cultural Relics" and "Better Telling Chinese Stories".

The first national census on movable cultural relics has lasted for 5 years, surveying 15,463 state-owned institutions above the level of street and township in Beijing. Finally, 339 of them were confirmed to be collection entities of movable cultural relics, with 145 belong to the central government, 59 belong to the municipal government, and 135 belong to the district government. During the census, another 208 entities were confirmed to be collection entities of movable cultural relics, with 99 belong to the central government, 17 belong to the municipal government, and 92 belong to the district government. As of Aug. 31st, 2016, we have registered 6,924,809 pieces / sets of cultural relics, among which 463,146 pieces / sets are precious relics. The number of movable cultural relics registered in Beijing has accounted for 18.93% of the country's total, and precious relics has accounted for 22.76%, topping the list in the whole country.

Beijing is a historic and cultural city with over 3,000 years of history. Numerous immovable cultural relics are nonrenewable, hence the preciousness. They are important carriers and media of Chinese traditional culture. The stories behind these cultural relics not only describe the experience of the relics themselves, but also tell the history to us. During the census, we found a huge number of valuable movable cultural relics with a wide variety. They are the crystallization of wisdom of our ancient ancestors in Beijing. They also witnessed the vicissitudes of Beijing as a city. There were many new discoveries during the census. Stories behind these relics not only contain the wisdom of the ancients, but could also bring us back to the ancient times. We could better understand the cultural value of these relics through the research and study on the history of these relics.

The 38 articles compiled in this book were out of first-hand information collected by front-line employees or journalists. Through these articles, we could formulate a general picture about the fruitful census from different perspectives. Thanks to authors' in-depth study and research, combined with their comprehensive analysis and thoughts, we could have the chance to read such lively, fresh, exciting, and interesting historical stories.

Upon the publication of this book, I wish to express my heartfelt thanks to everyone involved in the work of the first national census on movable cultural relics in Beijing! I would also like to extend my gratitude to all 339 collection entities for your positive participation and great support!

目录

第一编　金石铮铮闻古声

第二编　玉瓷润泽触古韵

第三编　纸卷墨香览古意

第四编　杂玩汇通品古味

First series : metal cultural relics

Second series: jade and porcelain cultural relics

Third series: paper cultural relics

Fourth series: others

金石铮铮闻古声
metal cultural relics

库藏徽章
——民国掠影

Emblems in Collection
—A Glimpse of the Republican Era

2015 年一个寻常的夏天，我和典藏部的同事一起，例行下库进行每天的可移动普查文物整理工作。当清理到一排密集架的角落时，发现了几个不起眼的黑色木盒，上书"二等嘉禾勋章"，心中不觉一动，冥冥中有如获至宝的喜悦和激动，当打开木盒的一瞬间，大家不约而同地发出了一声惊叹，因为木盒内不仅仅静躺着嘉禾勋章，更有多枚不同时期却同样精致无比的徽章随着盒盖的开启全部展现在我们面前。随后，我和同事共清点出 103 枚徽章，这些徽章均为民国时期所授，以国内所授为主，也有同时期国外颁授之奖章。这一枚枚徽章，以丰富的种类、广泛的颁授缘由，诉说着民国时期政治、军事、经济、文化等方方面面惊心动魄的故事。

徽章是用以表示身份、职业、荣誉或用以纪念某一事物的特殊标志，

In summer 2015, I went to the storage room as usual to continue the daily task of conducting the census of cultural relics with my colleagues from the Collection Department. When we came to the corner of the shelves, we found several black wooden boxes with the characters "Erdeng Jiahe Xun Zhang (Second-grade Emblem of the Golden Grain)on them." I had the feeling in my heart that I must have found some treasures. Everyone was awed into silence at the moment when we opende the box. There were fully 103 pieces of delicate emblems from different time periods in it. Most of them were granted by the Chinese Republican government but a few were awarded by foreign countries. These emblems from a wide range and variety could tell some exciting stories of politics, military, economics and culture during the Republican era.

Emblems are designed to identify a person's social status, position and

民国二十三年（1934）第十八届华北运动会徽章
the emblem of the 18th North China Sports Meeting, the 23rd
year of the Republican era

一般分为国徽、证章、奖章、纪念章等。[1]我部门收藏的这两枚徽章，纪念的是同一事件，虽然它们并非库藏军事类勋章，但我们依然可以从中领略当年激情燃烧的岁月。徽章正面刻有文字"第十八届华北运动会""中华民国二十三年十月十日"，图案为华北运动会会场正门。徽章直径4.4厘米，合金材质。第二枚徽章长4.2厘米，厚1.5厘米，铜质。正面上端印一个"华"字，下方印3行小字，分别为"纪念""第十八届华北运动会""河北省政府主席于学忠赠"，图案为北方长城卧于巍巍群山中，

rewards or commemorate a special event. Generally, they could be divided into national insignias, badges, rewards and memorable medals and so on.[1] The two emblens in our department are just in memory of the same event. Although they were not military medals, we could reimage the thrilling war times from them. On the front side, there inscribes "The 18th Sports Meeting in the North China" and "10th October, the 23rd Year of the Republic of China." There is also an image of the front gate at the venue for the meeting. The emblem is 4.4 cm in diameter and it is made of alloy metal. The second medal is made of copper, which is 4.2 cm long, 5.9 cm wide and 1.5 cm thick. On the upper front it writes "Hua," another name for China. Below the character there are three lines of small characters, "In Memory of", "The 18th North China Sports Meeting", and "Gifted by Yu Xuezhong, President of the Hebei Government". On the backside, the medal reads "Held in Tianjin, Hebei province," "Memorable Medal," "Held in the 23rd Year of the Republic of China." The image on the medal is the Great Wall residing in the mountains.

Based on the characters and images, two medals are closely related to the North China Sports Meeting which was

[1] 张立:《徽章》,辽宁教育出版社,1999年, 第1页。

[1] Zhang Li, *Emblems*, Liaoning Education Publishing House, January 1999, p. 1.

徽章背面刻有文字"河北省天津举行""纪念章""民国二十三年十月十日"。

从徽章的文字和图案可知，徽章与华北运动会有密切关系。华北运动会是中国近代体育史上影响力最大、持续时间最长的区域性运动会。该运动会由著名教育家张伯苓先生创建于1913年，几乎每年举行一届，至1934年，共举行了18届，而尤以第18届因其参与人数之巨、省份之多、比赛项目之广，引起了社会各界的广泛关注。当时天津为河北省政府的省辖市，省主席于学忠对于人民强身健体非常

华北运动会纪念章（正面）

the memorial medal of North China
Sports Meeting (front side)

the most influential and lasting regional sports event in modern Chinese athletic history. The activity was initiated in 1913 by Zhang Boling, a famous educator, and was held almost once a year. By the end of 1934, altogether 18 meetings had been held. And the 18th meeting attracted wide attention of the people from different social background thanks to the huge numbers of athletes and provinces that participated, and the wide range of sports activities. Tianjin at that time was the capital city of Hebei province. In addition, Yu Xuezhong as the provincial president cared about people's health and fitness, and thus he participated in the preparation work for the meeting in person. Even though people suffered significant financial difficulties, a well-designed and appropriate-structured stadium was built under the collaboration of the government and people.[1]

The 18th Sports Meeting was held after the Mukden Incident in 1931 and before the Marco Polo Bridge Incident in 1936. Because the conflicts between Chinese people and Japanese imperial invaders escalated and people's patriotism ran unprecedentedly high, this sports

[1] The Editing Committee of Culture and History for the Tianjin Council of the Chinese People's Political Consultative Conference, *Cultural and Historical Materials of Hedong District, Tianjin, vol. 1*, Tianjin People's Publishing House, December 1988, p. 123.

重视，亲自主持筹备事宜，经过当时政府与民间上下一致的努力，天津市在当年财政十分困难的情况下仍建造完成了一座布局合理、设计新颖的体育场。[1]

第18届华北运动会举办之时，正值1931年九一八事变之后与1936年七七事变之前，这一时期中国人民与日本帝国主义侵略者的矛盾日益激化，大众爱国热情空前高涨，由此引发了此次运动会中一幕幕令人难忘的瞬间。

第18届华北运动会的召开共发生了两件振奋人心的大事。一件是比赛开始之时，以南开大学学生为主的天津学生们手举彩旗，打出了"毋忘东北""毋忘国耻""勿忘九一八""收复失地""还我河山"等一幅幅巨型标语，瞬间点燃了全场几万人同仇敌忾之情，群情沸腾。而另一件则是九一八事变东北沦陷后，在东北体育协进会的努力下，东北组织了一支庞大的体育代表队参加此届运动会，当写有辽、吉、黑、热四省的大旗伴随着几百名东北运动员进入会场时，场面令人为之动容。队长刘

meeting had some impressive moments.

There are two most exciting moments in the meeting. The first one took place before the competition began. Tianjin students led by those from Nankai University raised the colorful flags written with huge slogans such as "Never Forget Northeast China", "Never Forget National Humiliation", "Never Forget The Mukden Incident", and "Retaking Lost Land", and"Returning My Country". These words aroused tens of thousand people's hatred against the enemies. Another touching moment was when a delegation of hundreds of athletics holding the flags of Liaoning, Jilin, Heilongjiang and Jehol poured into the stadium. It was a huge delegation organized by Northeast Sports Institute after the Mukden Incident. When the team leader Liu Changchun[1] walked around the stadium with the flag, the audience cried out for joy with thunderous applause. The scene enraged Kawagoe Shigeru, the Japanese consul general, who sat on the stage at that time. He protested towards the host and asked shamelessly for the Northeast delegation to leave the stadium immediately. But Yu Xuezhong, the provincial president and famous Northeast general, did not response to his request. Japanese consul

---

[1] 中国人民政治协商会议天津市委员会文史资料委员会：《天津市河东区文史资料第一辑》，天津人民出版社，1988年，第123页。

[1] Liu Changchun, the only person in Chinese Sports Delegation who participated 100-meter race at the 11th Olympic Games in Los Angeles, 1932.

长春[1]举旗绕场一周后，全场欢声雷动，掌声经久不息。这种情景触怒了在主席台上的日本驻天津总领事川樾，他向主办运动会的当局提出抗议，并无耻地要求东北四省代表队立即退出会场。当时的河北省主席、东北军名将于学忠也坐在主席台上，他对日本总领事川樾的抗议置之不理。日本总领事愤怒地说："你们不停止摆字，我立刻将大炮对准南开大学。"于学忠强硬地回答："你的大炮能对准南开大学，我的大炮就能对准日本租界总领事馆。"川樾愤而退场，这样，东北四省代表队照常参加了运动会。[2]

文物不仅是文化的载体，更是民族精神传承的载体。摩挲着这两枚徽章，我可以遥想当年运动场上人声鼎沸、激情澎湃的情景，可以感受到面对日本侵略者，中华儿女不屈抗争的精神，面对时局之困，炎黄子孙依然自强不息的态度。这就是我们的民族精神，这就是我们的脊梁！中华文明需要代代传承下去，但是曾经的屈辱

华北运动会纪念章（反面）
the memorial medal of North China
Sports Meeting (backside)

general was infuriated and shouted, "If you do not stop raising the slogans, our cannons will face towards Nankai University." But Yu Xuezhong responded toughly, " If your cannon can be aimed at Nankai University, mine could be targeted at Japanese Consulate General", making Kawagoe Shigeru leave with anger. In this way, the delegation of the four provinces from Northeast could participate the sports meeting as usual.[1]

Cultural relics are not only the carrier of culture but also the bearer of cultural

[1] 刘长春：中国体育代表团参加 1932 年美国洛杉矶第 10 届世界奥林匹克运动会时唯一的百米短跑选手。
[2] 中国人民政治协商会议天津市委员会文史资料委员会：《天津文史选辑（2000 年第三辑）》，天津人民出版社，2000 年，第171 页。

[1] The Editing Committee of Culture and History for the Tianjin Council of the Chinese People's Political Consultative Conference, The Selective Work of Tianjin's Culture and History 2000 (3), Tianjin People's Publishing House, October 2000, p. 171.

与苦难更需要作为后人的我们铭记，时刻鞭策、提醒我们，这是中国和平崛起的动力。每次进入库房，我都有一种时间停止的错觉，寒来暑往，一代代文物工作者老去，而我们守护的文物一直静静地躺在那里，诉说着它们曾经经历过的故事。

高山流水
北京市文物局图书资料中心

spirits. Touching these two emblems, I could imagine how passionate and excited the crowds were in that sports meeting, and also I could feel the unflagging spirits of Chinese people in the face of Japanese invaders. This is exactly our national spirit, the cornerstone of a nation! Chinese civilization needs to be passed on generation by generation, but more importantly, the younger generations should remember the humiliation and sufferings of the previous people, which could remind ourselves of the history. This is the driving force of our great rejuvenation and peaceful rising. Whenever I went into the storage room, I had the feeling that the time seemed to be stagnant. The season changes, the people who work for cultural relics age, but the relics we protect lie there quietly, telling us their stories.

Gao Shanliushui , Literature Center of Beijing Municipal Administration of Cultural Heritage

铜钱背后的故事

The Story Behind a Copper Coin

2015 年夏天，刚刚从学校完成学业的我参加了北京市公园管理中心组织的招聘考试，来到了天坛公园管理处。刚参加工作的我还没有来得及体验初入职场的兴奋和喜悦，就参与到天坛公园可移动文物普查工作当中。八月份的天气非常炎热，我和天坛公园可移动文物普查小组的同事们一起忍受着夏季的酷热，对公园保藏的万余件文物逐一进行了整理和清点。在普查工作中，我得以近距离地观察文物，这不仅使我将自己学到的知识结合到实践当中，而且加深了我对文物保护工作的认识。

在普查工作当中，一件名为"清宽永通宝铜钱"的文物引起了我浓厚的兴趣。这件公园旧藏的文物是一枚圆形方孔铜钱，只见这枚铜钱面背平整，内外郭宽窄均匀，面文"宽永通

In the summer of 2015 when I graduated from the university, I passed the recruitment exam organized by the Beijing Parks Management Center, and became a member of the Management Office of Temple of Heaven Park. I had no time to experience the excitement of entering the professional world, but went directly into the work of the national census on movable cultural relics in the Temple of Heaven Park. It was really hot in August. Together with the coworkers, we sorted out and counted tens of thousands of artifacts collected in the park in the extreme heat of summer. During the census, I got the chance to closely observe and touch these relics, not only allowing me to apply my knowledge into practice, but also deepening my understanding of the preservation of these treasures.

During the census, a common artifact named "Qing Kuanyong Tongbao Copper Coin" greatly interested me. This artifact collected in the park is a round

宝"四字楷书顺读，素背。虽然表面存在一些锈蚀的痕迹，但是依然可以看出这枚铜钱外观的精致。据我的了解，清代的铜钱多为年号钱，清朝共经历了 12 位皇帝，这其中没有一位皇帝曾以"宽永"作为其在位时期的年号。这不禁使我产生了一个疑问：这枚铜钱究竟是在什么时期铸造、使用的呢？

带着对这枚铜钱的好奇，我盼望着工作间歇时间快些到来。文物一件一件地被搬出库房，我和同事们继续对文物逐件进行整理、清点、登记和拍照，大家将手头的工作告一段落后，终于盼到了工作休息的时间。我和其他同事纷纷结束了自己的工作到阴凉处休息，休息时我顾不得夏天的暑热和满头的汗水，悄悄地向一位老师傅身边移动，在老师傅身旁坐定后，我向他说出了我对那枚圆形方孔铜钱的疑问，并请教了关于"宽永通宝"的事情。老师傅用毛巾擦了擦脸上的汗水，给我讲起了这枚圆形方孔铜钱的大致情况。我从老师傅的讲述中了解到：宽永通宝是日本铸造的一种钱币，极有可能是在中日贸易的过程中流传

宽永通宝铜钱（正面）

front side of Kuanyong Tongbao
copper coin

copper coin with a square hole right in the middle. It is plain and smooth on both sides. The outer and inner edges are of evenly thickness. On the front side, there are four characters namely Kuan Yong Tong Bao. The back side is blank. Although there are some rusts on the surface, the delicate appearance of this copper coin can still be appreciated. According to my knowledge, the Qing dynasty copper coins were mostly reign title coins. In Qing Dynasty, there were 12 emperors in total, but none of them had the reign title as "Kuanyong". Then when was this copper coin casted and used?

Out of curiosity on the copper coin, I was looking forward to a break so that I could be able to discover the story behind this coin. The artifacts were taken

到中国来的。听完老师傅的讲述，出于好奇心的驱使，我更想了解这枚陌生铜钱的详细信息了。下班回家之后，我到网上搜索了一下有关"宽永通宝"的信息。根据网上的资料可知，"宽永"是后水尾天皇的年号，宽永通宝始铸于宽永二年即1625年。在之后的200余年当中，宽永通宝成为日本国内主要流通的货币，直到明治维新之后才被废止。宽永通宝流通的这段时间正是中日贸易的繁荣阶段，这种铜钱也因贸易的繁荣而大量流入中国。

了解了宽永通宝的来龙去脉，我的眼前仿佛出现了当时中日贸易的繁

宽永通宝铜钱（背面）

the backside of the Kuanyong
Tongbao copper coin

out one by one from the storage house. The coworkers and I continued to sort out, count, register and photograph these relics. After finishing part of the work, we finally got a break. We put down the work at hand and went to take a rest in shady places. During the break, despite the heat of summer and the sweat on my face, I quietly moved toward an elder colleague. I told him my doubts against the round-shape square-hole copper coin, and asked him about the "Kuanyong Tongbao". The colleague wiped the sweat on his face with a towel, then began to talk about the facts related to it. According to him, "Kuanyong Tongbao" is a kind of coin casted in Japan, and it probably came into China through the Sino-Japanese trades at that time. After that, I became even more curious about the detailed information in this strange coin. After work, I went home and started to search for related information on the Internet. According to the online sources, "Kuanyong Tongbao" was first casted in the 2nd year of Kan'ei (in Chinese: Kuanyong) of Emperor Go-Mizunoo (1625 CE). In the subsequent two centuries, "Kuanyong Tongbao" became the major currency in Japan, and was abolished after the Meiji Reform. "Kuanyong Tongbao" flew over into China when Sino-Japanese trade was in its height.

荣景象，来自日本的商人们用宽永通宝换取清王朝琳琅满目的货物，使得宽永通宝由遥远的日本漂洋过海来到中国，又随着中国外贸商人在各地的贸易而遍布全国。

根据网上的查找，再结合老师傅的讲解，我对于宽永通宝圆形方孔铜钱有了一定的了解，由于是先遇到了问题，而后通过各种渠道找到了解决的办法，使我对这枚铜钱蕴藏的历史信息印象深刻，收获很大，这些知识是我在学校书本上根本学不到的。

天坛公园的这次可移动文物普查使我和其他同事进一步掌握了公园所藏可移动文物的基本情况，为今后更好地保存和保护文物提供了依据，积累了经验。同时，可移动文物普查工作为我们提供了更多了解文物背后故事的机会，每一件文物都在向我们诉说着它们背后的故事，每一次对文物的触碰都是我们与文物的一次心灵的沟通。一件件文物在库房的角落里悄无声息，可在文物的背后却有着讲不完的故事，有着不为人所知的奥秘。

这次可移动文物普查还让我对天坛公园的可移动文物有了系统的了解，

After knowing the history of "Kuanyong Tongbao" copper coin, in front of my eyes there seemed to be an emerging prosperous scene of Sino-Japanese trade in the late Ming and early Qing periods. The merchants from Japan traded the various glittering goods of the Qing dynasty with the "Kuanyong Tongbao" copper coins, which crossed the ocean from distant Japan to China, and went around the country through the hands of Chinese foreign trade merchants who travelled to everywhere.

Combining the findings on the Internet with the words of my elder colleague, I learned quite a lot of knowledge about the "Kuanyong Tongbao" round-shape square-hole copper coin. During the process, I came up with a question at first and then started to find the answer by various means. This study was impressive for me. I gained a lot of knowledge which I could never learn from the textbooks.

This census on movable cultural relics in the Temple of Heaven Park made the coworkers and I further understand the general information of movable relics collected in the park, and allowed us to accumulate experience and knowledge that will benefit for the future preservation. In the meantime, the census offered us more opportunities

对文物背后隐藏的故事进行了清晰的梳理，借着这枚宽永通宝圆形方孔铜钱，我获得了一些关于铜钱的知识，并且对明清时期的中外贸易有了进一步的了解，通过与普查小组同事们的研究以及在网络上的查找，我了解了隐藏在宽永通宝背后的故事。

刘　毅

北京市天坛公园管理处

to get to know the stories behind these artifacts. Every artifact is telling us its unique stories. Every touch on the artifact is a spiritual communication between the relic and us. Pieces of artifacts laid in the corner of storage house in quiet, but the untold mystic stories behind them are inexhaustible and limitless for us to explore.

Through this census on movable cultural relics, I acquired a systematic knowledge of the movable artifacts in the Temple of Heaven Park, and had a clear understanding of the story behind the artifact. By this "Kuanyong Tongbao" round-shape square-hole copper coin, I acquired knowledge relate to copper coins, and a deeper understanding of the foreign trades in Ming and Qing periods. Through the study with the coworkers and the research on the Internet, I got to know the story hidden behind the "Kuanyong Tongbao" round-shape square-hole copper coin.

Liu Yi, Temple of Heaven Park
Management

圆明园梵香楼遗珍
——"地天母"铜像

Statue of Mother of Heaven and Hell
— the Lost Treasure

清朝统治者尊崇藏传佛教，力图通过藏传佛教的影响力治理蒙藏地区。圆明园作为清帝长期居住、理政的御园，更是梵刹林立，其中的藏传佛教建筑，其内部装饰及陈设、供奉，遵照藏传佛教教义布置，神像、佛塔、佛经和法器，数量多，用料讲究，工艺精湛，有富丽华贵的皇家气派。目前圆明园出土的清宫廷造像以中小型为主，材质有铜、玉、石、瓷，其中铜造像数量最多，艺术水平也最高。含经堂出土的"地天母"铜像是其中的精品，而且具有明确的出土地点，它的制作、供奉、损毁还有一段跌宕起伏的故事。

含经堂位于长春园中心地带，是乾隆帝为自己归政后预修的养老之所。梵香楼在含经堂西配殿西侧，是清乾隆年间所建的 8 座六品佛楼之一。乾隆二十二年至四十七年（1757—

Rulers in Qing Dynasty worshipped Tibetan Buddhism, and expected to control Mongolia and Tibetan area through the influence of Tibetan Buddhism. The Yuanmingyuan Park, as the place where emperors spent a long time to live in, was full of temples. There are many Tibetan Buddhist architectures, interior decoration and furnishings, offerings, statues, pagodas, and Buddhist scriptures decorated according to Tibetan Buddhism doctrine. These decorations were of fine quality, dainty materials, and exquisite workmanship, representing the royal style. Statues unearthed in the Yuanmingyuan Park are mainly small and medium-sized, made of bronze, jade, stone, porcelain, among which bronze statues account for the largest portion. The statue of Mother of Heaven and Hell was unearthed in the Tripataka Hall is one of the high-quality goods. It could show us a twisted story in its production,worship and damage .

Located in the center of Changchun Park, the Tripataka Hall was a resort for his own senior care center built by

含经堂梵香楼遗址鸟瞰

overlooking the ruins of Incensation
Pavilion in the Tripataka Hall

1782），乾隆帝先后在紫禁城和北京其他地区、承德的皇家园林中建有8座六品佛楼：紫禁城建福宫花园内的慧曜楼、中正殿后的淡远楼、慈宁宫花园内的宝相楼、宁寿宫花园内的梵华楼、长春园含经堂的梵香楼、承德避暑山庄珠源寺的众香楼、普陀宗乘寺大红台西群楼、须弥福寿寺妙高庄严西群楼。"六品佛楼"的名称源自清宫档案，是一种藏传佛教的佛楼规制，六品佛楼是供奉相应的佛像、佛经、佛塔及法器的建筑。梵香楼是继楼。据清宫《内务府造办处活计档》记载，梵香楼的内部陈设以慧曜楼为范本，局部略做改动。

梵香楼平面呈"凹"字形，是一座两层转角楼。其中西房7间为明间，左右北房与南房各3间，前有檐廊，

Emperor Qianlong. The Incensation Pavilion was on the west side of west palace. It was one of eight Liupin Buddha Pavilions built during Qianlong's reign. From the 22th year to 47th year of Qianlong (1757-1782), the emperor had constructed 8 Liupin Buddha Pavilions in the Forbidden City and imperial gardens in Beijing and Chengde. They are Huiyao Pavilion in the Forbidden City, Danyuan Pavilion behind the Zhongzheng Pavilion, Baoxiang Pavilion in the Garden of Cining Palace, Fanhua Pavilion in the Garden of NIngshou Palace; Incensation Pavilion in the the Tripataka Hall of Changchun Garden, Zhongxiang Pavilion in Zhuyuan Temple of Chengde Summer Resort, Dahongtai Xiqun Pavilion in Zongcheng Temple of Putuo Mountain, Miaogaozhuangyan Xiqun Pavilion in Xumifushou Temple. The name of "Liupin Buddha Pavilion" derived from the palace archives of Qing Dynasty. These Pavilions worshipped corresponding figures of Buddha, Buddhist scriptures, pagodas respectively. The Incensation Pavilion was the second Buddha Pavilion established inside the Forbidden City following Huiyao Pavilion. According to "Working Journal of Construction Department of Inter Affair Ministry", workers had used Huiyao Pavilion as the template, when designing the internal decoration of the Incensation Pavilion, merely making some slight changes.

The Incensation Pavilion is a

地天母铜像，2001年圆明园含经堂出土，通高15.4厘米
Mother of Heaven and Hell was unearthed in the Tripataka Hall of the Yuanmingyuan Park in 2001

其发掘结果与历史文献记载相符。[1]室内正中有天井连通上、下楼，楼上、楼下两室合为一品，共六品间。梵香楼一楼明间供释迦佛，周围墙壁供唐卡。明间之外的6室分别供奉金、银、铜、珐琅、紫檀、玻璃制成的形制各异的佛塔。6座佛塔样式仿慧曜楼，但尺寸较慧曜楼塔提高7寸，其中制作金塔所需"八六色金三千四百两"，

[1] 北京市文物研究所：《圆明园长春园含经堂遗址发掘报告》，文物出版社，2006年。

"concave" shaped two-story turrets. The seven west room are outer rooms, and there are both three rooms in the north and south respectively. There was an eaves gallery in front of the architecture, which is consistent with historical documents.[1] The indoor patio connected the two stories. Two rooms were called "Pin", therefore, there are in total Six Pin (Liupin). An outer room was used to worship the Buddha in the Incensation Pavilion, with walls decorated by thangka. Other 6 rooms were worshiping different shapes of the pagodas made of gold, silver, copper, enamel, red sandalwood, and glass. Six stupas imitated that in the Huiyao Pavilion, but they were seven inches higher. A gold stupa required 3400 liang (50g) of gold. And it was 7 inches higher, so it required more 300 liang of gold.[2] The crescent on the stupa were made of white jade which weighed 27 liang.[3] You could imagine the large budget to build these stupas. As a result, since the 3rd Buddha Pavilion, Zhongxiang Pavilion, stupas in the Liupin Buddha Pavilions still followed the format of Huiyao Pavilion and the Incensation Pavilion, while all adopted the enamel as

[1] Excavation Report on the *Tripataka* Hall, Changchun Park of *Yuanmingyuan* Park, compiled by Beijing Research Institution of Cultural Relics, Cultural Relics Publishing House, 2006
[2] First Historical Archive of China: *Yuanmingyuan Park*, Volume 2, Shanghai Classics Publishing House, 1991, Page 1410
[3] First Historical Archive of China: Yuanmingyuan Park, Volume 2, Shanghai Classics Publishing House, 1991, Page 1411

后因放高 7 寸又追加"八二色金三百两"。[1] 金塔上月牙由一块重一斤十一两的白玉剖开制成,[2] 花费之多可想而知。正因为如此,从第三座六品佛楼众香楼开始,之后所建的六品佛楼中的六塔形制虽仍照慧曜楼和梵香楼的样式,但材质全部改用掐丝珐琅工艺。梵香楼的六座佛塔虽已不存,但在体量和用料价值上可以说是六品佛楼中空前绝后的。二楼正中明间供奉白檀香宗喀巴像,左右的 3 间中,正中供案上供 9 尊大铜像,两边墙上所嵌的佛格下层供每品主要的法器和佛经。佛格上层的 61 个小龛内各供小铜佛一尊,每室共有小铜佛 122 尊。这些小佛像莲台正面上沿铸有"大清乾隆年敬造"款,下沿刻汉文尊名,背后刻所属品间的名号,这尊出土的"地天母"铜像就是其中之一。

地天母原是古印度之神,后成为藏传佛教中镇地和保佑国土丰饶的神灵。这尊佛像结半跏趺坐于莲座之上。一面二臂,头戴五叶冠,葫芦形发髻,耳后有束发缯带,长发披于双肩。面

materials. The six stupas had no longer existed, but they were unprecedented in terms of scale and the value of their materials. On the second floor, the statue of Tsong Khapa from sandalwood incense was worshipped. Nine great bronze Buddha were worshipped in the middle, with major multiplier and Buddhist scriptures in the embedded shelves on the walls. There were 61 small niches with a bronze statue of Buddha in each niche. There were in total 122 statues in every room. On the lotus-shaped pedestal was carved "Made during Qianlong Period, Qing Dynasty", followed by the Chinese name of the Buddha and its Pin room. And the statue of emperor's mother was one of them.

Mother of Heaven and Hell was originally an Indian God, and later became the god blessing on the prosperity of a country in Tibetan Buddhism. This statue of Buddha sat cross-legged on the Indus. She had a face and two arms,

[1] 中国第一历史档案馆:《圆明园(上册)》,上海古籍出版社,1991 年,第 1410 页。
[2] 中国第一历史档案馆:《圆明园(下册)》,上海古籍出版社,1991 年,第 1411 页。

莲座背后錾刻"根本"

behind the lotus throne carved "fundamental"

相方圆端正，额头宽阔，鼻梁高挺，修眉细目，嘴唇刻画生动。右手置于胸前托宝瓶，左手护持，身躯略向侧扭，姿态优雅。身上佩饰为耳珰、项链、臂钏、手镯、脚镯，肩披帛带，腰束长裙，衣褶起伏自然流畅铺于座面上，身姿曼妙，神态刻画入微。莲花座为单层覆式，莲瓣圆润，排列规整。莲座上缘饰有3道连珠纹，中间原应铸有"大清乾隆年敬造"楷书阳识，现因锈蚀严重已模糊不清。莲座下缘正面錾刻"地天母"佛名，背后錾刻"根本"。莲座底部内壁錾刻有"十五"字样，是工匠铸造过程中使用的计算件数或铸造次的简便符号。

含经堂出土的这尊"地天母"铜像由于长期深埋地下，出土时已没有六品佛楼小佛像"见肉泥金，发顶扫青"的特征，但莲座上錾刻有佛名和所属品间名号，而且与紫禁城宁寿宫

莲座正面下缘錾刻"地天母"

on the edge of lotus throne carved "Mother of Heaven and Hell"

wearing gourd shape bun with hair belt behind ears. Her long hair was hanging over her shoulders. Her face was round and organized, with wide forehead, high-bridged nose, thin eyebrow and long eyes. Her lips were carved vividly. Her right hand was holding the sacred bottle in the chest, with her left hand protecting it. Her body slightly leaned to the side and looked gracefully. She wore earrings, bracelets, anklet, necklace, etc. She was wearing a belt on her shoulders, a long skirt, with smocking naturally and smoothly covering the pedestal. Her body shape was beautiful, and her expression was vivid. The single covered lotus was neat and beautiful. lotus throne fringe was decorated with three alignment lines, between which there should be a regular script of "made in Qianlong Period ", while it was too corroded to be recognized. On the edge of lotus throne was carved "Mother of Heaven and Hell ", and behind the lutus throne was carved "fundamental". On the wall of the lotus throne was engraved with the word "15", which was a number representing the order or the total number of stupas made by craftsmen.

The bronze statue of Mother of Heaven and Hell unearthed in the Tripataka Hall had lost the feature of "paste gold and blue top", while the name of the Buddha and its Pin room were carved on it. Besides, it was almost the same with the statues of Mother of Heaven and Hell worshipped in Fanhua

梵华楼内所供的"地天母"佛像造型相同，只是体量略小，由此可确定这尊佛像原应供于梵香楼二层德行品间的佛龛中，是梵香楼700余尊小铜像中唯一幸存的。

梵香楼曾经辉煌气派，梵音缭绕。然而咸丰十年（1860）英法联军洗劫、焚毁了圆明园，建筑被野蛮的战火吞噬，陈设被侵略者践踏、强占，这尊铜像也从此尘封于地下。虽然它只是昔日圆明园珍宝中的沧海一粟，也难觅昔日风采，但它不仅与紫禁城中那些堂皇富丽的清皇家文物同根同源，更是圆明园兴衰荣辱的历史见证。

陈　辉

北京市海淀区圆明园管理处

Pavilion in the Forbidden City, only a slightly heavier. Then we can determine that the statue should be the only existing one of the over 700 statues originally worshiped in the small niches on the second floor of the Incensation Pavilion.

The Incensation Pavilion was once glorious with Vatican curling upwards. Unfortunately, the second series was destroyed when the Yuanmingyuan Park was burnt by the British and French forces in 1860 (the 10th year during Xianfeng's reign). Architectures were swallowed up by a brutal wars and our treasures were trampled by invaders. This bronze statue was sleeping underground since then. Although it is just a drop in the ocean of the Yuanmingyuan Park treasures, and had already lost its original beauty, it still shares the history with the royal cultural relics kept in the Forbidden City. What's more, it is a witness of the vicissitudes of the Yuanmingyuan Park.

Chen Hui, Management Office of
Yuanmingyuan Park

月牙钱

Crescent Coin

2015 年年初，应北京市文物局要求，北京古代钱币展览馆将馆内藏品逐一做了可移动文物普查，将 7000 多件文物分门别类，进行了拍照和测量，并将数据一一记录，为文物们建立起了各自的"名片"。我有幸参与了这一工作，在工作中，接触到了丰富的馆藏钱币，饱览了诸多难得一见的珍品。一些钱币孤品和稀缺类型的钱币

At the beginning of 2015, at the demanded of Beijing Municipal Administration of Cultural Heritage, we implemented the census on movable cultural relics in the Museum of Ancient Coin in Beijing, sorting out, photographing, and registering over 7,000 pieces of collections, setting up the "identification card" for every piece. It is a great honor for me to participate in this work. During the census, I got the access to a rich collection

唐早期开元通宝

details of Kaiyuan Tongbao coin

更是令我记忆深刻。在这钱币的海洋里，许多钱币背后都有自己的故事和传说，它们见证着历史，经历了风雨，诉说着沧桑，以自身的钱文和图案，勾勒出一幅幅历史的画卷。在这诸多有故事的钱币里，有一种钱币以它独特的富传奇色彩的历史背景深深吸引了我，让我不禁在工作之余关注起它的来历和故事，它就是开元通宝。

开元通宝版别众多，普通版本存世量大，馆藏量充足，藏品保存相对完整，是唐朝统治289年中的主要流通货币，主要为铜质材料铸成，规格为直径2.4厘米。开元通宝影响了中国之后1000多年钱币的形制、钱文模式和十进位衡法。开元通宝最大的特点就是多数开元通宝背有甲痕。如果您仔细看唐玄宗时期的开元通宝，就会发现，在它的背面都有一个月牙形的印，其位置或在穿上，或在穿下，或在穿角，因此又有"穿上望月""穿下俯月"等名称。这究竟是怎么回事呢？古人有两种说法。唐朝人郑虔《荟萃》、薛珝《唐圣运图》皆将此月牙形印附会为李世民文德皇后的甲痕，而宋朝人刘斧《青琐高议》则附会为唐玄宗贵妃杨玉环的甲痕。

of coins with different categories and forms. It was a precious opportunity for me to take a close look at our treasure from history. Some coin vintage impressed me a lot. Among these coins, many of them have their own stories and legends. They have witnessed the history, and represented it with their own designs and patterns. During the census, I was deeply impressed and attracted by a kind of coin due to its unique history, making me spend more leisure time studying it.

There are many versions of Kai Yuan Tong Bao Coin. There are lots of the common versions of this coin now kept in the museum, with relatively complete body and of fine quality. The main feature of this coin is that there is a crescent mark behind the coin, sometimes on the upper edge, sometimes lower, and sometimes beside the square hole which is used to link many coins in a string, hence its names of "looking up at the crescent" or "looking down at the crescent" according to different linking directions. Why is there a crescent mark on the back of the coin? There are mainly two stories, *Assemble* (《荟萃》) written by Zheng Qian in Tang Dynasty and *The future of Tang Dynasty* (《唐圣运图》) written by Xue Dang. They both believed that the crescent mark was the nail mark of Queen Wende of Li Yuan; While in *Qing Suo Gao Yi* (《青琐高议》) written by Liu Fu in Song Dynasty, it was said to be the nail mark of

先从唐玄宗和杨贵妃的传说说起。

唐代皇帝崇尚道教，唐玄宗也不例外。相传开元时期，他把宰相宋璟举荐的道士陈善通视若座上宾。一个初秋的夜晚，唐玄宗与杨贵妃又开始了《霓裳羽衣舞》的排练并邀请李善通前来观看。排演进行了3遍，杨贵妃已是香汗袭人。忽然，她喊道："着火了！"在场的都起了身，果然看到西方一片通红。高力士有经验，说既是起火，咋不见浓烟，皇宫也是处变不惊；李善通更是镇定，说道："不忙，莫慌，让贫道前去看个究竟。"言毕，闭目端坐，神态安详。约摸一杯茶的工夫，李善通睁开双眼，起身并整了整衣冠，笑道："一场虚惊，此乃户部在浇铸开元通宝。"在场的人都将信将疑。为验证道士的话是否属实，杨贵妃便向唐玄宗提议，要看看开元通宝的样品。唐玄宗即命高力士传话，让户部铸钱监速速送来。铸钱监送来一枚开元通宝蜡样。唐玄宗仔细端详了通宝蜡样，又给杨贵妃看。可是杨贵妃的指甲太长，竟在蜡样背面留下了一个指甲印。只见那印纤纤细细，一如夜空中的弯月。杨贵妃灵机一动，向唐玄宗说："臣妾特意在

Lady Yang, Concubine of Emperor Xuanzong.

Let's start with the story between Concubine Yang and Emperor Xuanzong.

Emperors worshiped and advocated Taoism during Tang Dynasty, and Emperor Xuanzong was no exception. It is said that during the Kaiyuan Period, Emperor Xuanzong treated Chen Shantong, a Taoist recommended by his prime minister Song Jing, as a guest. One night in early autumn, the Emperor and the Concubine Yang began their rehearsal of *Rainbow Skirt and Feather Garment Song*（《霓裳羽衣舞》）. And Emperor Xuanzong invited Li Shantong to watch their rehearsal. After rehearsal for three times, Concubine Yang got sweaty. She rested against the jade railings, breathing out. Suddenly, she cried: "Fire!" Every one present stood up and the sky in the west was indeed red. Gao Lishi was well experienced, saying that if that was a fire, why wasn't there any smoke? And there was also no warnings in the palace. Li Shantong was even calmer and said: "Don't worry, let me go there to check it out." Then he closed his eyes serenely. Just after a little while, Li Shantong opened his eyes, stood up, and adjusted his clothes and then laughed. "A false alarm! The Ministry of Revenue is making the Kai Yuan Tong Bao Coins!" Every one was skeptical about his explanation. To verify whether Li was true, Concubine Yang suggested to look at

通宝背面留了一个指甲印，一来让老百姓都知道金钱来之不易，不能坑蒙拐骗偷，要靠双手劳动挣来；二来让它作为今晚舞会的纪念！"唐玄宗听后，觉得有道理，立即传旨让户部照此样儿熔铜制钱。之后，开元通宝背面，都有一个指甲印，当时民间都知道那是贵妃娘娘的指甲印，金代著名文学家李俊民，还曾写过"金钗坠落无因见，藏得开元一捻痕"的诗句呢。

然而，这只是一个美好的传说，是人们将美好的愿望寄托在这枚带新月的钱币上。宋朝人刘斧《青琐高议》中把传说的文德皇后的故事篡成了唐玄宗李隆基与杨贵妃的故事，说是杨贵妃的甲痕，是把开元通宝的"开元"与唐玄宗年号的"开元"混为一谈了。其实，宋朝刘斧未必不知两个"开元"并不是一回事，可能是出于文学艺术的需要故做此说。因杨、李二人的爱情故事在当时社会已有广泛影响，传为佳话。经考，文德皇后是李世民的皇后，李渊铸开元通宝时，李世民尚未当太子，更谈不上立皇后的事，又怎么会有文德皇后的甲迹呢？

除文献记载外，从当时钱币铸造工艺程序来看，所谓的"甲痕"也

the samples of Kai Yuan Tong Bao Coin. Emperor Xuanzong then ordered Gao Lishi to pass on a message to the Ministry of Revenue, making them send a coin sample to the palace as soon as possible. And a waxy sample was delivered. Emperor Xuanzong took a careful look at the sample before giving it to Concubine Yang. But the nails of Concubine Yang were too long, and she indeliberately left a nail mark on the back of the sample, which looked like the crescent in the sky. Concubine Yang thought for a while and told the emperor: "I have left a nail mark on the back of the coin to remind the common people that money are hard to make. Therefore, they should not make money by stealing or cheating. They should earn a living with their own hands. And it could also become a souvenir for tonight's rehearsal!" Emperor Xuanzong thought it reasonable and asked the Ministry of Revenue to make coins according to the sample with a crescent mark on the back. After that, all Kai Yuan Tong Bao Coin had a crescent mark on its back. And all folks knew that the mark was the nail mark of the Concubine. And some one even wrote a poem: " The hairpin fell down and we couldn't see it. And there is a nail mark on the back of Kai Yuan Tong Bao Coin (金钗坠落无因见，藏得开元一捻痕)."

However, this was just a beautiful story, where people attached their wishes to the coin with a crescent mark. Liu Fu in

是不可信的。有论者已指出，如果在蜡样上掐出指甲痕，应为下凹的阴文，经制模后铸造的铜钱上也应当是凹纹，但现在所见的唐开元通宝月纹均为凸起的阳纹，可见所谓"文德皇后的甲痕"云云纯属无稽之谈。这是有道理的。根据我国古代铸造钱币的工艺程序，无论采取怎样的铸造方法，样钱都是作为铸造钱币的最初样本。铸造钱币时，以样钱为本，仿制一定数量的母钱颁发至各铸钱部门制范开炉铸造。如果说开元通宝钱背的仰月纹是在蜡样上由某一皇后用指甲所掐下的痕迹，并经过皇帝钦定，那么其他任何人都是不能随意更改的，钱币上的月牙纹应当是凹下去的阴文，而不是凸现出来的阳文。但是，现今所见到的开元通宝上的仰月纹，均为凸出的阳纹。

总之，无论是文献记载，还是从钱币铸造工艺程序分析，说开元通宝钱背的仰月纹与文德皇后、杨贵妃等人的"甲痕"有关，都是不正确的。可以说，这些说法均为传言、附会而已，并无实据。

那么，开元通宝背上的月牙纹究竟代表什么呢？中国传统观念中，

Song Dynasty changed the story of Li Yuan and his queen, Wende, replacing the original protagonists with Emperor Xuanzong and his concubine Lady Yang, claiming that the mark was left by Lady Yang. It seemed that Liu Fu had confused the word "Kai Yuan" in "Kai Yuan Tong Bao Coin" with the Emperor Xuanzong's reign tile "Kai Yuan". In fact, Liu Fu might know about the differences between these two "Kai Yuan", and he merely wrote the story in this way for the sake of literature and art. Because the romantic story of Emperor Xuanzong and Concubine Yang had become eternal, imposing extensive influence on the society at that time. According to the proved history, Queen Wende was the queen of Li Shimin, Emperor Taizong. When Li Yuan was making Kai Yuan Tong Bao Coin, Li Shimin had yet to be the crown prince, let alone having any queens. How could it be the nail mark of Queen Wende?

From the perspective of the real history and standard procedure of coin casting, there is also no ground for the "nail mark theory". Some researchers argued that the crescent mark was left by nails, then there must be a dent too. According to casting process at that time, no matter what way of casting was adopted, it should be based on samples. And then same coins casted would be distributed to each money-casting department as a template. The design of sample coin was decided by the emperor,

以新月象征"新生""向上""初始"之义。李渊取得政权，扫除隋弊，开辟了新的纪元。大凡开国君主无不希望"从新更始"，李渊何尝不是如此？不但新君如此，百姓也有同样的愿望。经过隋末大乱，饱尝战乱饥荒痛苦的人民，也一定希望翻过历史的一页，开辟新的纪元。因此，大书法家欧阳询在制钱文时便取名"开元通宝"，并得到李渊的赞同。既然是开辟新纪元，开元钱自然也应当区别于前代钱币。那么，除了钱名不同外，还应留下些什么标记呢？于是，铸钱使等便在钱背上留下了新月形以表新王朝新生兴旺、蒸蒸日上之意。

根据唐代以前货币所铸背文或为装饰、或为铸造地地名、或为铸钱炉别记号的特点看，开元通宝钱背的仰月纹，肯定不是地名，那么只剩下两种可能，一是作为装饰，一是作为铸钱炉别记号。从"开元通宝"钱背所铸"仰月纹"的情况看，其具备部位规范、整体布局协调、线条粗细匀称、弧度大小适中、两端浑圆的特点，使人观之既无夸张之感，又无添足之嫌，显而易见是由人专门设计铸造所致。因此，可以认为开元通宝钱背的仰月

and no one could arbitrarily change it. Characters were cut in intaglio. If someone indeed accidentally left a mark on the sample coin, then the mark on Kai Yuan Tong Bao coins should be cut in intaglio. But actually the mark was protruding, which was not in line with the previous assumptions. Therefore, the nail mark theory was only a legend instead of a historical fact.

So, what does the crescent mark on the Kai Yuan Tong Bao Coin mean? I have made several wild judgments both emotionally and historically after referring to the background of coin-casting culture. The crescent represents the newborn and a fresh start in China. The founding emperor, or Emperor Gaozu, anticipated to usher into a new era and longed for the bright future with great ambition and infinite possibility. And all ordinary people also longed for peace and a new start after wars at the end of the Sui Dynasty. Hence, Ouyang Xun, a great calligrapher, proposed the "Kai Yuan Tong Bao" which represented a fresh start, and got approval from by the emperor. Apart from the words on the coin, what else could they do to differentiate their own coins with those in previous dynasties? Therefore, the crescent mark was left on the back of the coin, representing the birth of a new regime, expecting it to prosper and improve day by day.

In fact, before Kai Yuan Tong Bao Coin, there were precedent of coins with

纹当是一种兼具装饰和炉别记号功能的纹饰。

本馆展出的开元通宝主要是铸造于唐代会昌年间的会昌开元。淮南（今扬州）节度使李绅率先铸造进呈一种背面铸有"昌"字的开元通宝钱，以纪年号"会昌"，于是朝廷下令各地州郡仿效淮南的做法，在钱币背面铸字，表示铸造地和其他纪念内容。会昌开元因铸造地不同而种类众多，背文记有"昌、京（长安）、洛（洛阳）、益（成都）、荆（江陵）、襄（襄阳）、蓝（蓝田）、越（绍兴）、宣（宣城）、洪（南昌）、潭（长沙）、兖（兖州）、润（镇江）、鄂（武汉）、平（昌黎）、兴（兴平）、梁（汉中）、广（广州）、梓（三台）、福（福州）、桂（桂阳）、丹（晋城）、永（零陵）"等23种，"永"字铸量最少，次为"丹""福""平""桂"等。

张　婧

北京市古代钱币展览馆

marks. The mark might be the casting place, or used as a pattern to differentiate furnaces. The crescent mark on the back of Kai Yuan Tong Bao Coin is definitely not a mark of casting place. In view of the format of the mark, the lines were moderate and so were the angles, with no exaggeration and redundancy. So they should be specially designed for casting and become a mark to differentiate the furnaces.

Our museum mainly exhibits the Hui Chang Kai Yuan Coin, casted during Hui Chang Period in Tang Dynasty. Governor in Huainan (now Yangzhou) Li Shen took the lead to cast a kind of coin with "Chang" on the back to commemorate the reign title "Huichang". And the emperor ordered other provinces to follow Huainan's lead. There are many kinds of Hui Chang Kai Yuan coins, and the characters on the back included "Lan (Lantian), Jing (Chang 'an), Jing (Jiangling), Luo (Luoyang), Run (Zhenjiang), Yue (Shaoxing), Yi (Chengdu), Tan(Changsha), Xiang (Xiangyang), Gui (Guiyang), Ping (Changli), Xuan (Xuancheng), E (wuhan), Hong (Nanchang), Guang (Guangzhou), Liang (Hanzhong), Yan (Yanzhou) and Xing (Xingping), Zi (Santai), Yong (Lingling), Fu (Fuzhou), Dan (Jincheng). Among the 23 types, Yong is the least, followed by Dan, Fu, Ping and Gui.

Zhang Jing, the Museum of Ancient

Coin in Beijing

千秋功绩话鲆镈

Stories Traced Back Thousands of Years Ago behind "Ling Bo"

在国家博物馆的古代中国展厅，有一件青铜器叫"镈"，是中国古代一种打击乐器，也是象征王侯贵族地位和财富的重要礼器。在本次可移动文物普查中出现在大家眼前的镈，是春秋晚期一位名为"鲆（ling）"的人铸造的，故称其为"鲆镈"。"鲆"是

鲆镈
Ling Bo

"Bo", an ancient Chinese percussion instrument made of bronze, is on display in the exhibition hall of National Museum of China. It is also an important ritual bronze instrument that symbolizes the high status and wealth of kings and nobles. This Bo, rediscovered in this year's national census on movable cultural relics, was made and named by "Ling" in late Spring and Autumn period. "Ling" was a grandchild of Bao Shuya, the famous administrator of the State of Qi in Spring and Autumn period. The 174-Chinese-character inscription on it revealed the achievements of Bao Shuya and the honor of him being awarded with fiefs by Duke Huan. In the inscription, the maker also encouraged himself to keep working hard and make prays to the ancestors, hoping that they will bless the family and the decedents and ensure the prosperity of the State of Qi.

Why could Bao Shuya earn such glory for his family? Let's start from how

春秋时齐国著名政治家鲍叔牙的孙子，而镈上的174字铭文记述了鲍叔牙的功业及齐侯赐予鲍家封邑的荣耀大事，同时勉励自己时刻奋发努力，祈祷先祖保佑鲍家子孙，祈求齐国国运昌盛。

鲍镈上的铭文

inscriptions on Ling Bo

而提及齐侯赏赐鲍家封邑，则必须从鲍叔牙帮助齐桓公即位说起。据铭文所载，众所周知，齐桓公是春秋时齐国第十五位国君，春秋五霸之一，在位期间强军富民，驱逐戎狄，三平晋乱，为时人及后人所敬仰。而在即位前，齐桓公也就是姜小白正赶上齐国

he helped Duke Huan of Qi take back the throne.

Duke Huan of Qi, the fifteenth monarch of the State of Qi in Spring and Autumn period, was a well-known historical figure in China. As he strengthened the national forces, enriched his people, and drove out the enemies during his reign, the state of Qi became one of the Five Hegemons of Spring and Autumn period. And due to these achievements, he was admired by later generations. But before all that, he was only Jiang Xiaobai, a prince among political chaos. He then fled to State of Ju under the protection of Bao Shuya, while his brother Jiu to State of Lu accompanied by Guan Zhong and Zhao Hu. At that time, the reigning Duke Xiang of Qi was dissolute and fatuous. He was killed by Gongsun Wuzhi who usurped the throne. But soon the usurper also died among the chaos. A kingdom can't sustain without a king for even one day. The two younger brothers in exile of Duke Xiang, Prince Jiu and Prince Xiaobai, upon hearing the news, rushed back their home. They both knew that the one that arrived at Linzi (capital of Qi) first would be the monarch to rule the country. Guan Zhong, who was Prince Jiu's advisor, led a force by himself and blocked the way from State of Ju to State of Qi, determined to kill Xiaobai,

国内政治混乱，管仲、召忽保护公子纠逃到了鲁国，而鲍叔牙保护小白逃到莒国。当时的齐国国君齐襄公荒淫无道，昏庸无能，公元前686年，公孙无知杀齐襄公，自立为齐国国君，然而不久后这个篡位者同样死于内乱。但国不可一日无君，齐襄公的两个弟弟，流亡在鲁国的公子纠和流亡在莒国的公子小白，闻讯后都急着赶回齐国。当然，两人都明白，谁能早到临淄，捷足先登，那他就是新的国君，掌管齐国国政。当时辅佐公子纠的管仲为了让自己辅佐的公子纠当上国君，亲自带领一支军队堵截住莒国到齐国的路，决意杀掉公子小白以除后患。管仲弯弓搭箭，瞄准小白，一箭射去，公子小白应声倒下。见心中大患已除，公子纠和管仲一行人等便放缓了前行的脚步，并派人向鲁国报捷。但令他们万万没想到是，管仲这一箭正好射在了公子小白的带钩上，机智过人的小白佯装中箭，骗过了公子纠和管仲。在鲍叔牙护卫下，他更换便装，抄近路抢先赶到临淄。在前朝大臣的支持下，公子小白如愿成为齐国国君，而公子纠的那支队伍花了6天时间才到

who would be a big obstacle preventing Jiu from being the monarch. Guan Zhong pulled the bowstring, aimed at Xiaobai, and shot the arrow. Xiaobai was hit and fell down.

Guan Zhong thought that Xiaobai had been put down, so they slowed down their pace, and informed State of Lu of the good news. To their surprise, the arrow only hit the waist belt of Xiaobai. Xiaobai was a clever man. He pretended death and both Prince Jiu and Guan Zhong were deceived by him. Under the protection of Bao Shuya, he put on ordinary clothes, and reached Linzi through a shortcut before Prince Jiu. With the support from the officials of the overthrown dynasty, he became the monarch as he had wished, while it took six days for Prince Jiu and his men to arrive at the capital.

Soon after he took the throne, Xiaobai led an army to attack the State of Lu. As Lu's army was weak, they were soon defeated and ran away. Duke of Lu was afraid of the powerful Qi, so he killed Prince Jiu and imprisoned Guan Zhong. Xiaobai, who was then Duke Huan, wanted to award people according to their contributions, so he appointed Bao Shuya as the Chancellor. But Bao rejected this idea in every possible way, and recommended Guan Zhong to Duke Huan. He said, "I was fortunate to have

达临淄。公子小白即位后不久，便发兵攻打鲁国。鲁国实力薄弱，很快败走。鲁国怕得罪于强大的齐国，杀了公子纠，并囚禁了管仲。而后齐桓公论功行赏，准备任命鲍叔牙为相国。谁知鲍叔牙百般推辞，并竭力推荐管仲为相国。他说："我很幸运地跟从了您，而君上您已经成为齐国的国君。我虽然对您忠心耿耿，但只是任用我，君上可能不会有更大的作为。如果您仅仅想治理好齐国，那么有当下群臣便已足够；可是您若想称霸诸侯，则非管仲不可。管仲在哪个国家，那个国家则一定会强大。"鲍叔牙之所以了解管仲，是因为他俩是多年的好友。他们一起长大，一起经商，一起从军，后来又一起从政，分别作了公子纠和公子小白的师傅。与管仲的长期接触，使他对管仲的为人、学识、才能、智慧和抱负都有深刻的了解。鲍叔牙深信，管仲是能助齐桓公干大事的人，只要有明主赏识，一定会干出一番惊天动地的伟业来。

齐桓公是位胸襟开阔、远见卓识的政治家，他摒弃前嫌，不记管仲的一箭之仇，听从了鲍叔牙的建议。他

followed you, your Majesty, and your Majesty have become the monarch. I will always be loyal to you, but I won't be very helpful if you want to make greater achievements. If your Majesty only aims to be a good ruler, then all the officials can already give enough support; however, if you want to be a dominant power, then you have to employ Guan Zhong. Any country under his administration is bound to be powerful."

The reason why Bao knew Guan so well was that they had been friends for many years. They grew up together, did business together, joined the army together, and entered politics together, with Guan being the teacher of Jiu, while Bao of Xiaobai. Years of interaction with Guan familiarized himself with Guan's personality, be it knowledge, abilities, intelligence or ambitions. Bao was well convinced that Guan had the ability to help Duke Huan achieve greatness that could shock the world, only if his value was appreciated by a wise master.

As an open-minded and far-sighted politician, Duke Huan accepted Bao's suggestion despite of what Guan had done to him. He threatened to kill Guan for revenge and sent someone to escort him back. Then he talked with Guan about how to become a Hegemon. He was delighted with what Guan said, so he

扬言要杀仇人，把管仲接回齐国，然后和管仲谈论霸王之术。听了管仲的霸王之术，桓公大喜过望，拜管仲为相国，尊为"仲父"，委以政事，鲍叔牙则心甘情愿地当起了管仲的下属。在管仲的辅佐下，齐国迅速由乱转治，由弱变强，君臣同心，励精图治，对内整顿朝政，厉行改革，对外尊王攘夷，存亡续绝。齐国成为诸侯中最强大的国家，北却戎狄，南拒强楚。而齐桓公也终于实现了自己的愿望，成为春秋时期的第一位霸主。所以说鲍家的荣耀起于鲍叔牙，他不仅辅佐齐桓公即位有功，而且淡泊名利、唯才是举。他因辅佐齐桓公有功而被封赏，他淡薄名利、唯才是举的行为更是成为千古美谈。鲍叔牙才干过人，在选拔官吏、内政外交等方面都有独到的见解，不得不说齐桓公称霸诸侯，鲍叔牙起到了很大作用。但鲍叔牙过于刚正不阿，管仲生病时齐桓公想让鲍叔牙为相，管仲极力阻止，他认为鲍叔牙为人清正廉明，但不愿当和事佬，不会讨好君上，长此以往恐怕渐渐会得罪齐桓公。所以管仲逝世后，齐桓公便没有任用鲍叔牙为相，而任用公

decided to appoint him as Chancellor, and called him "Father Guan" for respect. Bao embraced the decision wholeheartedly. With Guan's assistance, Duke Huan turned State of Qi from a chaotic and weak country to a well-governed and powerful one. They worked together, and went all out for the prosperity of the country. In terms of domestic affairs, they consolidated the monarch's position by carrying out revolution; regarding foreign relations, they expelled the barbarians to ensure the longevity of the sovereign. As a result, Qi became the most powerful state at that time, which was able to banish barbarians from its northern territory and resist the strong state of Chu to its south. And Duke Huan also realized his dream - he was the first hegemon of Spring and Autumn period.

Bao Shuya had brought glory to his family, not just because he helped Duke Huan of Qi gain the throne, but also because, rather than only seeking fame and wealth for himself, he recommended whoever he thought was competent. His story was thus told again and again through ages. Bao Shuya himself was also a competent official with an insight into foreign affairs and personnel recruitment. He had played a significant role in the process of gaining dominance of Duke Huan.

孙隰朋。但一个月后，公孙隰朋逝世，齐桓公坚持让鲍叔牙为相，鲍叔牙答应下来，但条件是齐桓公得先远离易牙、开方、竖刁3个小人。齐桓公开始同意了，但后来又想念易牙、开方、竖刁三人，把他们征召回来。不久，鲍叔牙因为此事郁郁而终。可见鲍叔牙不怕得罪主上，是一位忠心耿耿又刚正不阿的大臣。

当然，治国安邦靠有用之才；然而贤才难得，荐贤、让贤更属不易，鲍叔牙举荐管仲的事成为千古佳话，他与管仲的交情也被称为"管鲍之交"。得到人才管仲后，齐桓公并没有忘记鲍叔牙举荐管仲的功劳，经常给他封赏，鲍家子孙也因此世代享受齐国的俸禄，得到封地的便有十几代。值得一提的是，鲍叔牙死后，他的子孙大多数仍是齐国著名的大夫，继续为齐国的富强奉献自己的力量。

如今两千多年过去了，鲍叔牙之孙"黼"铸造的这件铸有长篇铭文的青铜镈还没腐朽，其上的铭文还清晰地告诉我们贤臣鲍叔牙的一系列功绩。其不朽之身如同鲍氏家族的丰功伟绩，让世人永远铭记。而鲍叔牙举贤让能的高尚品

When Guan was sick, Duke Huan wanted Bao to replace him, but Guan did his best to stop him. In Guan's opinion, Bao was such an honorable man that he would not make peace with the despicable, and Guan was afraid that he would displease Duke Qi if things continued this way. In the end, Duke Huan appointed Gongsun Xipeng as Chancellor instead of Bao after Guan died. However, Gongsun also died just one month after he took over the position. So Duke Huan insisted that Bao should take the offer. Bao finally accepted on condition that Duke Huan distanced himself from Yiya, Kaifang, and Sudiao from their positions. At the beginning, Duke Huan agreed with the condition, but later he sort of missed these three persons, so he called them back. Bao was so unhappy about that and he died in gloom soon. We can see that Bao was a loyal and upright official, never stooping to flattery.

Indeed, able and competent talents are necessary for the governance of a country. It's difficult to find such men, but it's even harder for a person to step back and give room to better men. However, this was exactly what Bao Shuya did. The story of him and Guan Zhong was passed down from generations to generations, and their friendship was specifically called as " The friendship between Guan

格以及对主上的忠诚，也随着这悠远的
镈声，在华夏大地上千古传颂。

郝爽君

中国国家博物馆

and Bao". Duke Huan didn't forget that it was Bao who recommended Guan to him, and rewarded him constantly. Later, Bao's decedents had received official's salary for many generations, and they were also awarded with fiefs. What's worth mentioning is that most of Bao's decedents were also renowned chancellors of Qi and had contributed a lot to Qi's prosperity.

Though more than two thousand years has passed, Ling Bo, created by Bao Shuya's grandchild Ling, hasn't been eroded by time, and the clear inscription on it keeps telling people the stories of Bao Shuya. This bronze ware will bring these stories into eternity, and make them remembered for ever. The virtues of Bao will be like the melody "Bo" plays, continuing to reverberate for the next two thousand years.

Hao Shuangjun, National Museum of China

永乐大钟三迁记

The Relocation of Yongle Bell

说起位于今天北京市北三环西路的大钟寺（觉生寺），您可能会马上联想到寺中收藏的那口体量巨大、庄严宏美的永乐大钟。可您知道吗？永乐大钟其实也是个"拆迁户"，并非

永乐大钟

Yongle Bell

When it comes to the Great Bell Temple (also known as Juesheng Temple) in the North Third Ring Western Road, Beijing, you may think of the big and solemn Yongle Bell there. However, what you may not know is that Yongle Bell was originally not collected in the Great Bell Temple. Actually it had been relocated for three times during Ming and Qing Dynasty. Its footprint could be seen in most part of Beijing.

Yongle Bell was created in the Bell Foundry to the northwestern of the bell tower in Beijing, Ming Dynasty. It boasts a history of roughly 600 years. Today, this place was still called Bell Foundry Alley. During Yongle's Rein in Ming Dynasty, many famous bells were made. Besides the Yongle Bell, Yongle Dageng Bell in the Bell Tower in Beijing, Yongle Bronze Bell in the bell tower in Zhai Palace in the temple of Heaven and Yongle Iron Bell in the Ancient Bell Musuem in the Great Bell Temple were all made in the Bell Foundry. They belonged to a same family.

一直悬挂在大钟寺，而是从其他地点经过二次辗转搬迁而来，这里面还有一段时间跨越明清、足迹绕遍大半个北京城的故事。

永乐大钟"出生"在明代北京城钟楼西北的铸钟厂，算来已有近600岁，今天北京还保留着铸钟胡同的地名。明代永乐年间的铸钟厂，可谓名钟辈出，除大钟寺收藏的这口永乐大钟外，今天北京钟楼上的永乐大更钟、天坛斋宫钟楼上的永乐铜钟，以及大钟寺古钟博物馆收藏的永乐铁更钟等都"诞生"于此，是永乐大钟的"同胞兄弟"。

永乐大钟在铸钟厂铸成后，由铸钟厂迁出，住进了位于今天景山公园东北的汉经厂，这里是明代皇家收藏汉文佛教典籍、并为皇帝举行佛事的场所。永乐大钟在汉经厂默默无闻地一住就是近200年。直到万历皇帝登上皇位后，其母李太后痴迷佛教，万历为讨母亲欢心，不但在西直门外为她修建了规模宏大的万寿寺，还将汉经厂的永乐大钟搬到了那里，每天派六名僧人，专门负责撞击它，传说钟声数十里外都可听到。万寿寺也因永乐大钟悠扬的声响而名声大振，京城的百姓与文人墨客纷纷来到万寿寺，只为一睹永乐大钟的风采，聆

Upon completion, Yongle Bell was removed from the foundry to the Hanjingchang, located to the northeast of today's Jingshan Park. Hanjingchang was home to Chinese version of Buddhist literature. Emperors would go there to practice Buddhist activities. And Yongle Bell had been there for nearly 2 centuries. After Emperor Wanli stepped into power, he wanted to play up to his mother, Empress Dowager Li, who was obsessed with Buddhism. Therefore, he built the Wanshou Temple outside the Xizhi Gate for his mother and then removed the Yongle Bell into Wanshou Temple from the Hanjingchang. And every day, 6 monks would go there to ring the Yongle Bell. It is said that the chime of Yongle Bell could be heard from far away. The Wanshou Temple was also famous for the chime of Yongle Bell, attracting many people, officials and scholars in Beijing to see and listen to the chime of the bell.

However, a decade later, Yongle Bell was removed from the bell tower when Emperor Tianqi, Wanli's grandson, ascended to throne, as he believed in the rumor that "the chime in the west part of Beijing will harm the rein of the emperor". As a result, Yongle Bell was put in the eastern yard of Wanshou Temple for over 100 years.

听那震撼心灵的钟声。

　　然而，十多年后，万历皇帝的孙子天启皇帝登上皇位，听信了坊间流传的"京城的白虎方（西方）鸣钟，对天子不利"的流言，于是下令将永乐大钟从钟楼上摘下。这永乐大钟在万寿寺院东的地上一卧就是100多年！

　　直到清乾隆初年，永乐大钟才重新进入皇帝的视野。经负责勘查风水的官员奏报，建议将永乐大钟安置在刚刚建成的觉生寺中，得到了乾隆皇帝的采纳。这年冬天，为永乐大钟"搬家"的工作正式开始了。

　　为什么"搬家"季节选在天寒地冻的冬季呢？这里面另有玄机。在没有大型起重搬运设备的古代，要想给永乐大钟这个重达46.5吨，高6.75米，底口直径达3.3米的庞然大物"搬家"，绝非易事。但聪明的古人却早已掌握了物理学中通过减小摩擦系数从而减小摩擦力的这个原理。在北京滴水成冰的冬季，搬运大钟的人们于万寿寺和觉生寺之间，每隔一里地打井一口，用井水泼地，使地面结冰，以减少移动过程中的阻力，然后用牛群拉动大钟在冰面上滑行。就这样永乐大钟"滑"到了觉生寺。乾隆皇帝还特

It didn't attract any royal attention until Emperor Qianlong ascended to throne. The official in charge of studying geomantic omen advised that the Yongle Beill should be put in the Juesheng Temple which was established recently back then and his advice was adopted by Emperor Qianlong. In the winter of that year, the relocation of Yongle Bell began.

But why did Qianlong choose to relocate the bell in such a cold winter? He had his own reason -- in the ancient time without any lifting equipment, it was very hard to relocate the Yongle Bell, a giant bell of 46.5 tons of weight and 6.75 meters of height. It is 3.3 meters in diameter. But our clever ancestors had already mastered in physics and managed to remove the giant bell reducing the friction coefficient. In the chilly winter in Beijing, they drilled a well every li (500 meters) between Wanshou Temple and Juesheng Temple, and then splashed water from these wells to freeze the ground. With the reduced resistance, the bell was moved to the Juesheng Temple by cattle. More specifically, it was slid to the Juesheng Temple. Emperor Qianlong also specially built a new "home", the Great Bell Tower, in the fifth courtyard in the temple, and made a poem for it. The poem was called Song of Big Tower,

意在觉生寺中第五进院落里，以天子才能享用的"天圆地方"式的建筑，为永乐大钟建了"新居"——大钟楼，并将永乐大钟的身世赋成一首名为《大钟歌》的长诗，御笔亲书，镌刻在上等汉白玉雕成的石碑上，也安置在大钟楼内，从此永乐大钟"定居"下来，成为名副其实的"钟王"，而觉生寺也因此得了"大钟寺"这一别名，甚至到今天我们只知道大钟寺而不知觉生寺了。

永乐大钟在大钟寺安顿下来后，便有了新的使命，成为清代皇帝祈雨的法器，只在遇到旱年举行祈雨仪式

and was inscribed by Qianlong himself on a white jade monument. From then on, Yongle Bell finally settled down and became the king of bells. And since then, Juesheng Temple was also named as Dazhong Temple (Great Bell Temple). Today, many people may only know its name as Dazhong Temple instead of its original name.

After settling down, Yongle Bell got another mission. It had become a sacrificial tool for emperors to pray for rain. It would only be ringed when there was draught. And this tradition lasted from the rein of Emperor Qianlong to the end

永乐大钟迁移示意图

the relocation route of the Yongle Bell

时才会敲响，这一制度从乾隆年间一直延续至清末。自 1985 年大钟寺古钟博物馆成立至今，大钟楼一直作为永乐大钟原状陈列展厅，保持了乾隆年间永乐大钟原本的悬挂状态。

2014 年 10 月，大钟寺古钟博物馆经过历时两年的修缮改陈，重新向社会开放。大钟楼在继续保持永乐大钟原状陈列的同时，有了一些新的变化——博物馆工作人员运用高科技 3D 扫描技术，对永乐大钟内外壁 23 万余字的铭文进行了系统的数字化扫描，不但整体掌握了永乐大钟铭文内容与分布规律，还运用计算机还原了永乐大钟的三维模型。在大钟楼内推出了"永乐大钟铭文电子拓片展"与"360 度看大钟"两大多媒体展示互动项目，观众还可以通过"幻影成像"技术"目睹"永乐大钟的铸造过程。

每年元旦子时，新年来临之际，在大钟楼举行的"鸣钟晚会"是大钟寺古钟博物馆的品牌民俗活动，至今已延续了 34 届。听，2017 年新年的钟声近了，永乐大钟的鸣声近了！

罗飞

北京日报

of Qing Dynasty. Since the establishment of the Ancient Bell Museum in Dazhong Temple in 1985, Yongle Bell was in display at its original status, hanged in the bell tower just like in the rein of Qianlong.

This October, after two years of restoration, the ancient bell museum was open to the public again. The Yongle Bell would still be maintained at its original status, but at the same time, there are some new changes. Staffs in the museum adopted the high-tech 3D scanning technology to digitalize all inscriptions containing over 230,000 characters both outside and inside the bell. They have not only grasped the distribution pattern of the inscription, but also established the 3d model of Yongle Bell. They have launched two multi-media interacted exhibition, namely "digital inscription on Yongle Bell" and "3D bell". Visitors could also see the casting process of the bell through the imaging technology.

On the eve of every new year, the "Bell Chime Party" would be held on the Big Bell Tower. As a brand of folk customs, the party has already been 34 years old.

Listen! The chime of 2017 is approaching! The chime of the Yongle Bell is approaching!

Luo Fei, Beijing Daily

克盉、克罍：揭开首位燕侯之谜

Ke He and Ke Lei: Revealing the Mystery of Lord of Yan

北京建城已有 3000 多年（今年北京建城 3061 年）历史，源头在房山琉璃河镇的西周古燕都。

周武王灭商后，在北方地区同时分封了两个诸侯国——封召公于燕，封黄帝之后（一说为帝尧之后）于蓟（今广安门一带）。燕国历史上的一桩悬案是：真正到燕地就封的第一代燕侯究竟是何人？

古今学者对召公姬奭是否去燕就封，多有疑惑。主要原因是根据《史记·鲁周公世家》的记述，周公虽被封于鲁，但因为需留佐武王，故由其长子伯禽到鲁国就封。而当时，"召公为保，周公为师，相成王左右"，与周公地位相当的召公，应该也是难以离开宗周而远赴封地的。近代学者多认为，召公和周公一样"亦以元子就封，而次子留相王室，代为召公"。

不过，这仅仅是推论，毕竟《史

Beijing enjoys a history of over 3,000 years (more specifically speaking, 3061 years) and the history originated from the capital of Yan State during the Western Zhou Period alongside the Liuli River, Fangshan District.

After King Wu of Zhou, also known as Ji Fa, defeated Shang, he granted two enfeoffments in the northern region at the same time. He granted Yan area to Lord Zhao, and granted Ji (today's Guanganmen area) to the decedent of Emperor Huang (or the descendant of Emperor Yao according to another theory). But who is the first term of Lord of Yan? It still remains a mystery.

Many scholars doubted whether Lord Zhao accepted the grant and then went to Yan area. According to Chronicles of Lord Luzhou in Shi Ji (Records of the Grand History), although Lu area was granted to Lord Zhou, Lord Zhou did not go there because he needed to stay and assist King

记》中没有明确记载，更无其他佐证。关于燕国的历史，文献上只有只言片语。假使召公真的未就封，那么代封之元子又是谁？

1986年，在房山琉璃河西周燕都遗址发现了第1193号大墓。此墓不仅是琉璃河遗址发现的最大的墓葬，而且有4条墓道。商周时期只有贵族的墓葬才设墓道，身份越高贵则墓道越多。考古人员判断此墓应是地位显赫的一代燕侯之墓。

尽管曾被盗掘，但1193号大墓仍出土各类随葬品两百多件，包括礼器、工具、兵器、车马器、漆器、货贝、装饰品等，可见最初这座墓葬中的随葬品相当丰富。众多随葬品中，最引人注意的便是它们俩——克盉（hé）

克盉
Ke He

Wu of Zhou. Instead, Lord Zhou's son went to the granted area. Back then, "Lord Zhao was the guard and Lord Zhou was the teacher. They assisted King Cheng of Zhou together." Therefore, just like Lord Zhou, Lord Zhao was unlikely to leave the capital and went to his granted area. Many modern scholars believed that Lord Zhao dispatched his eldest son to his granted area just like Lord Zhou.

But this is only an assumption. After all, there weren't any specific recordings about this part of history and there wasn't any other evidence either. Few words recorded the history of Yan State. If Lord Zhou did not go to his granted area, then which son of him took his place?

In 1986, in the site of capital of Yan State during the Western Zhou Period alongside the Liuli River, Fangshan District, Beijing, we discovered the No.1193 tomb. It is the largest tomb discovered in this site, boasting 4 tomb passages. Only tombs of the noble during Shang and Zhou Period would have tomb passages. The nobler this person was, the more passages his tomb would boast. Therefore, archeologists believed that the tomb should belong to "a noble Lord of Yan State".

Although the tomb had been partly stolen, we still found over 200 pieces

与克罍（léi）。

盉与罍都是青铜酒器。

盉，一般前有长流，后有鋬和盖。1193号大墓中出土的克盉，圆顶盖，盖顶正中置半环形钮，盖沿处置一半环钮，上有环链与鋬（pàn）相连。侈口、方唇、直颈，前有管状流，后有兽首鋬，鼓腹、分裆，下接四圆柱足。盖钮两端各有一对凸目和角组成的兽面，盖沿及颈部均饰以云雷纹为地的四组长尾凤鸟纹，腹部光素。盖与器口内壁各铸有相同的43字阴文铭文。

罍，一般为深腹圆鼓，平底圆足，流行于商至西周。前不久通过海外拍卖回归的皿方罍，使这一相对少见的器型的知识得到普及。克罍，圆顶盖，盖顶正中置圆形捏手、平沿、方唇、

of funerary objects inside including sacrificial vessel, tools, weapons, chariots, horses, lacquer, cargo shells, and decorations. And among all, Ke He and Ke Lei are the most notable ones.

He and Lei are both bronze drinking vessel.

He generally has a long mouth, a cap and a handle. Ke He unearthed in the No.1193 tomb has a round cap. And in the center of the cap attached a half ring button connecting with the handle. The mouth is wide and the lip is square. The spout is like a tunnel and the handle is beast-head featured. The belly is protruding under which connected with four round-shaped feet. On the either side of the button on the cap is carved a pair of beast face with protruding eyes and horns. The rim of the cap and the spout are decorated with four pairs of phoenix and cloud-pattern and thunder-pattern. The belly is polished. Inscription containing 43 characters were carved on the cap, mouth and inside the belly.

Lei, normally with general deep and circular abdomen and round-shaped flat foot, was popular during Shang and Zhou Dynasty. Recently, we bought back the Minfang Lei in an overseas auction, enriching our knowledge about this rare kind of vessel. Ke Lei has a round cap. In

克罍
Ke Lei

短颈、圆肩，肩部两侧置半环状兽首耳，衔环。鼓腹下收，圈足微外撇，底内凹，下腹部一侧有兽首形鼻钮。盖与器肩部均饰有涡纹，颈部饰有两圈突弦纹，腹部涡纹下则有一周凹弦纹。盖与器口内壁各铸有相同的43字阴文铭文。

克盉、克罍的铭文字数相同，内容也相同，仅个别字的写法和行款字数有别，是目前琉璃河墓地出土文物中铭文最长的。铭文大意是说：周王说，太保，你用盟誓和清酒来供奉你的君王，我非常满意你的供享，命克做燕地的君侯……克到达燕地，接收了土地和管理机构，为纪念此事做此祭祖彝器。

多数学者根据铭文内容，结合史籍记载研究认为，两件铜器铭文中的"克"字，应指人名，即召公奭的元子，亦是这两件青铜礼器的做器者和拥有者，因此这两件青铜器便以他的名字冠名，分别称克盉与克罍（也可合称"克"器）。两件"克"器的发现殊为重要，如果学者对铭文的释读无误，那么它解决了两个重大历史问题：一是受王命实际到燕地就封的第一代燕侯，确实不是召公奭本人，

the center of the cap is carved a circular handle. The rim is flat, mouth square, spout short, shoulder round. On either side of the shoulder are carved two beast-head featured ears with a ring in the mouth of each beast. The upper part of the belly is bigger than the lower part and the feet are stretching outwards. On one side of the belly is carved a beast-shaped button. The cap and shoulder of the vessel are decorated with swirl-pattern. The neck is decorated with two rings of protruding string-pattern, and under the belly is carved a ring of sunk string-pattern. Inscription containing 43 characters were carved on the cap, mouth and inside the belly.

The inscriptions on Ke He and Ke Lei contain the same content and same characters. There are only small differences in the writing style of some characters. The inscriptions are the longest unearthed alongside the Liuli River. In the inscription, King of Zhou said: "Lord, you have served the king with commitments and wine, and I am very satisfied with your treatment. Therefore, I grant Yan area to you as an enfeoffement..." After Ke arrived Yan, he took over the land and administrative branches there and then built the vessel to honour the grant.

Most scholars and researchers believe that, according to the content of

使史界所持召公"亦以元子就封"的观点得到印证；二是召公奭的长子名"克"，他便是代召公奭到燕国实际就封的初代燕侯，填补了文献对西周燕国历史记载的不足。

赵婷
北京日报

the inscriptions and historic literatures, Ke should be the name of Lord Zhao's eldest son. Ke should also be the builder and owner of the two vessels. Therefore, the two vessels were named after him as Ke Lei and Ke He, or Ke wares. The discovery of the two "Ke wares" is very important. If scholars' interpretation of the inscriptions is correct, then it solved two major historical problems: first, Lord Zhao was not the first term of Lord Yan. Instead, his son, took his place and accepted the granted area. It proved the theory of "Lord Zhao's son took his place"; Second, Lord Zhao's son was called Ke. He was also the first term of Lord of Yan, making up for the rare recordings about the history of Yan State during Western Zhou Period.

Zhao Ting, Beijing Daily

北京城最早的美丽见证者：伯矩鬲

The Witness of the Beauty in Beijing: on Boju Li

伯矩鬲（lì），全名"牛头纹带盖伯矩鬲"，小名"牛头鬲"，被誉为中国最美的青铜器之一。

它身高约30厘米，在青铜器家庭里算不上"大块头"，但造型独特，工艺精美得令人惊叹，"牛气"十足：高

Boju Li (an ancient cooking tripod with hollow legs), also known as "Boju Li with ox-head pattern and a cap" or "Ox-head Li", is regarded as one of the most beautiful bronze wares in China.

It is about 30cm tall, relatively small compared to other bronze wares unearthed in China, while it is unique and exquisite with amazing craftsmanship. It is "bullish": the combination of perfect decoration of seven different styles of ox-head pattern, with two realistic ox-head statute as handles on its cap. These two oxes are mythical creatures with fangs, and the scale pattern above the horns showed the sacredness of majesty. Another three taurens were decorated in the round-shaped feet, with curled-up horns, gazing eyes, protruding noses, even making the ware more solemn.

Although ox may seem silly and dumb, it was the symbol of power during the Western Zhou Period. It

伯矩鬲
Boju Li

浮雕和浅浮雕相结合，通体装饰 7 个风格各异的牛首兽面纹——两个写实的牛首相背而立组成盖钮，居高临下；器盖的两个牛首则为神兽，口中獠牙及角上鳞纹都显现出不同凡物的威严；另有 3 个牛头装饰于浑圆的足部，长角上翘，巨眼圆睁，大鼻突起，更显庄重霸气。

看似憨拙的牛在商周时期作为力量的象征，是最高等级的祭品，其肩胛骨也常用来占卜，因此牛首是商周青铜器兽面纹中比较常见的题材。但如伯矩鬲这般多达 7 个牛首的造型却极为罕见，其高浮雕的立体风格也迥异于常见的平面化兽面纹。纹饰如此复杂的铜器一次浑铸成型，反映出西周时期极为高超的青铜冶铸水平，堪称燕国青铜艺术与工艺的巅峰之作。

更重要的是，伯矩鬲的盖内及颈内壁分别铸有相同的 15 字铭文："在戊辰，燕侯赐伯矩贝，用作父戊尊彝。"大意是，在某年某月的戊辰这一天，燕侯赏赐贵族伯矩海贝，伯矩为了纪念这一荣耀而铸造了这件尊贵的铜器，用于祭祀父亲戊。

商周时，南海出产的热带海贝因珍奇而被作为货币使用，赐贝就相当

was the best sacrifice, and its shoulder blades were commonly used to practice divination. Therefore, ox-head pattern was commonly-seen in the bronze ware made during Shang and Zhou Dynasty. Boju Li, with 7 ox-head statutes on it, was very rare and its pattern were carved in embossment. The complicated decorative pattern reflected the extremely high level of bronze casting during the Western Zhou Period, marking the culmination of bronze casting in Yan State at that time.

And, more importantly, same inscriptions containing 15 characters were both carved inside the pottery and inside its cap, read: "At Xuchen, the Lord of Yan State granted shells to Boju and Boju casted the Li to sacrifice to his father". It means: "at Xuchen (a time point during a day), the Lord of Yan granted Boju, a noble man at that time, some shells. And Boju built the bronze ware to sacrifice to his father."

During Shang and Zhou Dynasty, shells from South China Sea were used as currency. Therefore, granting shells means granting money. Nowadays, although there wasn't much literature about Boju, we could roughly identify Boju as a noble man at that time, as he built over 20 pieces of bronze wares when he was alive. He might be the relative of the royal in Yan State.

于赐钱。虽然没有更多文献资料能揭示这位伯矩何许人也，但目前发现的伯矩铸造的青铜礼器已达20余件，据此判断伯矩应贵为公卿，有可能是燕侯的亲族。

鬲是古代炊煮器，用于煮鱼、肉或粥，有圆体和方体两种，形状像鼎，特别之处在于其腹部和中空的足部相连接成袋状，既加大了容量，也扩大受火面积而容易加热。陶鬲是极具中原文化特色的器物，新石器时代已普及。铜鬲出现于商代，盛行于西周。西周时期，鬲也是标志贵族等级身份的重要器物，有时可代替鼎。

20世纪60年代，房山琉璃河一名村民在自家菜地挖菜窖时，无意中刨出了两件青铜器。此后经过20多年的考古发掘，不仅发现了燕国城址，还有贵族墓葬区，并出土了一批带有燕侯铭文的青铜器，从而确定这里就是西周时期燕国的都城所在。今天，我们说北京有三千年建城史，琉璃河便是开疆拓土的第一章，而这里出土的伯矩鬲以及堇鼎、克盉、克罍等珍贵文物，便是历尽沧桑而不变的恒久见证。

伯矩鬲收藏于首都博物馆，并曾

Li was used for cooking fish, meat or porridge in the ancient time, either in circular or square shape. And its main feature lies in the package-like connection between its belly and feet, expanding the volume and the area being heated. Pottery Li was featured by cultural characteristics in the central part of China and it was popular since the neolithic period. Bronze Li was first made during Shang Dynasty and got popular in the Western Zhou Period. During the West Zhou Period, Li was also a ware demonstrating the identity of a noble man and sometimes it could be used to replace Ding.

In the 1960s, a villager living by the Liuli River in Fangshan District in Beijing, inadvertently dug out two bronzes. After more than 20 years of archaeological excavations, we have discovered not only the site, but also the tombs of noble men in Yan State and unearthed a batch of bronze wares with inscriptions inside. And we believed this site to be the capital of Yan State during the Western Zhou Period. Today, we often say that Beijing enjoys a history of over 3,000 years, and the origin of the history was unveiled alongside the Liuli River. Boju Li, Jin Ding and Ke He and Ke Lei are all witnesses to this period of history.

Boju Li has been collected in the Capital Museum and was once in

长期展出，最近因展览调整而暂时撤下，不久就将回到展厅。目前在它的"娘家"——房山琉璃河西周燕都遗址博物馆，可以见到精美的复制品。

赵婷

北京日报

display. Rencently, it was removed from the display due to some adjustments. It will soon be back in the exhibition hall. Now we could see the replica of this masterpiece in the Site Museum for the Capital of Yan State in the west of Liuli River, Fangshan District, Beijing, where the bronze ware was originally unearthed.

Zhao Ting, Beijng Daily

小钱币，大艺术

Small Coins with Great Art

古代铜质辅币，也就是老百姓俗称的铜钱，是指秦汉以后的各类方孔圆钱。方孔圆钱的铸造时期一直延伸到清末民初，大多数是以铜合金为材料铸造的，是我国古代钱币中最常见的一种。本次文物普查收获的这枚古钱币流通于北宋徽宗崇宁年间（1102—1106），因而称为崇宁通宝。它在当时社会生活中所起的作用就不赘述了，

Ancient copper fractional currency, commonly known as the copper coin, refers to the various circular coins with a square hole in the middle after Qin and Han Dynasty. The coinage of this kind of coins did not disappear until the beginning of the Republic of China (1912 - 1949), or about in the late Qing dynasty. Most of them were made of copper alloy. Circular coins with a square hole are one of the most commonly seen ancient currencies. The piece of coin we found during the census on cultural relics was once circulated during Chongning Period under Huizong's reign in Song Dynasty. (FIG. 1-1) Here we are not going to give you more details about its role at that time. Today, we will appreciate this piece from an aspect of art.

In terms of shape, the coin is circular with a square hole in the middle. It seems not special at all. But in China, circle is regarded as the most beautiful thing in the world. The ancient believe that all the beautiful things are circular. They could only be

崇宁通宝

Chongning Tongbao

今天我们仅从艺术的角度对它进行一番欣赏。

从造型上看，外面一个圆，中间一个正方形，似乎没有什么。但在中国，则把圆看作美的最高境界。古人认为，"天体至圆，万物做到极精妙者，无有不圆。……以至一艺一术，必极圆而后登峰造极"。圆的出现，会令人想到完美、和谐、无限和包容。

方形，给人坚实、明确、庄严、秩序的感觉，同样是中国文化的重要象征符号。中国的一些重要建筑如宫殿、庙宇，以及许多吉祥图案，都有方形元素在内。

这枚崇宁通宝，巧妙地将圆与方结合在一起。内部的正方形端庄典雅，给人以稳重的安全感；而外部包环的圆边，又给人流动统一的视觉感受。静中有动，柔中见刚，既符合货币的特性，也给人以视觉上的享受。

再来看看钱币的布局。

对称和平衡在中国传统美学中具有不可替代的作用。这枚钱币以方孔的四条直线为基准，每个边都对应一个汉字，上下匀称，左右和谐，给人以平衡、周正的艺术美感。

这枚方孔圆钱给我们带来造型和

beautiful after they become circular. Circle means perfect, harmonious, infinite and inclusive, while square means solid, specific, solemn and regulation, making it another important cultural symbol in China. Some of China's important architectures, such as palaces, temples and many auspicious patterns, contain squares as an important designing element.

And this coin cleverly combined circle and square together in one piece. The square hole in the coin could give us a sense of security and the circular modelling would make us feel the beauty of flowing. We could see dynamism in the stationary coin and softness in the clean-cut square hole, which is not only in line with the characteristics of the currency, but also brings about visual enjoyment.

Now let's take a look at the layout of the coin.

Symmetry and balance have played an irreplaceable role in Chinese traditional aesthetics. This coin is symmetrical with a Chinese character next to each side of the square hole in the same distance, making it harmonious with the art of equilibrium and geometric aesthetic feeling.

The shape and layout of the circular coin with a square hole is beautiful, but it has even more implications. What is

布局很美的感觉，但这仅仅是它的外在表现形式。艺术是什么？艺术是用形象来反映现实但比现实有典型性的意识形态。外圆内方钱币的统一制型，始于秦始皇时期，因而深深打上了天圆地方宇宙观的烙印。这个宇宙观认为，皇帝是圆，是天，即天子；臣民是方，是地。"主执圆，臣处方。方圆不易，国乃昌"，反映了帝王期望江山永固的社会意识形态。中国帝制存在了两千多年，外圆内方的货币也流通了两千多年，直到最后一个封建王朝清朝灭亡后才退出历史舞台。

中国是世界上最早使用钱币的国家之一，有四千年的历史。最早的货币是自然界的海贝，春秋战国时又出现了以生产工具镈、刀、纺纱轮（或玉环）为原型的布币、刀币、圆钱等青铜铸造的货币，在秦朝被统一为外圆内方的制型。从崇尚镈、刀、纺纱轮等具体形态，到改用方、圆几何图形，从美学角度讲，是认识上从具象到抽象的深入，实现了艺术上的一大跨越。

我们从古钱币造型、布局中领略了形态美和布局美，但如将历朝历代的钱币集中在一起就会发现，这些形

art? Art is to use image to reflect the ideology which stems from but goes beyond the reality. A square earth and spherical heavens. The modelling of the coin could be dated back to the rein of the first emperor in Qin Dynasty. Therefore, it is a vivid reflection of the world view of "a square earth and spherical heavens". According to this world view, the emperor is the circle, namely the heaven, and his subjects are the square, namely the earth." The emperor is the circle and his subjects the square. If this is not changed, the country will be in peace." The poem reflected the feudal ideology of perpetual reign. The Imperial China existed for 2000 years, and so did the circular currency with square hole. It did not disappear until Qing Dynasty, the last feudal dynasty in China.

China is the world's first country to use coins. The currency circulation in our country enjoys a history of about 4,000 years. The earliest currency included seashells collected from the Nature. And during the Spring and Autumn Period and the Warring States Period, cloth coin, knife-shaped coin and circular coin as the prototype of tools such as knife, spinning wheel (or yuhuan) appeared. And in Qin Dynasty, all kinds of currencies were unified into the same modelling, namely circular coins with square hole. The shift from advocating specific shape

状完全一致，大小几乎相同的铜钱给人们的视觉感受竟然是那么不同。不同之处是上面的文字，与西方以图案图像来装饰钱币不同，中国一开始用青铜制钱，就与文字结下了不解之缘。钱币上的文字被称为"钱文"。

钱文集中国书法之大成，有笔法圆融平正的篆书，有韵味十足的隶书，有气势浑厚的楷书，有放纵流动的行书，还有豪迈奔放的草书，自然给人的感受不一样。

文字是要靠书写发挥作用的，而能把书写发展成艺术的民族，在世界上寥寥可数。中国书法就是跨越几千年的古老艺术。书法，是在洁白的纸和其他可书写的载体上，靠毛笔运动的灵活多变和水墨的丰富性，通过线条、结体、章法等展现出千姿百态的美感。

作为一种表现性艺术，书法家个人的生活感受、学识、修养都会通过运笔的疾厉、徐缓、飞动、顿挫，将情感、情绪悄悄地折射出来，极具个性化。秦朝李斯书写的"秦半两"篆书钱文纤细有力，气韵飞动；王莽书写的悬针篆钱文细挺劲健，骨力中含；唐朝欧阳询写的"开元通宝"，文体

such as knife, spinning wheel, etc. to the geometry of square, circular, from the aesthetic point of view, is the deepening of recognition from the concrete to the abstract, registering a large step forward of art.

When we appreciate the beauty of the shape and layout of the ancient coins, we would have different feeling when comparing coins of same shape from different dynasties. The characters carved on the coins are different from each other. In the west, coins were often decorated with images, while in China, characters were adopted. Characters on the coins were called "Qian Wen" (literally: coin character), which means inscriptions on the coin.

Coin character is the crystalization of calligraphy, integrating seal character with rounded strokes, clerical script with lasting appeal, regular script with great power, wild running-hand script, and bold cursive script, each representing a different feeling.

Characters were only meaningful when written down, and rare countries could turn calligraphy into an art. And Chinese calligraphy is an art lasting for thousands of years. When practicing calligraphy, one should take a piece of white paper, and write on it with a flexible brush and rich ink. Through the strokes, structure and style of characters, we could see the rhyme of beauty.

刚劲峻拔，结构开朗，既是书法的杰作，也是古钱币中的珍品。

再来看看这枚"崇宁通宝"，这四字钱文是北宋皇帝徽宗赵佶用瘦金书亲笔题写。赵佶虽然治国无能，葬送了北宋江山，但在书画上却颇有造诣。他糅合了唐人薛稷、褚遂良、宋朝黄庭坚等大书法家之长，自创出了这种"瘦金体"，在中国书法史上占有一席之地。

从这枚崇宁通宝可以看到，瘦金书的特点是横画收笔带钩，竖画收笔带点，撇如匕首，捺如切刀，竖钩细长，连笔处好像游丝行空，接近行书，给人一种曼舞轻歌、清新优美之感，所谓"天骨遒美，逸趣霭然"；又具有强烈的个性色彩，"如屈铁断金"。这种书体，在前人的书法作品中未曾出现过。赵佶的瘦金体在当时就大受好评，他题写的"崇宁通宝""大观通宝""政和通宝"一面世就很受欢迎。在蜀中，竟然出现了人们因为太喜欢这些御书钱而藏匿不出，造成铜钱匮乏，不得不加紧铸造铁币补充流通不足的局面。一首诗记载了当时的情形：

When practicing the expressive art, calligrapher's personal life experience, knowledge, accomplishment could be seen in the flowing stokes, which is highly personalized. Li Si in Qin Dynasty wrote the characters "Qin Ban Liang" on the coin in seal script with great nicety. While Wang Mang's calligraphy seems more powerful. Ouyang Xun in Tang Dynasty wrote "Kai Yuan Tong Bao" on the coin at that time, which is not only a masterpiece of calligraphy, but also a masterpiece of coinage history.

Let's take a look at the "Chong Ning Tong Bao". These four characters were written in slim style font by Zhao Ji, also known as Emperor Huizong, in the Northern Song Dynasty. Although Zhao Ji was not competitive at all as an emperor, he was quite gifted for calligraphy and Chinese painting. He drew on the strengths of other calligraphers including Xue Ji and Zhu Suiliang from Tang Dynasty, Huang Tingjian from Song Dynasty and created the unique slim style font, gaining a ground in the history of Chinese calligraphy.

Seen from the "Chong Ning Tong Bao", we could see that the characteristics of the new kind of script is the sharpness. And the connection between strokes is like thread, just like the running-hand script, generating a sense of beauty and rhyme. Just as people put it, "the slim

风流天子出崇观，

铁画银钩字字端；

闻道蜀中铜货少，

任凭顽铁买江山。

今天，瘦金体依然影响着我们的工作和生活。有人研究后认为，现代汉字字体中的"宋体"就是模仿瘦金体的神韵而演变出来的。

据传在宋代的公文来往中，来自全国各地的公文字体不统一，大臣秦桧认为这样不够严谨、规范，于是动了心思，加之他特别对徽宗赵佶的瘦金体研究颇深，在赵佶字的基础上创造出了一种独特字体，横细竖宽，工整划一，简便易学，这便是后世的"宋体"了。随后，秦桧开始用自己创造的新体字誊写奏章，引起了赵佶的注意。徽宗由此下令秦桧将其新体字的书写模板发往全国各地，要求全国统一按模板字体写公文，这种字体很快得到了推广。这种字体最初曾称为"秦体"，后世百姓虽唾弃秦桧为奸臣，但没人愿意放弃秦桧发明的稳重、端庄、秀丽的字体结构，便改称"宋体"。

直到清朝末年，钱塘人丁辅之、

style font is strong and interesting.", the new style of font is very unique, and it seems to be "strong enough to cut up a gold bar". Prior to Emperor Huizong, no one wrote in such a style. Therefore, this font was very popular at that time. The "Chong Ning Tong Bao", "Da Guan Tong Bao" and "Zheng He Tong Bao" written in this font were very popular too. In the central part of Shu area (today's Sichuan province), some people would hide these coins because they liked this font too much, leading to a paucity of this currency in the market. Just as the poem put it:

"The distinguished emperor wrote the characters on the coin and his calligraphy is so beautiful and powerful.

In the central part of Shu area, people will hide the currency because they like the writing, and they could only buy things with metal."

Today, slim style font still influences our work and life. According to some researches, Song typeface comes out of the slim style font by imitating its charisma.

It is said that at the beginning of Song Dynasty, fonts used in official documents are completely different. And Qin Hui, a minister, believed that they should be more rigorous and standardized.

丁善之等人集宋代刻本，仿刻了一种印刷活字字体，横竖粗细相等，字呈长方形，清秀美观，这便是"仿宋体"。有宋一代的书法对后世的影响也由此可见一斑。

本次文物普查发现的这枚小小的钱币，不禁令人感叹它的造型、设计、书法等各个方面都蕴含着古人对世界观的认识，对哲理的阐述，以及对美的感受。

郝爽君

中国国家博物馆

Therefore, he studied Emperor Huizong's slim style font and created a new font, which is known as Song typeface nowadays on the basis of slim style font. Later, Qin Hui started to write in the new font, attracting Emperor Huizong's attention. Then Emperor Huizong announced a decree to promote the new font created by Qin Hui and required that all documents nationwide should be written in this new font. The font was initially called "Qin typeface". Although people spitted on Qin Hui, no one would abandon this solid, beautiful, prudent, dignified font created by him. Therefore, they renamed the font as "Song typeface".

At the end of Qing Dynasty, Ding Fuzhi, Ding Shanzhi etc. from Qiantang (in today's Zhejiang province), collected many block-printed editions and created a new font based on Song typeface, known to the future generation as "the-imitation-of-Song-Dynasty-style typeface". We could clearly see the influence of calligraphy in Song Dynasty on the future generations.

During the national census on cultural relics, we could see our ancestors' philosophies, sense of beauty and their world view through the small piece of coins from the angle of shape, design and calligraphy on it.

Hao Shuangjun, National museum of China

第二编
Second series

文物背后的故事

玉瓷润泽触古韵
jade and porcelain cultural relics

"没有金刚钻，别揽瓷器活"
——记首都博物馆文物普查中发现的几件早期锔瓷工艺实物

"Without Diamond, One Should Not Mend the Porcelains"
— On Porcelains Mended with Ju Craft Discovered During the National Census on Cultural Relics

锔瓷，是一种古老的瓷器修补手艺，是指将残破的瓷器碎片以金属锔钉接合，使瓷器拼合完好并能够继续使用的技艺。锔瓷的具体方法，是先将破碎的瓷器碎片依其原始状态拼对、接合完好，并用绳子捆扎牢固，根据瓷器的破损程度和具体情况，在瓷器外壁接缝两侧等距离相对应处，设计好若干组打眼位置，然后分别用金刚钻在预设位置打出成组的孔眼（孔眼深度须掌握好，不可将瓷器钻透），再将书钉形状的金属锔钉的两脚，分别敲入接缝两侧成组的两个孔眼中，根据打孔的多少分别依组敲入，使金属锔钉将瓷器破裂的两部分连接，固

Ju, an ancient porcelain mending craft, refers to using metal nails to joint the broken fragments of the porcelain, thus to renovate the porcelain for future use. Firstly, the broken porcelain pieces should be jointed according to its original status and then tied up by ropes. According to the damage degree and the specific situation of a porcelain, groups of drilling positions should be marked on the joint of both sides on the exterior walls of the ware in corresponding equidistance. Then drill the marked positions on both sides with a diamond drill (The drilling depth must be carefully controlled, lest the porcelain is drilled through). Then fix the staple feet of the metal nails into the holes drilled by the diamond on both sides of the joint to firmly connect two

定牢固，最后用以白瓷泥、石灰粉、糯米汁、鸡蛋清等调制而成的白泥，将铜钉与孔眼之间可能出现的孔隙抹平、填实，待干燥后起到进一步补漏、紧固的作用。瓷器锔补完成后，可做到盛水而不漏，基本不影响正常使用。锔瓷在旧时又称"锔盆"或"锔碗"，是三百六十行中重要的手艺行当之一。锔盆碗的匠人们，通常挑着担子走街串巷，吆喝买卖。担子两头分别挑着带有抽屉的小木柜，里面装有锤子、剪刀等工具，以及必不可缺的一把钻子。因钻头是以金钢石做就，且锔盆碗最重要的工具非它莫属，故俗话有"没有金刚钻，别揽瓷器活"一说。

fragments of the porcelain. Finally, we should use the white mud mixed by white porcelain clay, lime powder, sticky rice juice, egg white to fill in and then float the gap possibly occurred between the holes and nails. Therefore, after the porcelain is dried, it was mended and fixed firmly. After mended, the porcelain would not leak and could be used normally. In the past, Ju porcelain, also called "Ju basin" or "Ju bowl", is one of important crafts among all traditional professions in China. Basin and bowl menders always wandered about the streets with their burdens, shouting to attract consumers. On both ends of the burden respectively hanged a small wooden cabinet with many drawers filled with tools such as hammers, scissors, as well as a diamond drill which was crucial to the mending. The drill was made of diamond, and it was the most important tool to mend a porcelain. Therefore, today there is a Chinese saying goes" without the diamond, one should not mend the porcelain". When mending the porcelain, the mender would clamp the porcelain with his two knees, with one hand firmly holding the drill pipe and fixing the drill to a certain point on the porcelain, and with the other hand pulling the drill horizontally, thus to allow the belt to drive the diamond to drill a small hole on the porcelain. The mending work requires meticulous patience, so most of

首都博物馆藏《三百六十行》画册中的锔瓷手艺人形象

image of porcelain mender in the *Traditional Chinese Professions Album* kept in the Capital Museum

匠人操作时，用两膝将瓷器夹稳，一手牢牢扶住钻杆，将钻头固定在瓷器上某点，另一手左右拉动弓钻，使皮带带动钻头快速旋转，在瓷器上打出小孔。因锔盆、锔碗需要细致耐心，所以在旧京从事这一行的多是老人，据说当年他们多居住在城南郊的永定门外。

由于中国古代文献对于手工业技艺记载的缺失，以至于我们很难从传世文献中找到锔瓷工艺究竟出现于何时。目前能够看到的最早提及中国古代锔瓷工艺的文献，均不早于明代。明代医药学家李时珍编写的《本草纲目》一书，在介绍"金刚石"时，有"其砂可以钻玉补瓷，故谓之钻"的描述。《本草纲目》成书于明万历六年（1578），是时已届明末，如果据此判断中国的锔瓷技艺始于明末，显然不能令人信服。在邻国日本的古代文献中，也提到过中国的锔瓷工艺，如江户时代一位名叫伊藤东涯的儒学家在1727年所著的《蚂蟥绊茶瓯记》中记载，日本室町时代的幕府将军足利义政（1436—1490）藏有一件南宋龙泉窑瓷碗，因碗上出现冲裂，便派

menders were old men in the past. They were said to live outside the Yongding Gate, in the southern suburb of Beijing.

Due to the lack of Chinese ancient literature for this handicraft skills, we can hardly find specific information about the exact origin time of this mending craft. And the literatures about this craft were all compiled no earlier than the Ming Dynasty. Li Shizhen, a medical expert in Ming dynasty, introduced the "diamond" in his masterpiece *Compendium of Materia Medica (《本草纲目》)*, describing it as "diamond grits can drill on jade and mend porcelains, and it's called diamonds". *Compendium of Materia Medica* was written in the sixth year under Emperor Wanli's reign in the end of Ming Dynasty (1578). Therefore, it was not convincing to define that the craft derived from the end of Ming Dynasty. The ancient literature in the neighboring country Japan also mentioned this mending craft in China. For example, during the Edo Period, a man named Ito Tokayi, a Confucianism wrote about an anecdote about the craft in his masterpiece *The story of the cracked tea cup (《蚂蟥绊茶瓯记》)* in A.D. 1727. Japan's Muromachi Period, Ashikaga Shogunate (1436-1490) had a porcelain bowl made in Longquan Kiln in Southern Song Dynasty. Due to

人将它带到中国，想再找寻同样的一件带回，无奈无法找到，使者只好请中国的锔瓷匠人将那只残碗锔补后带回日本。足利义政复见此碗，看到硕大的金属锔钉如同蚂蟥一般趴附于碗的外壁，不由连呼"蚂蟥蚂蟥"，并大为赞赏其精妙的锔瓷技艺，从此该茶碗便被称为"蚂蟥绊"，并因此名震东瀛。作为一件传世国宝，"蚂蟥绊"茶碗现在日本东京国立博物馆珍藏至今。足利义政时代相当于我国明朝的正统至成化时期，属明代前期。这则典故，恐怕是目前能够看到的文献记录中对中国古代锔瓷工艺的最早描述了，并有存世实物印证，因此它至少确证无疑地将中国锔瓷技艺存在的时间节点推进到了明代前期。然而，

日本东京国立博物馆藏南宋龙泉窑"蚂蟥绊"碗
"leeches" bowl made in Longquan Kiln in Nansong Dynasty, now kept in the National Museum in Tokyo

the cracking appeared on the bowl, he ordered some one to bring the bowl to China and hoped to get a same one back but finally failed. Out of choices, the emissary had to ask a porcelain mender to mend the bowl and then brought it back to Japan. Ashikaga saw the big metal nail covering on the exterior wall of the bowl, and he couldn't help shouting "Leeches! Leeches!". He highly praised the subtle porcelain-mending craft. And the bowl was henceforth referred to as "leeches teacup", and became famous in Japan. As a national treasure passed down from ancient times, leeches teacup has been now kept in National Museum in Tokyo, Japan. When Japan was reigned by Ashikaga, China was during Zhengtong period and Chenghua Period, the early stage of the Ming dynasty. The allusions might be the earliest literature recorded to describe this craft with the culture relic as physical evidence. Therefore, at least it confirmed that the craft was created no later than the early stage of the Ming Dynasty. However, we still don't know the exact time when this craft was created.

And we haven't seen any porcelains mended in this way before the Ming Dynasty. Here we have to make it clear that the time when the porcelain was mended is not necessarily the same with the time when it was made. For example,

文物背后的故事
stories behind cultural relics

铜瓷技术最早出现于何时，仍然难觅其踪。

目前存世早于明代的、经过铜补的瓷器尚能见到。但这里需要特别说明的是，当面对一件经过铜补的瓷器时，我们不能草率地将瓷器的修补时间，与其制作年代混为一谈。前文提到的日本国宝——被称为"蚂蟥绊"的南宋龙泉窑青釉瓷碗，即是制作于南宋，铜修于明代。类似的例子还有不少，天津博物馆收藏有一件元代青花缠枝牡丹纹兽耳大罐，器身上留有条带状的铜孔（铜钉已被摘除），由于是传世品，这件残损元代瓷器的具体修补时间已无法确知，只能凭借经验，对铜钉孔的设置方式、铜钉孔内残留物的氧化状况等进行综合分析后予以判断——其铜补的时间不会很早，可能在清代甚至更晚。文物具有传世性，后人可对前人留下的物品不断传承使用、代代相延，尤其对于某些被认为比较珍贵的前朝器物，一旦在后世使用的过程中发生损坏，通常不会将其遗弃，而是加以修补并继续保藏，这种现象在瓷器传世的过程中不在少数。有经验的文物工作者都知道，从

the above mentioned leeches teacup was made in Longquan Kiln during the southern Song Dynasty while mended during Ming Dynasty. Similar instances are numerous. For example, stipe-shape drills could be found in a blue-and-white peony-pattern tank decorated with beast ears (Nails have been removed). The specific mending time of the porcelain could not be determined as it was handed down from generation to generation. According to our past experience, we comprehensively analyzed the setting of nails and the residue oxidation condition in the drill hole and concluded that it was mended in Qing dynasty or later. Cultural relics could be handed down from generation to generation. When they were worn out, people would not easily abandon them especially those made during previous dynasties which were normally considered more precious.

天津博物馆藏元代青花缠枝牡丹纹兽耳大罐

blue and while peony-pattern tank with beast ears made in Yuan Dynasty, kept in Tianjin Museum

实践来看，当下无论在博物馆，还是在民间藏家手中，我们所能见到的锔瓷实物，多属传世品而非科学发掘品。这些传世的锔补瓷器，经手锔补的时间多为清代或近代，其中即便有怀疑是明代甚至更早时期锔补的瓷器个例，亦因缺乏科学客观的有关锔补时代判定的参考证据，难以被确证并采信。基于此种原因，我们要找寻锔补时代早于明代的、能够反映早期锔瓷工艺发展状况的实物，以求进一步找到中国古代锔瓷工艺出现时间的线索，只能寄主要希望于考古发掘材料。然而这样的考古实物资料，我们能找到吗？

事情出现转机，竟得缘于近两年在全国范围内广泛开展的国有可移动文物普查工作。2015 年是国家第一次可移动文物普查工作在北京地区的大力推进之年，作为北京地区最大的地方综合性历史类博物馆，为保质、保量、圆满完成本单位文物普查的总体工作目标，首都博物馆的可移动文物普查工作在这一年中紧锣密鼓、有条不紊地紧张开展。由于历史原因，首都博物馆收藏有一批北京地区历年来出土发掘的地下文物，在此次普查

Instead, people would mend these wares and continued to preserve them, which was not a rare case for porcelains. Experienced antiquarian would infer that, from our practice, all the porcelains mended with this craft no matter they are in the museum or in the hands of private collectors, were handed down rather than discovered from archaeological discovery. And most of these porcelains were mended in Qing Dynasty or even later in the modern time. Even though there were indeed several porcelains mended in Ming Dynasty or even earlier, but it was not evident because of the shortage of scientific and objective historic materials. For this reason, if we wanted to find any physical evidence which could reflect the development of mending craft earlier than Ming Dynasty and lead us to the exact time of the birth of this craft, we could only rely on historical materials from archaeological discovery. However, could we be able to find such materials?

A turnaround finally occurred in the national census on moveable relics during the past two years. 2015 witnessed the endeavor of the first national census on movable cultural relics census work. The Capital Museum, as the largest local comprehensive museum of history in Beijing has carried out the national census in an orderly manner, in order to ensure

前一直未及详细清理和进行完善的登记入账工作，它们被集中存放在馆外库房的旧木箱中，"尘封"多年。在2015年开展的可移动文物普查工作中，这批出土文物首先得到细致的清点和整理，并严格依照相关标准开展登记入账工作。笔者在参与整理这批出土文物的过程中，竟有幸从中意外发现了几件珍贵的能够反映早期锔瓷技艺具体工艺状况的实物资料。它们的发现对于中国瓷器锔补工艺出现时间的探索和推定，具有重要意义。

故事还须从1969年说起。这年11月，在位于北京房山县良乡镇南街的县药材批发部院内，因动土施工，在距地表3米深处发现一处元代窖藏，从中共出土瓷器35件、铁器13件、铜器4件。在出土的35件瓷器中，有元代钧窑瓷器共14件，其中1件为双耳瓷罐，1件为瓷钵，其余12件均为瓷盘。该窖藏的发现及出土文物情况，已在《考古》1972年第6期以简报形式发表，简报标题为《北京良乡发现的一处元代窖藏》。

时隔46年之后，在首都博物馆新馆的某间库房内，上述元代窖藏出

the quality and the successful completion of national census on movable cultural relics. Due to historical reasons, some cultural relics were kept in the Capital Museum without clear registration after they were unearthed. Before the census, they had been kept in old wooden cabinets in warehouse outside the museum, covered by dust for many years. During the national census on movable cultural relics in 2015, this batch of cultural relics were firstly checked and sorted out and then registered in accordance with relevant regulations and standards. I also participated in the census and it was my luck to find some pieces of physical evidence to reflect the development of the mending craft in the early stage. They were of great significance for us to determine the exact time when this craft was created in China.

The story could be dated back to 1969. In November of that year, a hoard of Yuan Dynasty was found 3 meters underground in a well in the Materials Wholesale Department of a county hospital, south street, Liangxiang County, Fangshan District, Beijing. In the hoard, we found 35 pieces of porcelains, 13 pieces of ironware and 4 pieces of bronze vessels. Among the 35 pieces of porcelains, 14 were made in Jun Kiln, 1 of them were double-ear porcelain, 1 of

土的 14 件钧窑瓷器中的 11 件，即瓷盘 10 件、瓷钵 1 件，被从旧木箱中小心取出，摆放在文物普查工作人员的面前（其余 3 件钧窑瓷器已于 1969 年 11 月办理了登记入库手续）。10 件钧窑瓷盘的形状基本相同，大小不等，敞口，矮圈足，口径 20~23.2 厘米，高 3.6~4.7 厘米，胎厚而釉浓。盘外下部近底处，大部分不挂釉，其中 4 件瓷盘的盘底外有墨书题记"兀剌赤王□"五字。当年的发掘简报对该五字题记及其所反映出的相关问题进行了介绍与讨论，简报认为，"'兀剌'按《华夷译语》鸟兽门译为驿马，'赤'为所有者或所掌者之意。《华夷译语》人事门译'兀剌赤'为马夫……可知'兀剌赤'乃指管理驿马者，亦即驿站中之小吏"，"很可能这个窖藏就是元代良乡驿站的小吏所埋藏的"。在今天看来，此结论无疑是中肯、合理的。几件带有墨书题记的钧窑瓷盘的发现，对于窖藏坑埋藏时代的判定及器物主人身份的推定，具有重要意义。

在对这 11 件钧窑瓷器进行整理的过程中，经仔细观察，首都博物馆的

them was a bowl and another 12 were plates. And this discovery was briefly published in the Issue.6 of *Archaeological Journal* in 1972, and titled: *Yuan Hoard was found in Liangxiang, Beijing.*

46 years later, in a room of the warehouse of the Capital Museum, 11 out of 14 porcelains made in Jun Kiln, namely 10 plates and 1 bowl, were carefully taken out of the old wooden cabinet, put in front of the personnel in charge of census in the museum (the other three pieces of porcelain had already been registered in November 1969). The 10 porcelain plates were all basically in the same shape with different sizes, open mouths and short ring foot. The mouth diameter was 20-23.2 cm, and the height was 3.6 to 4.7 cm. The body of porcelain was thick and the glaze was also thick. The lower part of the plates near the bottom almost wore no glaze. 4 pieces of plates had inscriptions outside the bottom, reading *"Wuci Chi Wang"* written with ink. And the briefing about the discovery in the Journal had introduced and discussed about the inscription and its meaning behind. According to the briefing, "Wuci" means "post horse" and "Chi" means "groom". Therefore, "Wuci Chi" could refer to "groom", namely the official in charge of the courier station. In the briefing, it was claimed that "The hoard

工作人员发现其中有3件瓷盘和1件瓷钵，原本已经残破，但器身上留有明显的铁锈块或锈斑痕迹。这些尚存的锈块应是铁质锔钉，虽然腐蚀比较严重，但有些仍完整地趴附于器物表面，骑跨在断裂瓷器的接口之上，仍然起着接合瓷片的作用；有些锔钉已锈烂无存，但器物外壁上的锈斑仍清

1969年房山县良乡镇南街药材批发部院内出土元代钧窑瓷盘中的一种

porcelain plate made in Jun Kiln during Yuan Dynasty, unearthed in 1969 in the yard of Medicine Wholesale Department, Nan Street, Liangxiang Township, Fangshan County, Beijing

晰可见，在器壁的接痕两侧留有对称的锔钉孔，孔内有锈渣。由此可以判定，这4件钧窑瓷器均是经过锔补的器物，它们是难得一见的元代以金属锔钉修补瓷器的重要实物。它们的发现，至少可将古代锔瓷工艺的出现时

was created by an official in the courier station in Liangxiang County during the Yuan Dynasty". And this conclusion is definitely objective and reasonable viewing from today. And later we also found some plates with inscription made in Jun Kiln, which were essential to determine the time of the hoard and the identity of the owner.

When sorting out the 11 pieces of porcelains, after careful observation, staff from the Capital Museum found that there were three pieces of porcelain plate and 1 piece of porcelain bowl already broken, while there were obvious traces of rust on the body of these porcelains. The remaining rust should be iron nails. Although they are heavily corroded, there were still several complete nails covering the surface of wares, which jointed the fragments of porcelain. Some nails had been completely corroded and thus disappeared, but the rust on the exterior wall of the porcelain was still clearly visible. And we also found symmetrical drill holes on both sides of the wall, with rust in these holes. Therefore, we could safely draw a conclusion that this 4 pieces of porcelain had been mended with the Ju craft, and they were very rare and important as they were physical evidence of porcelain mended with this craft during the Yuan Dynasty. The discovery of this

间上推至元代。

无独有偶，在工作中经查阅相关资料，笔者发现在北京地区近年的考古发掘中，居然也有类似的发现。如北京市文物研究所于 2006 年 10 月发掘了平谷区马坊镇河北村西的 5 座元墓，在部分墓葬中出土了器物上带有锔钉孔的瓷器。其中 1 号墓中出土一件天蓝色釉钧窑碗（M1：4），碗上有锔钉孔 6 处（3 组）；2 号墓出土一件磁州窑白地黑花碗（M2：5），碗壁上有锔钉孔 6 处（3 组）；8 号墓出土一件白地黑花"清净道德"文字四系瓶（M8：8），瓶身上有锔钉孔 18 处（9 组）。这些出土文物及前述首都博物馆藏元代锔瓷实物的发现，意外填补了早期锔瓷工艺研究上的资料空白，这无疑让文物工作者们兴奋、雀跃。

通过对首都博物馆藏元代钧窑锔瓷实物做近距离的细致考察，并结合前述其他相关出土文物的发现情况，我们可对元代锔瓷技术的整体发展和具体工艺状况试做分析与讨论，并得出初步结论。第一，在首都博物馆整理的这批 11 件元代钧窑瓷器中，其中

batch of porcelains had pushed the exact time of the birth of Ju craft back to the Yuan Dynasty.

Similarly, when looking for related materials during the census, the author found similar discoveries in recent archaeological excavations in Beijing. For example, in October 2006, the Beijing Municipal Institute of Cultural Relics unearthed 5 tombs of Yuan Dynasty in the west of Hebei Village, Mafang Town, Pinggu District, Beijing. In these tombs, they had found some porcelains with nails on them. In the Tomb No.1, an azure-glazed porcelain bowl made in Jun Kiln (M1:4) was unearthed. There are 6 drill holes on them. In the Tomb No.2, a white porcelain bowl with black-flower pattern made in Cizhou Kiln (M2:5) was unearthed. There are 6 drill holes (3 pairs) on it. In the Tomb No.8, a white porcelain bottle with black-flower pattern and characters "Serenity and Morality" was unearthed (M8:8). There are 18 drill holes (9 pairs) on it. These unearthed relics mentioned above in the Capital Museum unexpectedly made up for the shortage of materials when studying the Ju craft in the ancient China. It made all antiquarians excited.

Through close and meticulous investigation on the porcelains which

有 4 件经过锔修，数量已非个别。结合锔补瓷器在元代墓葬中亦被多次发现的情况，种种迹象表明，对毁损的某类瓷器进行锔补修复、使之能够继续使用的行为，在元代并非偶然现象，似乎在一定程度上已成为市井习俗、社会传统。第二，根据观察，首都博物馆所藏经过锔修的这 4 件钧窑瓷器，其锔合方式一致，并且与明清时期广泛采用的以铁质锔钉进行锔补的方法相比，二者基本已无明显差异，由此看来，明清时期的锔瓷技术是由元代直接继承、发展而来，并且这种锔补技术在元代已经发展得比较成熟，得到较为广泛的应用。第三，在首都博物馆收藏的几件元代锔补瓷器的断裂接口处，以及锔钉孔周围等位置，发现了以白色瓷泥填补的痕迹。这种情况说明，元代的锔瓷工艺已使用了以白瓷泥进行缝隙填补和加固的方法，这与明清时期相比亦无较大差异，工艺的传承性十分明显。第四，清代锔瓷实物的存世量较大，通过观察与对比可以发现，清代对一件瓷器的锔补，通常使用的锔钉数量较多，锔钉的设置比较密集（故有"蜈蚣钯"之说，

were mended with Ju craft created in Jun Kiln during Yuan Dynasty and by combining with other materials about related unearthed relics, we could preliminarily define the overall development and specific process of Ju craft in Yuan Dynasty. Firstly, 4 out of the 11 pieces of porcelain discovered in the Capital Museum during the census were mended with the craft, which means the mending craft was not rare at that time. Besides, there were many porcelains mended with this craft discovered in tombs of Yuan Dynasty. All of these traces could lead a conclusion that in Yuan Dynasty, porcelain mending was not a coincidence, but rather a custom in the society. Secondly, the four porcelains mended with same Ju craft, which were no different from the mending craft using iron nails during Ming and Qing Dynasty. Therefore, the Ju craft in Ming and Qing inherited from the Yuan Dynasty. And the craft had already been mature and widely adopted as early as in Yuan Dynasty. Thirdly, traces of white clay were found around the joint and around the drill holes on the porcelains kept in the Capital Museum. It shows that in Yuan Dynasty, craftsmen had already used white clay to fill the cracking and consolidate the joint, which was similar to that in Qing Dynasty, highlighting the strong inheritance of the craft. Fourthly,

其描述十分形象）。而从元代锔瓷实物来看，通常锔钉设置比较稀疏，使用锔钉相对较少，体现了早期瓷器锔补工艺的时代特点。第五，从目前发现的元代锔补瓷器实物的窑口品种来看，包括钧窑、磁州窑等，这些瓷器最为显著的共性即是器壁较厚，尤其钧窑瓷器，因釉水与胎壁均很厚，并且胎质相对疏松，适于以钻打孔且不易钻透，因此目前发现的元代锔补瓷器中以钧窑器的数量最多，它们应当是较早采用以铁质锔钉方式进行锔合的瓷器品种。而在元代得到空前发展的景德镇窑的青白釉瓷器或青花瓷器，因其胎体致密、器壁较薄，容易钻透，在当时的技术条件下可能尚难以采用同样的锔补工艺。

文物虽无言，但它们发出的声音却振聋发聩。锔瓷行当的产生，是与中国瓷器的发展以及相关手工业技术和技巧的进步有着密切联系的。中国古老的锔瓷行业最初起源于何时虽尚难精确考证，但从现有的实物证据考察，其发展历程恐已跨越了千年，这是基本可信的。要探究锔瓷工艺的缘起，笔者推测，它可能与更加古老的、

the amount of porcelains mended with Ju craft during Qing Dynasty was relatively large. After comparison and observation, one could easily find that in Qing Dynasty, craftsmen preferred using more nails, hence its name as "centipede rake". While in Yuan Dynasty, craftsmen would use less nails, which demonstrated the characteristics of the Ju craft in an early stage. Fifthly, porcelains mended with Ju craft in Yuan Dynasty discovered so far were mostly made in Jun Kiln and Cizhou Kiln. And a common feature of these porcelain is the thick wall, especially those made in Jun Kiln. The glaze and the body of these porcelains are very thick. Therefore, they are easily to be drilled but not easy to be drilled through. As a result, so far most porcelains mended with Ju craft in Yuan Dynasty were made in Jun Kiln. And this kind of porcelains was among the earliest to adopt the mending craft with iron nails. In comparison, green or blue and white porcelain, made in Jingde Town in the Yuan Dynasty rarely adopted the craft due to the thin body and glaze.

Cultural relics cannot speak, while they are impressive. The creation of Ju craft is highly related to the development and progress achieved in handicraft industry and porcelain industry. Although the exact time of the creation of this

中国传统"玉作"技艺有着密切的关联，此是后话。谜团尚待彻底破解，或许更加令人惊奇的破冰发现就在不远之处，让我们拭目以待。

李　健

首都博物馆

craft has yet to be known accurately, it is evident that the craft should enjoy a history of over 1,000 years. To explore the origin of Ju craft, the author assumes that it may be related to a more ancient and traditional Chinese "jade craft" , but this is another story. Mystery is yet to be thoroughly cracked. There may me more amazing discoveries ahead of us awaiting. Let's look forward to it.

Li Jian, the Capital Museum

铜胎掐丝珐琅六角扁瓶的诞生

The Birth of the Flat Hexagonal Vase in Cloisonné Enamel on Copper Body

16 英寸铜胎掐丝珐琅六角扁瓶是北京市珐琅厂有限责任公司原总工艺师钱美华先生 1965 年设计的景泰蓝精品，器型古朴典雅、构图疏密有致。

16 英寸铜胎掐丝珐琅六角扁瓶

the works of Master Qian Meihua,

16 inch flat hexagonal vase

The 16-inch flat hexagonal vase in cloisonné enamel on copper body was designed and made by the former chief craftsman Qian Meihua of the Beijing Enamel Factory in 1965. This quality piece has an elegant shape with balanced decorations. Master Qian threaded six panels of decoration into an entity. The upper part of the scenic painting is surrounded by the traditional cloud patterns which are sublime and beautiful. Every detail in the six pictures was made by hand which embodies high craftsmanship. In the pictures, mountains afar roll continuously, trees grow exuberantly, flocks of deer rest with ease and comfort, mandarin ducks play in the water, and lotus leaves float on the water. The whole picture forms a perfect combination of tranquility and vitality, presents simple and elegant colors, and displays a harmonious image between the tradition and nature. Therefore, Master Qian took this as an interior world, with joys in tranquility.

作者将瓶身中间的六面纹样连为一体，风景图的上方被传统的回纹所环绕，严谨美观。画面中的每个细节都是手工掰制，表现了制作技工的高超技艺，画面中远山连绵，树叶繁茂，群鹿悠闲自在，鸳鸯在水中嬉戏，荷叶在水面飘动着，动静交织、清幽安详，体现了传统与自然的和谐之美。钱美华先生称其为：洞天乐园，静中幽趣。

钱美华大师1951年6月于中央美院华东分院毕业，分配到北京特艺进出口公司，9月被选送到清华大学营建系深造，师从梁思成、林徽因，主研工艺美术，抢救濒于灭绝的景泰蓝。当时，北京仅存的几家作坊和景泰蓝厂子大都处于倒闭边缘，新、老艺人青黄不接，所制作的景泰蓝图案单调，缺乏创新，而要拯救这一濒临灭绝的民族艺术，最关键是调整生产结构，全面更新设计，才能使景泰蓝起死回生。

当时用于景泰蓝的图案只有荷花、牡丹花和钩子莲几种，几百年来一直没有太大的变化，而中国的装饰图案始终在千变万化地发展着。林徽因找出了珍藏的历代装饰图案，让大家学习研究。后来他们又多次到景泰蓝作

Master Qian Meihua graduated from the Central Academy of Fine Arts in Eastern China in June 1951 and was assigned to work for Beijing Special Crafts Import and Export Company. She got a chance to further her study in Tsinghua University in September of the same year. She studied with two famous scholars, namely Liang Sicheng and Lin Huiyin, focusing on arts and crafts, especially the all-but-varnished cloisonné technique. At that time, the only few enamel workshops and factories were on the verge of closedown due to the lack of qualified craftsmen and creativity in design. The key to renovating this craft was to rearrange the structure of production, and to update the design and technique.

The patterns used in cloisonné for hundreds of years were limited to only a few images such as lotus flowers, peony, and lotus intertwined with branches and leaves while decorative patterns in China went through changes all the time. Professor Lin Huiyin found out the decorative patterns for the collected pieces from each time period for her students to study. Later they conducted several field trips in enamel workshops in order to observe the old craftsmen to familiarize themselves with the process of making, making the enclosures with thin

坊调查研究，从掐丝、点蓝、烧蓝、磨光、镀金，一道一道工序跟着老艺人干活，熟悉每一个工艺流程。

在林徽因的指导下，美术组为景泰蓝设计了一批具有民族风格的新颖图案，突破了以往单调的荷花、牡丹图。特艺公司还在崇文门外喜鹊胡同3号成立了研究、制作景泰蓝的国营特艺实验厂，将许多散落民间的景泰蓝艺人请进厂参加实验。当时有几位老师傅之前被迫改行拉黄包车了，被请回厂时激动得热泪盈眶。

在清华学习期间，梁思成、林徽因大师的学识和思想境界对钱美华的影响非常大，也奠定了她终生追求的目标。她遵循导师的遗愿，"一定要把景泰蓝传承发展下去"，因此，当1958年工贸分开时，她毅然选择了基层，来到北京珐琅厂从事景泰蓝专业设计工作，一干就是60多年，为景泰蓝艺术奉献了自己的青春年华和毕生心血。初入工厂的钱美华见识到了景泰蓝工艺的纷繁复杂。她把车间的每一道工序列出来制成了表，经她统计，车间大工序分制胎、掐丝、烧焊、点蓝、烧蓝、磨光、镀金7道，小的流程共有108道，而每一道流程，又

钱美华先生
Master Qian Meihua

wire, filling the blue glass paste, firing the paste, polishing and gold-gilding.

Under Lin Huiyin's guidance, the crafts group designed a series of new patterns with Chinese characteristics for cloisonné, which diversified the previous designs. Additionally, the Special Crafts Company set up a state-owned experimental factory and invited many folk enamel artisans for researching and experimenting cloisonné at No. 3 Xique Hutong outside the Chongwen Gate. Some artisans had already been forced to pull the rickshaws to make money, so they were so excited that they burst into tears

铜胎掐丝珐琅六角扁瓶技术档案说明卡

illustrations for the technic archive

分为很多个细节。当时，为了解景泰蓝的发展历程，梁思成给钱美华推荐了一位老师——中国历史博物馆研究

钱美华与沈从文

Qian Meihua and Shen Congwen

when being invited back to the factory.

During the study in Tsinghua University, Professor Liang Sicheng and Lin Huiyin had a great impact on Qian Meihua, which also laid the foundation for her career goal. She followed her professors' last wish, "cloisonné technique must be further developed and passed on." Therefore, when the industry and trade were separated in 1958, she chose to work at the Beijing Cloisonné Enamel Factory and stayed there for over 60 years. Thus, she devoted her life to the cloisonné enamel craft.

When she started to work at the factory, she came to realize how complicated the cloisonné technique was. She created a form to incorporate every

员沈从文先生。沈先生是著名的考古学家，当时在故宫博物院兼职工作，任陈列部织绣研究组业务指导。沈先生告诉钱美华，故宫的景泰蓝很多，有几个房间甚至都摞到了房顶，他给钱美华出了个点子，让她去故宫临摹图案。故宫存放景泰蓝的珍宝馆一般不对外开放，钱美华就和故宫工作人员商量好，把自己反锁在里面，清早进去，晚上出来，一干就是连续10多天，她终于掌握了传统纹样的规律，找到了不少失传的图案。到北京珐琅厂担任设计师的钱美华，首先对景泰蓝的造型进行了规格化，按图生产。早先的作坊里都是师傅带着徒弟拓样，点蓝师傅们也还有点保守思想，都是在手心里调色，不肯将经验全部告诉徒弟。有规矩也要有突破，突破单调的图案和颜色，便是钱美华着手做的，用她的话说，就是"工艺美术也要解放思想"。1950年前后，敦煌壁画来到北京做展览，钱美华他们根据敦煌壁画的素材设计了反弹琵琶和飞天的图案。她还发现敦煌壁画有很多具有装饰性的特点，即颜色都是复色，不是大红大绿，很符合现代人的审美，她为此指导工厂分配来的两名美校学

process in each department. According to her statistics, there are 7 major steps including building the copper body, enclosing with thin wire, filing the glass paste, firing the paste, polishing and gold-gilding together with 108 sub-procedures. Each procedure could be divided into several detailed movements. In order to better understand the historical development of cloisonné, Liang Sicheng introduced her to Mr. Shen Congwen, a researcher at the Museum of Chinese History. Mr. Shen was a well-known archaeologist who had a part-time job at Palace Museum, providing guidance for the textile research group at the Exhibition Department. Mr. Shen told Qian that there were so many cloisonné pieces in the Palace Museum that they were piled to the rooftop. He provided an opportunity for Qian to copy the enamel patterns there. Because the treasure room that stored cloisonné pieces was not open to the public, Qian Meihua told the colleagues at the Palace Museum to lock her in the room in the morning and unlock the door after work in the evening. She copied continuously for ten days and finally mastered the order of traditional patterns. She was also able to find some lost patterns. Working as a designer in the enamel factory, Qian Meihua firstly regularized the shapes of enamelware which shall be strictly followed during

1958年钱美华大师来到北京市珐琅厂从事景泰蓝专业设计
in 1958, Master Qian Meihua came to work at the Beijing Enamel Factory as a cloisonné designer.

生进行配色，并与釉料车间的技术人员一道开发出了很多新的釉色，有珊瑚红、碧玉这样的仿宝石色，也有国画里的花青色，其中还有一种颜色叫"地儿绿"，似透非透，蓝中透绿，很美。

这一时期，钱美华编写了我国第一部景泰蓝创作教材《景泰蓝创作设计》，并毫无保留地教给大家造型、纹样规律和配色方法。1958年，珐琅厂成立设计室，钱美华开始景泰蓝专业创作，发明了设计图纸"三步法"：第一先设计胎型图，然后再设计丝工图，最后是色彩图，三者完成后，再进行制作。当时，钱美华先生率领设

production. Previously, in the workshops, because of the apprenticeship that the apprentice would copy what his master did, masters were somehow reserved and not willing to share all the techniques with his apprentices. Therefore, the masters would use their palm as the palette in case their apprentice see how to make the blue glass paste. The rules had to be broken. What Qian wanted to do was to renovate the patterns and colors. In her words, "arts and crafts need to be emancipated from minds as well." Around 1950, the frescos in Dunhuang Cave were shipped to Beijing for an exhibition. Qian Meihua designed the patterns of "playing the Pipa without looking at it" and "Flying Apsaras" based on the frescos. She also found out that Dunhuang frescos were decorated mostly in tertiary colors that meet the modern aesthetic concept, rather than in the primary colors like bright red or green. Therefore, she asked two students from the Academy of Fine Arts to mix the colors. With the help of the craftsmen in the material department, a lot of new enamel colors were created, including those imitating the visual effect of gemstones like coral red and jade green, as well as others that imitate the optical effect of ink paintings such as an "earth green," which is a beautiful translucent bluish green.

计人员设计创作了众多精美的景泰蓝作品，游乐喜寿尊和铜胎掐丝珐琅六角扁瓶的设计图稿是现存年代最早的。

王建章

北京市珐琅厂有限责任公司

During this period, Qian Meihua edited the first textbook for cloisonné making in China—Jingtailan Chuangzuo Sheji (The Design and Making of Cloisonné). In the book, she shared without reservations how to design the form, understand the rule of patterns and the method to match colors. In 1958, the enamel factory set up a studio for design. Thereafter, Qian Meihua started to focus on the making of cloisonné. She invented the "Three Steps Method", the first step is to draw out the pattern of the shape, the second step is to design the decorative patterns, and the last step is to fill in the colors. After finishing the three steps of design, the craftsman then started to make Ms. Qian and her design team created a large number of fine cloisonné works. But most of the designs were lost during the Cultural Revolution. You Le Xi Shou Zun (Bottle with Joy, Happiness and Longevity) and Liu Jiao Bian Ping (Flat Hexagonal Vase in Cloisonné Enamel on Copper Body) are the two earliest design drafts.

Wang Jianzhang, Beijing Enamel Factory Co. Ltd.

水月观音
——元大都城址内出土的重要文物

One of the Important Cultural Relics Unearthed in the Site of Dadu of Yuan Dynasty

— on Bluish White Glazed Carving of Water-Moon Avalokiteshvara in Yuan Dynasty

　　元景德镇窑青白釉水月观音菩萨坐像，1955 年北京西城区定阜大街出土，是元大都城址范围内出土的重要文物之一。它以优美的艺术造型，精湛的烧制工艺，独特而完美的艺术风格，展现了元代雕塑艺术、佛教造像艺术和景德镇窑瓷塑烧制工艺的最高水平，为首都博物馆典藏的重要瑰宝之一。

　　这尊水月观音像通高 65 厘米，头戴宝冠，冠的正面有一小化佛（残），广额丰颐，眼睑低垂，神态安详。观音跌足而坐，右腿支起，左腿下垂，右臂搭于右膝上，左手支于身体左侧，姿态优美大方，给人自然闲适之美感；上身着双领下垂式袈裟，下身着长裙，胸前饰网状连珠式璎珞，袈裟及下裙上亦垂挂连珠式璎珞，装饰繁缛，雍

The bluish white glazed carving of Water-Moon Avalokiteshvara made in Jingdezhen Kiln during Yuan Dynasty was discovered in the Dingbu Street, Xicheng District, Beijing, in 1955. It is one of the important cultural relics discovered in the site of Dadu of Yuan Dynasty. Its graceful art, exquisite craft, unique and perfect artistic style all represented the highest level of Buddhist sculpture art and porcelain craft. It was one of the most important collection in the Capital Museum.

The statue stands at 65 centimeters, with a crown on her head. On the front of the crown is carved a small Buddha (residue), with wide forehead, downcast eyes and serene facial expression. The Avalokiteshvara sits with her bare feet, wearing a piece of pearl necklace. His right leg is bending, and left leg sagging. Her right arm is putting on the right knee,

容华贵。全身肌肉柔软细腻，其中面部及手足的肌肉尤其生动，在青白色釉料的映衬下，更显优雅温婉。而最为引人注目的是其慈祥悲悯的眼神，意在观照水中圆月，又似俯视芸芸众生。

此像胎质洁白细密，通体施青白釉，釉色白中泛青，色润柔和，制作工艺无与伦比。首先是塑像整体塑造精准大方，采用了塑、捏、压、琢等不同手法塑造头部、身体和四肢等部位，然后对不同部位进行细致修整，最后对菩萨面部及神态进行刻画。局部塑造也一丝不苟，而尤为突出的是宝冠，正面安有一尊小化佛（阿弥陀佛坐像），为观音菩萨身份的标识，冠的背面是一朵瓷塑的莲叶；宝冠为单独烧造，可以取下，又大大增添了烧造的难度。另外，此像的右肘搭于右膝上，整个右臂悬垂于膝前，这一细节也是工艺精湛的重要体现——同时代、同材质的水月观音像以膝支撑手臂之处均靠近腕部，而此像改悬腕为悬臂，不仅制作难度更高，整体造型也更为优美。

水月观音这一造型样式在早期佛教经典中并无记载，是佛教与中国本

and left hand on the left side of the body. She looks elegant and generous, bringing us a natural aesthetic feeling of leisure. She wears a sagging cassock, and dressed a long skirt, with a web of jade and pearl necklace on her chest and skirt, making her looks more luxurious and elegant. Her muscles look soft and delicate, and her face is especially vivid. She looks more elegant in the bluish white glaze. Her eyes full of kindness. It seems that she is looking down at the moon reflected in the lake, or looking at all human beings.

The bluish white glaze is fine and mild. The craft is unparalleled. First the overall shape is precise and elegant with the adoption of different methods, such as, shaping, pinching, pressing and carving to make his head, body and limbs. Then, different parts of the Buddha were modified, and finally bodhisattva face and expression was vividly depicted. The shape of small parts is also meticulous, especially its crown with a small statue of Buddha carved on it. It is the identification of Avalokitesvara. On the back of the crown is carved a porcelain lotus leaf. The crown was independently made, and it could be removed, increasing the difficulty of making it. Besides, the Avalokitesvara's right elbow is on her right knee, and her right arm hangs in front of her knees. This detail is also an

土文化融合而产生的。据《历代名画记》记载，这一形象最初由唐代著名画家周昉创塑。此后，水月观音即受到世俗社会的广泛崇信与青睐，一直盛行不衰，而宋元时流行尤甚。

水月观音是汉地自行创造并流行起来的一种造像题材与造型，但其风格明显受到了当时藏传佛教造像艺术的影响，体现了汉藏艺术融合的鲜明特点——此像全身结构匀称，比例适中，特别是腰部有明显的收缩，这些即体现了明显的藏传造像特点。而同一时期的中原造像大多体态丰腴，躯体结构不甚讲究，与藏传造像迥然不同。值得一提的是，类似汉藏风格的元代瓷质造像还有上海博物馆的元青白釉观音坐像、北京艺术博物馆的元代景德镇窑青白釉加漆描金释迦牟尼佛坐像等，由此可见汉藏融合的现象在当时陶瓷造像业中较为普遍，已成文化艺术潮流。元代我国重新实现大一统的政治局面，统治者对各种宗教采取兼容并蓄的政策，而对佛教尤其尊崇，这给佛教和佛像艺术提供了较大的发展空间。正是由于国家的统一和统治者的大力扶持，元代的佛教造像艺术焕发出新的生机与活力，展现

important embodiment of the exquisite craftsmanship. To compare with other contemporary statues of avalokitesvara, this piece represented higher level of craftsmanship and beauty.

Actually, there is no record of Avalokitesvara in the early Buddhist classics. It is the integration of Buddhism and Chinese local culture. According to famous paintings in all previous dynasties, the image of water-moon Avalokitesvara was initially created by Zhou Fang, a famous painter in Tang Dynasty. Since then, the water-moon Avalokitesvara was widely worshipped by the secular society and was popular especially in Song Dynasty and Yuan Dynasty.

The water-moon Avalokitesvara was created in Han area but its style was obviously influenced by the Tibetan Buddhist statue arts, embodying the distinctive characteristics of Sino-Tibetan art integration. The systemic structure with an obvious shrinkage in the waist embodies the obvious characteristics of Tibetan statues. While over the same period of time, statues made in the central part of China were mostly fleshy, and few attentions had been paid to the structure, which is different from those made in Tibetan area. It is worth noting that similar statues of Sino-Tibetan style

出新的时代艺术特征。元代藏传佛像艺术的传入丰富了内地佛像艺术的形式和风格，也极大地促进了汉藏佛像艺术双向的交流与融合。

武俊玲
北京日报

made in Yuan Dynasty include the bluish-white glaze Avalokiteshvara collected in Shanghai Museum, the green white glaze Shakyamuni Buddha statue with lacquer paint made in Jingdezhen Kiln during Yuan Dynasty collected in Beijing Art Museum, etc. Therefore, we could see that the Sino-Tibetan integration was quite common in terms of porcelain craftsmanship. It had already become a trend at that time. During Yuan Dynasty, the unification of the political situation was realized in China, and the then-rulers adapted the inclusive policy of various religions and paid special respect to Buddhism, leaving Buddhist arts and craftsmanship larger development space. It is because of the unification and the vigorous support from the rulers, the art of Buddhist statue during Yuan Dynasty was invigorated, showing unique artistic features of the new era. At the same time, the introduction of Tibetan Buddhist art in Yuan Dynasty enriched the mainland Buddhist art forms and styles, meanwhile also greatly promoted the Sino-Tibetan art communication and integration.

Wu Junlin, Beijing Daily

文物背后的故事
stories behind cultural relics

遥望金代父子驸马的风光
——青玉荷叶龟游佩

Green Jade Pendants with the Pattern of Lotus Leaf and Swimming Turtles
— Looking Back to Wugulun Family in Jin Dynasty

在许多北京人的认知里，金人是反面角色，是民族英雄岳飞的对手。然而北京正式作为皇都的历史，恰是从金中都开始的。

1980 年，北京市丰台区王佐乡米粮屯村先后发现了金代名臣乌古论元忠夫妇墓以及其父乌古论窝论的墓葬。后者是北京地区首次发掘的带有明确纪年的金代贵族墓，为研究金代历史提供了珍贵的实物资料。

In the eyes of many Beijing people, people of the Jin country during Song Dynasty are rivals to Yue Fei, a national hero in Song Dynasty. And Beijing had not formally become the capital of China until being occupied by Jin country.

In 1980, the tombs of Wugulun YuanZhong couple and Wugulun Wolun, famous ministers during Jin Dynasty, were discovered in Miliangtun Village, Wangzuo County, Fengtai District, Beijing. The latter tomb was the first tomb of nobleman in Jin Dynasty with specific chronicle evidence, providing precious materials for us to study more about the history of Jin Dynasty.

Then who are these three people buried in the tombs?

Wugulun was an important tribe in Jin Country. And their family was

青玉荷叶龟游佩

green jade pendant with the pattern of lotus leaf and turtles swimming in between

这对夫妇以及这位父亲，这三位墓主是何许人也？

乌古论部是金代女真重要部族之一，乌古论窝论家族又是金初的名门大户，其名声之显赫，从墓志的撰写人、书丹人、题额人皆极一时之选就可见一斑。

这父子二人皆是驸马，父亲窝论曾随金太祖完颜阿骨打一起征战，娶了金太祖的二女儿。但儿子元忠更为有名，"公生十年，仪冠颖异"，金世宗将最喜爱的长女许配给了他。这位鲁国大长公主是金世宗完颜雍与明德皇后乌林答氏所生。

金代帝后中最传奇的莫过于金世宗完颜雍与乌林答氏了。乌林答氏不仅容貌端庄秀丽，而且聪颖过人，完颜雍未登帝位之时，在宫廷的血雨腥风中，她曾几次设计保护丈夫免遭金熙宗和海陵王的毒手。后来，海陵王召乌林答氏前往中都（一说是垂涎其美貌，一说是要乌林答氏去做人质）。去则辱名，不去，海陵王可以抗旨不遵之名杀掉她的丈夫。乌林答氏留下给夫君的书信后整装前往，行至良乡固节时自尽。后来，完颜雍乘海陵王执意南下伐宋之际夺取了皇位。他称

regarded as noble at the beginning of Jin Dynasty. We could see its crucial influence from the inscriptions on the memorial tablet within the tombs, which were written by famous people at that time.

Wugulun Wolun and his son were both emperor's son-in-law. Wolun accompanied Emperor Taizu, Wanyan Aguda, in the military, and married Aguda's second daughter. And Wolun's son, Yuanzhong was even more famous than his brilliant father. "When Yuanzhong was ten years old, he was so handsome." And Emperor Shizong married his big daughter to him. The princess was the daughter of Emperor Shizong, Wanyan Yong and Queen Mingde, Wudalin.

Shizong and Wudalin were the most legendary couple in the history of Jin Dynasty. Wudalin was dignified, beautiful and intelligent. When Wanyan Yong ascended the throne, she helped him get rid of the crafty plots from Emperor Xizong and Lord Hailing. Once, Lord Hailing summoned Wudalin to Zhongdu, today's Beijing (As for the reason of this summoning, there are mainly two theories. One theory claims that Lord Hailing was attracted by Wudalin's beauty; and another claims that Lord Hailing wanted to hold Wudalin as his hostage). If Wudalin chose

帝后未再封后，意在将皇后之位永远为乌林答氏保留。

乌林答氏自杀时，公主才14岁。据公主的墓志所载，从那时起金世宗便"以家务付之"，后来更认为她"识虑深远，可用决疑，凡宫中之事皆咨焉，多所裨益"。

能娶这样一位公主，元忠自然不是一般人，他与皇帝可以彻夜促膝长谈，有小尧舜之称的金世宗"倚之为股肱"。据元忠墓志记载，大定二年（1162），兵部尚书可喜密谋趁金世宗前往房山的金陵朝拜列祖列宗时，"欲拒门为不轨"，却走漏了风声。完颜雍命元忠守卫寝殿大门。夜半时分，可喜发难，双方激战。面对刀光剑影，完颜雍和元忠聊着天，"语如平素"。最终自然是完颜雍安然返回中都。墓志中的寥寥数语，既尽显完颜雍的镇定与周密，又可见元忠跟皇上的亲近及受到的倚信。

这件青玉荷叶龟游佩出自乌古论窝论墓。

佩成对，为一块玉料对剖制成。材料为青玉，玉质温润细腻，抛光极佳。椭圆形，以浮雕、透雕技法琢出

to go to Zhongdu, it would be a tarnish to her reputation. If not, Lord Hailing could kill her husband for disobeying the decree. Therefore, Wudalin left a letter to her husband and committed suicide when she arrived Gujie, Liang County, near Zhongdu. Later, Wanyan Yong stepped into power when Lord Hailing was dedicated to conquering the Southern Song. After Wanyan Yong crowned, he never married another queen. Wudalin was his only queen.

When Wudalin died, her daughter was only 14 years old. According to the epitaph of the princess, after Wudalin died, Emperor Shizong would allow her to take charge of all internal affairs, and later, the farther fully recognized her daughter's intelligence and vision. He would discuss with the princess about all the difficult problems during his reign.

Yuanzhong could marry such a brilliant princess, and this shows that he must be special too. Emperor Shizong could discuss about internal affairs with Yuanzhong for a whole night and regarded him as his best assistant. According to Yuanzhong's epitaph, in the 2nd year of Dading period, Ke Xi, minister of military, plotted to stage a coup when Emperor Shizong went to Fangshan to worship his ancestors. But the plan was

荷叶、茨菰及水草纹，以单阴线刻出荷叶的叶脉。两荷叶中心各凸雕一小龟，颈长伸，相对爬行，以双阴线琢出六角形龟甲，背面仅以简练的刀法

青玉荷叶龟游佩

green jade pendant with the pattern of lotus leaf and turtles swimming in between

雕出植物的枝梗。我国古人认为龟是"通灵之物"，不但象征长寿，还与"贵"谐音，寓意富贵；而莲花则是廉洁、清高的化身。此玉佩不仅构思巧妙，而且琢制精细，将龟游弋在荷叶之上的画面表现得极为生动，且富有灵性，是目前出土的金代玉器的代表作。

虽然青玉荷叶龟游佩目前在库房中，难见真颜，但乌古论墓出土的耀州窑月白釉刻花卧足钵、耀州窑月白釉鋬铅洗、青釉葫芦式执壶等文物都在展出中，可以在首博的通史厅和瓷器厅找到。更为珍贵的是，墓葬中还

known by the emperor. Wanyan Yong demanded Yuanzhong to guard the palace. In the middle of that night, Ke Xi staged the coup and had a fierce fight with the emperor's guards. In the face of swords, Wanyan Yong chatted with Yuanzhong, just like nothing happened. And finally, Wanyan Yong won and safely went back to Zhongdu. From the short epitaph, we could see the calmness and vision of Wanyan Yong and Yuanzhong's trust and loyalty to him.

The pair of green jade pendants with the pattern of lotus leaf and swimming turtles was discovered in the tomb of Wugulun Wolun.

The pair of pendants was made out of green, fine, and well-polished jade. It was oval, with lotus leafs and water grass carved on it. And the vein of leafs was incised. In the center of each lotus leaf was carved a small turtle, with its neck stretching out. The hexagonal tortoise shell was incised. And in the back of the pendant, veins of plants were simply carved. In China, the ancient believed that turtle is the symbol of longevity, and Gui (turtle) sounds like "dignity" in Chinese; while lotus is the embodiment of integrity and loftiness. The pendant was designed cleverly and carved nicely, representing the vivid picture of turtles swimming

出土了三合墓志，长达数千字，为研究金代初年的历史提供了可靠的文字资料，甚至在某些方面弥补了《金史》之不足。透过这些文字与文物，我们得以遥望 800 多年前金代皇室的爱情与忠诚、背叛与杀戮……

赵婷
北京日报

in the water between lotus leafs. It is a representative of jade ware in Jin Dynasty.

Although the pair of pendants has not been displayed, the pale blue porcelain bowl with flower pattern carved on the body made in Yuezhou Kiln, pale blue porcelain brush cleaner made in Yuezhou Kiln, green calabash-shaped porcelain kettle with two ears could be found in the display hall of general history and the porcelain hall. More importantly, we also found epitaphs containing around 1,000 characters in the tombs, providing reliant historical materials for us to study the history of Jin Dynasty and, to some extent, making up for the Chronicle of Jin Dynasty. Through these words and cultural relics, we could clearly see the love, loyalty and cruelness in royal life.

Zhao Ting, Beijing Daily

从碎片中重生的蓝凤凰

——元青花凤首扁壶

Rebirth from the Debris of Blue Phoenix

— Blue and White Porcelain Pot with Phoenix-Head Pattern Made in Yuan Dynasty

元青花凤首扁壶壶身不是浑圆而是扁圆，昂起的凤首作流，卷起的凤尾作柄；展开的双翅垂于壶身两侧，而凤身之下一丛缠枝莲花茂盛向上，生机盎然。

元代景德镇官窑的青花瓷采用一种进口的钴料绘制，这种彩料的成分高铁低锰，高温烧制后青翠浓艳，并形成含铁的结晶斑，过烧则出现晕散，形成类似于水墨画的效果。青花瓷在元代中期开始大量烧制，其中用于外销的产品如大盘、大罐、梅瓶等，器型高大，纹饰繁密，带有浓厚的伊斯兰风格；而供给元代宫廷及贵族使用的大部分器型较小，纹饰疏朗，元大都出土的元代青花都属于这一类。

元青花这些年名气很大，由于存世稀少，为国际、国内各著名博物馆争相收藏。然而，首都博物馆收藏的

The pot's body is not perfectly round but elliptical. The raised head of phoenix serves as a spout and rolled-up tail as handle. The two sides of the pot are just like the spread wings of the phoenix, under which a branch of lotus is flourishing.

The blue and white porcelain was produced in Imperial Kilns of Jingdezhen in Yuan dynasty. Cobalt blue was imported from Iran with rich Fe and few Mn, probably in cake form. It was ground into a pigment, which was painted directly onto the leather-hard porcelain body. The piece was then glazed and fired and it will be extremely green with Fe. It will be smudged later and looks like a brush painting. A large amount of blue and white porcelains were produced in the middle of Yuan Dynasty. Porcelains shaped like huge plates, bottles and prunus vase were exported abroad. They are huge porcelains with intricate lines of Muslim's styles. Emperor and noble families in Yuan Dynasty tended to use smaller porcelains with sparse lines. The blue and white porcelains made in Yuan

文物背后的故事
stories behind cultural relics

这件精美绝伦的元青花凤首扁壶，却是历尽磨难而重生。

1970 年初春，旧鼓楼大街豁口，北京标准件四厂的工人正在城墙下挖土摔砖坯。一个周一的上午，一名铁路巡道工人打电话给北京市文物管理处反映说，在北城墙下面发现了青花白地的瓷器。

考古队的小于悄悄对 25 岁的小黄说："北城墙建造于明洪武初年，那底下可是元代地层。这里发现的青花瓷至少是洪武年间的，可能更早，很重要，咱们一定得去。"

二人赶紧向军宣队负责人请示，得到的答复是："你们这些挖坟头儿的，一、三、五不抓革命，二、四、六拿啥促生产咧？"

没办法，只好第二天再去了。

周二，赶到现场的小黄和小于惊呆了——由于晚来了一天，这批文物已经被"破四旧"了，碎片就扔在两边的土堆里。

"用 8 磅大铁锤砸的呀！"回忆起当时的情景，小黄的语气中依然充满无尽的痛惜和遗憾。

于是二人决定就是筛也得把它们筛出来！由于单位规定每周一、三、

Dynasty that were unearthed from Yuan Dynasty all belong to the latter.

Blue and white porcelain made in Yuan Dynasty has gained a great deal of popularity these years. International and domestic well-known museums have lined up to collect these relics due to the scarceness. However, this fabulous blue and white porcelain pot made in Yuan Dynasty collected in the Capital Museum has suffered a lot to rebirth in the very end.

In the early spring of 1970, at Houkou, Jiugulou Dajie, workers from Beijing Standard Parts NO.4 Factory was digging fallen bricks under the wall. On a Monday morning, a railway track inspector called Beijing Municipal Administration of Cultural Heritage, claiming he discovered blue and white porcelain under the north wall.

Yu, from the archeological team told the 25-year-old young man Huang: "The north wall was built in early years of Hongwu Period in the Ming Dynasty, so the strata can be traced back to Yuan Dynasty. The discovered blue and white porcelain could be a treasure from Hongwu Period, or even earlier. It's extremely important. We have to go there."

They asked for permission from PLA propaganda team without any hesitation but only got an negative reply like this: "All that you guys think about is digging tombs. You'd better focus on revolution so

五要抓革命（学"毛选"、学"社论"），只能周二、四、六去筛。小黄和小于找来铁锹，借来筛子，用 3 天时间把这两堆土过了一遍，把碎片装在箱子里用自行车驮回了办公室。考古队的同事们你一片我一片帮忙拼对，有盘子、碗、盏托……十几件瓷器中最精美的便数这个扁壶了。可是，48 块大大小小的碎片，大的如扑克牌，小的似指甲盖，只能拼出一半，其余的部分只好由美术师用石膏修补，正面的青花纹饰用粉质颜色粗略接笔，背面的花纹则未作处理，呈现石膏原色。由于大家都是考古人员而非专业修复师，黏合并不精细，接缝清晰可见，大伙儿开玩笑说，这是二凤的姐姐——大凤（缝）。在随后的 30 多年里，元青花凤首扁壶便以这残缺的样貌出现在《考古》杂志里、邮票上、展览中，却依然引来无数惊叹。当时国内对元青花的研究尚少，经考古发掘出土的元青花极为珍稀，这批元大都遗址上出土的青花瓷便有了不同寻常的价值。

2004 年，首都博物馆将扁壶送交修复专家蒋道银先生，进行了历时 13 个月的修复。今天，展现在我们面前

that production can be promoted. "

They had no other choices but to wait for the next day.

On Tuesday, Huang and Yu got shocked when they arrived at the spot. The treasures had already been ruined by "breaking the four-olds" event. The destroyed fragments were thrown away everywhere on the sides of the hill.

"They smashed that with a eight-pound hammer! " Huang said that with a belly of grievances and pity when he recollected what had happened that day.

They will make every effort to sift those treasures out! People were supposed to learn revolution theories (Selected Works of Mao Zedong and Socialism Theories) on Monday, Wednesday and Friday so they could only do the sifting work on the other days. Huang and Yu brought shovel and sieve and spend three days filtering all the earth. They put the remaining pieces into boxes and transported them to the office by bikes. Colleagues from them archaeological team were trying very hard to piece them together. Those fragments became plates, bowls, trays and etc., of which the flat pot was the most fabulous one. Among all these forty-eight pieces, some were as big as poker cards while some were like fingernails. Only half part of the flat pot can be pieced up. The rest part had to be revamped with gypsum by the artist Wei.

的凤首扁壶宛若新生，可以让我们更真切地体会到它的美丽与珍贵——此器吸收了北方游牧民族的扁壶造型特点，壶流采用模制成型，壶柄以捏塑成型，壶身为雕镶成型，最后合成整体，制作工艺繁缛。造型构思别具匠心，整体画面饱满，纹饰生动流畅，釉质莹润。青花料采用进口苏麻离青料，发色绚丽浓艳，略有晕散，铁锈斑特征非常明显。它是中原文化与草原文化、青花图案装饰与造型工艺相融合的体现，是元青花瓷的代表作之一。

元青花凤首扁壶

blue and white porcelain pot with phoenix-head pattern made in Yuan Dynasty

The blue and white lines in the front side were polished a little bit while the reverse side was not given any treatment. The adhesion was not perfect so every particle of seam was obvious since archaeologists were not professional about this. People were joking: This is the big Feng, sister of Er Feng (Feng is a female name which sounds like the word "seam" in Chinese). In the next 30 years, this blue and white porcelain with phoenix-head pattern made in Yuan Dynasty appeared in magazine *Archaeology*, stamps and exhibitions as incomplete shape, arising great admiration. Researches about blue and white porcelain made in Yuan Dynasty were scarce in China then, making unearthed blue and white porcelain made in Yuan Dynasty even more priceless. The treasures that could be dated back to Yuan Dynasty had their special meanings.

In the year of 2004, Jiang Daoyin, an antiquity restoration expert at Capital's Museum's request spent 13 months to repair this flat pot. Thanks to that, people now are able to admire its marvelous beauty and value profoundly. This blue and white porcelain with phoenix-head pattern made in Yuan Dynasty is fabulous after its rebirth. The shape resembles the flat pot of northern nomadic tribes in ancient China. The spout was molded, and the handle kneaded and the body are sculptured to make the final piece. The whole process was complicated and burdensome. This masterpiece of ingenuity has awesome shape, vivid lines

根据已知的资料，青花凤首扁壶存世仅两件。2009 年 3 月，在首都博物馆举办的"青花的记忆——元代青花瓷文化展"上，展出了一件藏于新疆伊犁哈萨克自治州博物馆的凤首扁壶，其器型与首都博物馆藏凤首扁壶相似，凤尾不同，壶流、壶柄亦有残损。这两件凤首扁壶一凤一鸾，从工艺水准看各有千秋。

赵婷

北京日报

with full color and flawless enamel. The blue and white was made of Su Ma Li Qing (Samarra-blue) so it has vivid color. It was smudged a little bit and has obvious traces of rust. It is the combination of Central Plain culture and Northern Prairie culture, blue and white decoration and formative technology, making it one of the representatives of blue and white porcelain made in Yuan Dynasty.

These are only two blue and white blue and white porcelains with phoenix-head pattern made in Yuan Dynasty existing in the world according to already-known information. On "The Memory of Blue and White - Blue and white porcelain made in Yuan Dynasty Porcelain Cultural Exhibition" held by the Capital Museum in March 2009, blue and white porcelain with phoenix-head pattern made in Yuan Dynasty, which was collected in Xinjiang Ili Kazak Autonomous Prefecture Museum was displayed. Its shape resembles the one in Capital Museum's blue and white porcelain with phoenix-head pattern made in Yuan Dynasty but the tails are quite different. One is shaped as phoenix and the other is Luan (a mythical bird like phoenix). Their spouts and handles have different levels of damages and they are equally important in terms of design.

Zhao Ting, Beijing Daily

第三编
Third series

文物背后的故事

纸卷墨香览古意
paper cultural relics

民国十三至十七年：见信如晤
——焦菊隐、石评梅与他们的时代

Letter of Friendship and Love during the 13th to 17th Year of the Republic of China
—on Jiao Juyin, Shi Pingmei and Their Era

坐落于王府井大街首都剧场四层的北京人民艺术剧院戏剧博物馆开放于 2007 年，其时正值中国话剧百年华诞，北京人民艺术剧院历时 5 年筹备，精选上千件舞台艺术珍存，成就了中国第一家展示话剧艺术的博物馆。

戏剧博物馆的"剧院创始人展厅"展示了曹禺、焦菊隐[1]等 4 位建院创始人的艺术历程。在总导演焦菊隐的展线中，陈列着一封民国时期女作家石评梅写给学生时代的焦菊隐的信札，在若干戏剧类展品中，它散发着独特的气质。经研究考据，此信写于民国

Located in the fourth floor of the Capital Theatre, Wangfujing street, Bejing Museum of People's Art and Drama opened in 2007, at the 100th anniversary of Chinese drama. After five years of preparation, the museum sucessfully selected thousands of precious stage artworks, making it the first drama museum in China.

In the Exhibition Hall of Founding Fathers, the art career of four founding fathers of this museum including Cao Yu and Jiao Juyin were on display. In the exhibition of Jiao Juyin's[1] art career,

---

[1] 焦菊隐（1905—1975）：北京人民艺术剧院创始人之一，副院长兼总导演，北京人艺演剧风格的奠基者和开创者。他致力于话剧民族化的探索，善于将中国古典戏曲艺术中的美学观点和表现手法有机地融入到话剧艺术创作中，其代表作《龙须沟》《茶馆》《蔡文姬》是北京人艺的保留剧目。

---

[1] Jiao Juyin (1905—1975): One of the four founding fathers of the People's Art Theatre, vice president and general director. He was also the foundation layer and innovator of the drama style in People's Art Theatre. He has devoted himself to the nationalization of drama and integrating the traditional Chinese aesthetic view and demonstration method into drama performance. His masterpiece *Dragon Beard Ditch* (《龙须沟》). *Teahouse* (《茶馆》), and *Cai Wenji* (《蔡文姬》) are repertoires of the theatre.

民国十五年（1926）石评梅给焦菊隐的信件
the letter written by Shi to Jiao in the 15th year of the
Republic of China (1912 - 1949)

there was a collection of letters written to Jiao, who was still a student at that time, by Shi Pingmei, a female author in the Republic of China (1912-1949). These letters demonstrated unique and distinctive temperament among other collections. Through the study, we found that the letters were written in the 15th year of the Republic of China (1927), nearly 90 years ago. On the white paper, a few lines demonstrated great connotation. The full text is:

十五年（1926），距今已经90年了。素白的信笺上，虽寥寥数行，细细读来却内涵丰富。全文为：

菊弟：

听晶清说你匆匆返津了。

看报很挂念你，和你的双亲妹妹！如平安时乞告我一声！这些天惊魂未定，吊死慰伤，真觉人间何世！我愿早瞑目，不闻不见这些事才好，然而天啊不许我。

祝弟弟的珍重！

梅姊

三月二十四号

打完电话后，这封信换了个信封仍寄给你。

梅姊又及

Bro Ju:

I heard from Jingqing that you hurried back to Tianjin.

After reading the newspaper, I miss you, your sister and parents very much! If you are safe, please let me know! These days I was freaked out. So many people got hurt or even died. What a hell! I hope that I could die earlier, then I could shut my eyes for these recurring tragedies. While I am not allowed to die.

Best regards to you!

Sis. Mei,
March 24th
PS: After calling you, I still send this letter to you.

焦菊隐自学生时代即爱好文学，他笔耕不辍，散文、诗歌屡见报端。1924 年初，正在高中毕业前夕的焦菊隐通过文学社团的活动结识了石评梅。石评梅比焦菊隐大 3 岁，出生于山西省平定县的书香门第。她是典型的新女性，当时刚从北京女子高等师范学校毕业，在北京第一女子学校任体育和国文教员，同时组织身边同好创立了"蔷薇社"，是京城文学圈中颇有名气的才女。焦菊隐钦佩石评梅的文采，他们熟识后以姐弟相称，时常通信，在信中互相倾诉对社会、文学、时政的看法。

1924 年秋天，焦菊隐以优异成绩升入燕京大学欧洲语系就读。入学之后，寒素的家境难以支撑他的学费，为维持学业，他先后为北京《晨报》副刊和《京报》副刊写文艺稿及评论，挣取微薄的稿费，与同为《京报》副刊编辑的石评梅不仅相聚北平，更有工作上的交集。大学四年，他发表了大量的散文诗和翻译作品、戏剧论文。1924 年的一首《七月十四日晚怀 C 姑娘》，倾诉了他对评梅的那份仰慕之情，其中写道：

Jiao Juyin fell in love with literature since he was a student, and he had kept writing. Many of his articles, essays and poems were published in newspapers. At the beginning of 1924, Jiao juyin met Shi Pingmei in a literary club activity before he graduated from high school. Shi Pingmei, 3 years elder than Jiao, was born in a scholarly family in Pingding county, Shanxi province. She was a typical new female at that time, who taught Chinese and physical exercise in the Beijing First Women's School after graduating from the Beijing Women's Higher Normal School. And she founded the "rose club" with some friends. She was a well-known talented woman in the literary circle in Beijing. Jiao Juyin admired the literary grace of Shi. After they got familiar with each other, they started to call each other as "bro" and "sis". They would exchange their ideas about the society, literature and politics in their letters.

In the autumn of 1924, Jiao Juyin was successfully admitted into Yanjing University to learn European languages. However, his shabby family could hardly afford his tuition. In order to keep studying in the university, he eared a few incomes through writing essays and commentaries for the supplement

我没有能力慰你孤伶冷寂，
更不能爱你，姑娘！
姑娘，你的笑声时时漫入心底，
你的活泼的神情时时跳动在眼前，
你的一笑一颦都添了我不少新愁，
和旧愁加在一起燃烧。
……

诚如此，他不单对他们共同的好友陆晶清说过："我崇拜梅姐简直到了爱她的地步。"亦曾对后来的夫人秦瑾提起过："有一次我从天津去北平看梅姐，她拉我去滑冰。我是一个大近视眼，戴了眼镜没法滑，只有坐在旁边看。她穿着白毛衣，戴着白帽子，滑得那么潇洒，那么飘逸，好像天下飞下来的白天鹅，我真的看醉了。"

然而，石评梅早在 1922 年就与山西同乡高君宇相识，高君宇对她展开热烈的追求，石评梅由于曾经感情受挫，不肯轻易接受高君宇的炽热感情，但她仍以各种方式支持着高君宇的革命活动，往来不断。作为小她 3 岁的焦菊隐，自然只能把这份仰慕之情深埋心底。

of *Beijing Morning Post* and *Beijing News*. At that time, Shi Pingmei was an editor of the supplement of *Beijing News*. Therefore, Jiao and Shi could have the opportunity to gather in Beiping and cooperated at work. During the four years in the university, he published a lot of proses and translation works as well as drama paper. On 14th July, 1924, he wrote a poem called "*Thinking about Ms. C at the night of July 4th*", expressing his admiration and love for Shi Pingmei, which wrote:

> *It is beyond my power to comfort you when you are feeling cold and lonely,*
> *and I can't love you, my dear!*
> *Dear, your laughter is always lingering in my heart,*
> *and your face is always in front of my eyes.*
> *Your smile added to my new sorrows*
> *which burn together with those old ones.*

He had expressed his love for Shi not only to their common friend Lu Jingqing: "I admire Sis Mei nearly to the extent of love." And he had also told

1925 年，石评梅迎来遭遇重创的一年。3 月初，年仅 29 岁的高君宇因病英年早逝，令一直抱定独身主义的石评梅后悔不迭，留下终生的遗憾，在当年她给焦菊隐的一封信中写道，

菊弟：

这些天我很心慌，老父今年整七十，我本预备同哥哥回去祝寿的。如今交通阻梗，也只好惕丧而返。

京中战事迫切，家乡也在那里跃跃欲试其十五年培养成的好身手，奈何？只是父母的惦念我，我又惦念他们。

晶清徐□□少爷都在校，她们到何处去呢？我天天抽空去看她们。

今天追悼会你去莫有？现在的这样混乱社会，牺牲真不值的。极其糊涂的被人打死称烈士，简直不如痛快的自杀！

你千万小心你自己，不要多在街上跑，不要多参加团体运动，不是怕，是千金之子，坐不垂堂。你一定听姐姐的话。

梅姊

三月廿九日 夜中

府上平安吗？有消息吗？

his wife Qin Jin: "One time I went to Beijing from Tianjin to see her and she took me to go skating. I am a big myopia, so I can't skate. I had to sit down and see her skating. She wore a white sweater and a white hat, skated so naturally and elegantly, just like a white swan. I was obsessed with this image."

However, as early as 1922, Shi Pingmei had already met Gao Junyu, who also came from Shanxi province. Gao Junyu chased after her enthusiastically. Shi didn't want to easily accept this emotion as she once got hurt during a relationship in the past. But she tried a variety of ways to support Gao Junyu and his revolutionary activities. Jiao Juyin, three years younger than her, could do nothing but bury the admiration and love in the bottom of his heart.

In 1925, Shi suffered a lot. In early March, Gao Junyu untimely died from illness at the age of 29. Shi Pingmei, previously clinging to celibacy, suffered a life-long regret. She wrote a letter to Jiao:

Bro Ju:
These days I am very confused. My father is seventy years old, and I had planned to

在字迹依稀可辨的信封上，邮戳显示为"十四年三月三十"，即1925年3月30日。恰在高君宇离世一周后的3月12日，孙中山先生在北京逝世，而在1924年的10月，高君宇还曾在广州作为孙中山的秘书协助其平息叛乱。之后数日，举国沉浸在哀悼孙中山先生的气氛中，信中所指"追悼会"，即国共两党组织各界民众进行的哀悼活动。与此同时，国内战事频仍，革命尚未成功，全国陷于北伐战争的前夜。身为弱女子的石评梅无力回天，痛定思痛，对时事保有了几许难得的冷静，信末那一句对菊弟的嘱咐，发自肺腑，诚若家姐在弟弟耳畔的切切叮咛。

1926年，焦菊隐加入燕京大学同

民国十四年（1925）石评梅给焦菊隐的信件
the letter written by Shi to Jiao in the 15th year of the
Republic of China (1912 - 1949)

go back home with my brother to celebrate his birthday. But due to the traffic clog, we had to give it up regretfully.

Wars are looming in Beijing, our hometown is also keen to experiment on the military trained for 15 years. Will that help? My parents miss me, and I miss them too.

Jingqing and Mr. Xu are both studying in the school, where would they go? I go to see them everyday.

Did you go to the memorial today? Given such social chaos, sacrifice is worthless! Instead of being killed by people and then billed as the martyr, I prefer committing suicide!

You must take care of yourself. Don't wander in the street, and do not participate in any activities. It's not cowardness. it just doesn't worth it. You must listen to me.

Sis. Mei
on the night March 29th

Are you and your families safe? Any news?

学读书会，开始阅读进步书籍，并继续施展着他的文学才能，他翻译发表了多部契诃夫的短篇小说，世界出版社出版了焦菊隐翻译的莫里哀的剧本《伪君子》，散文诗集《夜哭》也在这一年出版发行。

3月18日，北平发生了震惊世人的三一八惨案，石评梅虽未亲临事件现场，但惨案中被杀害的女学生刘和珍以及受伤的陆晶清都是她的好友。第二天，石评梅即赴医院看望受伤的好友，其后的一周内，她一边在报纸上发表文章斥责段祺瑞政府的残暴，一边忙于对伤亡友人的抚慰和凭吊，心情十分低落。

回到文章开头这封信，石评梅首先对焦菊隐表达了关切之情，之后便是对这连续发生的事件的无奈和深重的哀怨。高君宇去世后这一年的时间里，悔恨和悲伤的情绪一直折磨着她。为了避免她触景伤情，焦菊隐约了几名好友到陶然亭公园高君宇的墓前植树，没想到却在那里碰到了正在凭吊的石评梅，可见她的悲伤心情并未平复，同时她也感受到了作为好友的焦菊隐对她和亡人的深厚友情，因此信

On the envelope, one can hardly recognize the postmark as "the 14th year of the Republic of China, March 30th", namely March 30th, 1925. A week after Gao Junyu died, on March 12nd, Sun Yat-sen died in Beijing. And in October 1924, Gao Junyu had quelled the insurgency in Guangzhou as Sun Yat-sen's secretary. After a few days, the country was immersed in the mourning of the Father of Nation. The "memorial" mentioned in the letter referred to the public mourning activities organized by the Kuomintang and the Communist Party. At the same time, wars were still unfolding, and revolution had yet to be successful. The country was preparing for the Northern Expedition. As a weak woman, Shi Pingmei was powerless in the face of the wars. But learning from these mistakes, she remained calm over the current affairs. Therefore, at the end of the letter, she warned her Bro Ju earnestly, just like a biological sister.

Jiao Juyin joined the students reading club in Yanjing University in 1926, and began to read books, continuing to display his literary talent. He published a number of translations of Chekhov's short stories, and the World Publishing Company published his translation of Moliere's play

中流露出对菊弟及其家人诚挚的惦念。

在信中，她甚至说出"我愿早瞑

陶然亭公园内的石评梅和高君宇雕像

the sculpture of Shi Pingmei and Gao
Junyu in the Taoranting Park

目"这样的言语，不幸一语成谶！两年后的1928年，石评梅因患急性脑膜炎去世，她的多愁善感使她始终深陷在高君宇离世的悲痛中难以自拔，宿命般殒落在那个纷乱的年代。

1949年，已然中年的焦菊隐带着

"*Hypocrite*". Besides, his prose poems "*Night Crying*" was also published in the same year.

On March 18th, "the 318 Massacre" took place in Beijing, shocking the whole world. Although not at the scene on herself, Shi was also very shocked as the died female student Liu Hezhen was her good friend. Another friend Lu Jingqing also got hurt during the massacre. The next day, Shi Pingmei went to the hospital to visit her friend. And then within a week, she published several articles in the newspaper blaming on the cruelness of the Tuan Chi-jui government. At the same time, she was also busy comforting and sending condolence to old friends.

Then she wrote the letter as shown at the beginning of this passage. She expressed her care for Jiao and then her grief for all these tragedies. During the year after Gao Junyu died, Shi had been afflicted by her regret and sadness. To avoid the sight stirring up her feelings again, Jiao Juyin and some of his friends went to the Taoranting Park to plant trees in front of Gao Junyu's grave, but he never expected to run into Shi Pingmei. She had not recovered from this grief. At the same time, she also felt the friendship between her, Gao and Jiao. Therefore,

新婚不久的妻子秦瑾，重访陶然亭公园的高、石之墓，看望他久别的梅姐，凭吊他们年轻时代共同的迷茫与忧伤，连同那一丝朦胧的、淡淡的情愫……

这批珍贵的信件共9封，字迹清晰，品相完好，由秦瑾女士于2005年焦菊隐诞辰百年之际向北京人民艺术剧院戏剧博物馆无私捐赠，成为馆内文稿类藏品中年代最久远的珍存。1924至1928年，作为民国四大才女之一的石评梅，宛若流星般地划过焦菊隐的青春时代，他们共同经历的人与事，给焦菊隐的一生带来深远的影响。遗憾的是，由于女作家的早逝，焦菊隐先生在同一时期写给石评梅的信件不知所终。每每翻阅那一页页不同字迹的信笺，虽泛黄了，但笔体清晰遒劲，话语殷殷，都恍觉百年不长，他

陶然亭公园内的高君宇与石评梅墓

the tomb of Shi and Gao in the Taoranting Park

in her letter, she expressed her sincere regards to Jiao and his families.

In the letter, she even said that she hoped that she could die earlier, which turned out to be an ill omen. Two years later, in 1928, Shi Pingmei died from acute meningitis. Her sentiment made it difficult for her to recover from the grief of losing Gao Junyu. She finally died during that tumultuous era.

In 1949, already middle-aged jiao juyin took his newly-married wife Qin Jin to revisit the tomb of in Taoranting Park, to see his Sis. Mei and mourn their confusion, sorrow and subtle feelings for each other of their youth...

This rare collection of letters only consists of a total of 9 pieces, all kept in good condition. It was donated freely by Qin Jin at the 100th birthday of Jiao Juyin in 2005. And these letters have become the oldest treasure kept in the Bejing Museum of People's Art and Drama. From 1924 to 1928, as one of four talented women of the republic of China, Shi Pingmei was like a meteor, shooting across the sky of Jiao Juyin's life. Their common experience had brought profound influence on his life. Unfortunately, due

们的对话犹在耳畔，他们的故事就在昨天。

刘　琳

北京人民艺术剧院戏剧博物馆

to the writer's early death, we could not find any letters written by Jiao to Shi. Going through those letters, we could still feel the sincerity behind these clear handwriting characters. It seems that their stories have just taken place yesterday.

Liu Lin, Bejing Museum of People's Art and Drama

参考书目及文章：

焦世宏，刘向宏：《焦菊隐》，中国戏剧出版社，2007 年。

王庆华：《石评梅传略》，《文史资料选编》，第十四辑，北京出版社，1982 年。

焦世宏：《父亲焦菊隐与石评梅、林素珊》，《传记文学》，2005 年第 9 期。

Bibliography and articles:

Jiao Shihong, Liu Xianghong: Jiao Juyin, China Drama Press, 2007.6.

Wang Qinghua: Brief Biography of Shi Pingmei; Issue 14. Extraction of Cultural and Historical Materials, Beijing Press, 1982.9.

Jiao Shihong: My Father Jiao Juyin and Ship Pingmei, Lin Sushan; Biography Journal, 2005.9.

救国公债上的华侨史

A History of Overseas Chinese behind National Salvation Bonds

1937 年至 1939 年中国抗日战争初期，国内投入了大量军队抵抗日军，国外的华侨纷纷以捐款、捐物资或直接回国参加抗战等形式支持祖国的抗日战争。以陈嘉庚为首的南洋华侨侨领于 1937 年 10 月成立了"马来亚新加坡华侨筹赈伤兵难民大会委员会"，1938 年 10 月又组织成立"南洋筹赈祖国难民总会"，这些组织号召当地华侨以募捐、义捐、认购债券等形式筹备抗战物资，还有大批青年华侨回祖国参加抗战。抗日战争时期，国内抗战所需战费及政费所需金钱的获得，与华侨有着密切的关系。1940 年，全年战费共 18 万万元，其中海外华侨汇款占 11 万万元，侨汇中南洋华侨的汇款占 7/10 左右，其余是美洲等处华侨汇款，[1]体现了南洋华侨为祖国的抗日战争做出的巨大贡献。*卢沟桥七七事*

In the early period (1937-1939) of the Chinese War of Resistance Against Japan (i.e. the Second Sino-Japanese War), massive Chinese army was mobilized to defend against the Japanese enemies. The overseas Chinese actively supported the homeland's resistance against Japan through donation of money goods and materials, or even directly coming back to join the army. Headed by Chen Jiageng, in October 1937, the leaders of overseas Chinese in the Southeast Asia founded the "Malaysia and Singapore Overseas Chinese Assembly Committee of Fundraising and Relief for Wounded Soldiers and Refugees". And in October 1938 they founded the "South Ocean General Assembly of Fundraising and Relief for Homeland Refugee". These organizations called upon the local Chinese immigrants to arrange provisions for the resistance against Japan through fundraising, volunteer donation, and purchasing defense bonds. There was also a huge amount of overseas Chinese youth who went back to join the army. During the War of Resistance, the money for military and government spending during the war had close relations with the overseas Chinese. The annual military spending in 1940 was 1.8 billion yuan,

---

[1] 陈嘉庚著，文明国：《陈嘉庚自述（下册）》，安徽文艺出版社，2013 年，第 314 页。

变后，中国全民响应抗日，国民政府为筹措战备资金也向海外华侨倡议经济援助，以陈嘉庚等为首的南洋华侨，与当时任国民政府财政部部长及中国自由公债劝募总会会长的宋子文多次进行电函，协商将钱款汇回国内的事宜。由于南洋华侨人数众多，募集钱款的活动频繁且范围广泛，当地的华人社团筹集了巨额金钱，并认购了大量的公债券，这些巨额钱款的流动引起了新加坡、马来亚等侨居国政府的关注，为了限制侨汇流回中国，侨居国政府有意对汇款征税。

陈嘉庚也因此多次与宋子文进行电函商讨，1938 年 1 月 24 日，陈嘉庚致宋子文电函中提到，马来亚政府有意限制华侨募捐钱款流回中国，对认购债券课以重税，并颁布了相关规定，即"限制每券最低须百元票面，须贴印税叻银四角五分，如五元、十元票面亦同此税费"[1]。马来亚政府的这些规定意在限制当地华侨对中国的战争汇款及援助，打压华侨抗日的热情和

with 1.1 billion coming from the overseas Chinese in general. Seventy percent of overseas funds were transferred from the Chinese in Southeast Asia. The rest of them came from the Chinese in South and North America.[1] The funds represented the great contributions to the homeland's War of Resistance made by the overseas Chinese. After the"Lugou Bridge Incident of July 7th" (also known as the Marco Polo Bridge Incident), all the Chinese people responded to the resistance against Japan. In order to further raise fund for the military, the Nationalist government also called the overseas Chinese for economic aids. The Chinese in Southeast Asia, headed by Chen Jiageng, contacted Song Ziwen for many times, who was the Secretary of Treasury in the Nationalist government and the Chairman for the Chinese General Assembly of Liberty Government Bonds Fundraising, to discuss the transfers of funds into the country. Due to the huge population of Chinese immigrants and the frequent fundraising activities in wide extents, the local Chinese communities raised enormous amount of money and purchased huge amount of government bonds. The huge flow of money arroused the attention of governments in Malaya and Singapore. In order to restrict the money from flowing into China, the local governments there had the intentions to levy tax on the transfers.

On this issue, Chen Jiageng discussed with Song Ziwen for many times through telegraphs. On January

[1] 中国第二历史档案馆：《宋子文与陈嘉庚为在新、马募集救国捐款事往来电函（1937 年 12 月—1939 年 7 月）》，《民国档案》2006 年第 3 期，第 28 页。

[1] *Chen Jiageng's Words, Volume 2*, Page 314, written by Chen Jiageng, compiled by Wen Ming-guo. Hefei: Anhui Literature and Art Publishing House, 2013.5

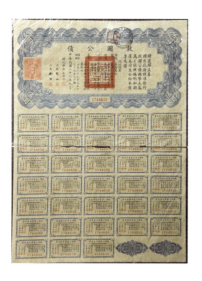

伍圆救国公债及局部放大图（1）

five yuan (face value) government gond of
national salvation, with zoom-in on the top part (1)

伍圆救国公债及局部放大图（2）

five yuan (face value) government bond of
national salvation, with zoom-in on the top part (2)

百圆救国公债及局部放大图

one hundred yuan (face value) government bond

of national salvation, with zoom-in on the top part

积极性。中国华侨历史博物馆收藏了 4 份贴有马来亚印花税票的救国公债，可以印证抗日战争时期马来亚等南洋当地政府对华侨汇款征收印花税的历史，每一份救国公债都体现了南洋华侨筹备战时资金的艰辛与不易。

这些救国公债都由新加坡华人收藏家陈来华先生无偿捐赠，是中国华侨历史博物馆的馆藏文物，属于可移动文物的纸制品票据类文物。其中有两份文物藏品虽然有磨损和污渍，但品相比较完好；另外两份在捐赠时就已经是断裂的状态，同样存在污渍和发黄的状况。4 份公债均是国民政府于 1937 年发行，尺寸都一样，均为纵 35 厘米、横 26.1 厘米，票面上都共有 33 张息票。其中前 3 份公债的面额为伍圆，编号分别为 1744060、1741574、1744632；第 4 份是百圆救国公债，编号为 514971。救国公债上的 33 张息票，每张的编号都相同，只是各自的领取利息时间不一样，第一张息票从民国二十七年（1938）开始可以领取利息，而第 33 张息票上写着领取利息时间为"民国五十九年"（1970），

24th,1938, in his telegraph to Song Ziwen, Chen Jiageng noted that the government of Malaya intended to restrict the Chinese money from transferring back into their homeland. The government levied heavy tax on the bond purchases, and issued respective rules: "a tax stamp of 4 dime (jiao) and 5 cent (fen) must be attached to every bond at the lowest note of one hundred yuan. If there are five yuan or ten yuan notes, the same tax fee applies."[1] The rules by the Malayan government were intended to restrict the local Chinese immigrants' donations and aids to China, and to suppress the Chinese immigrants' enthusiasm in the resistance against Japan. The Chinese Historical Museum of Overseas Chinese collected four government bonds of national salvation, with the Malayan tax stamps pasted on. They have proved the history of stamp taxation by Malayan and other Southeast Asian governments on the money transfers of local Chinese immigrants during the War of Resistance Against Japan. Every bond of national salvation demonstrates the hardships and difficulties experienced by the Chinese in Southeast Asia, in their fundraisings during the war.

These government bonds of national salvation were all donated without reimbursement by the Chinese Singaporean Collector Chen Laihua. They are now in the collection of Chinese Historical Museum of Overseas Chinese, classified into the bill notes category of paper products, movable artifacts. Among them there are two artifacts with

[1] Second Historical Archive of China: *Telegraphs between Song Ziwen and Chen Jiageng on fundraising in Singapore and Malaya*(1937.12 – 1939.7) *Republic Profile*, Issue 3, 2006, Page 28.

领取利息的时间从第 1 张息票开始至第 33 张息票逐年递增。息票上写有"凭此息票於民国 年 月 日向各地中央银行或其委托机关领取到期利息，国币贰角整"。

4 份救国公债特点是都贴有一张马来亚印花税票，伍圆救国公债上贴的是 10 分税额的税票，百圆救国公债上贴的是 25 分税票。这些税票有两个共同点，首先是税票上图案都一样，均为马来亚巴生清真寺建筑风景图；其次税票上均盖戳有"KUALA LUMPUR""1938"等字样。经查证，"KUALA LUMPUR"的中文译名为"吉隆坡"，简称 KL，位于马来亚雪兰莪州内，是马来亚首都。"KUALA LUMPUR""1938"字样是指救国公债于 1938 年在马来亚 KUALA LUMPUR（吉隆坡）盖戳纳税，即为完税证明。

为了避免因为纳税而遭受损失、将捐款最大程度地汇回中国支援抗日战争，侨领陈嘉庚给宋子文发电函商讨对策，并提出了避税的 4 条建议，兹抄录如下：

abrasions and stains, but still in good conditions. The first three government bonds have denominations of five yuan, serial number: 1744060, 1741574, and 1744632. The fourth one is a one hundred yuan government bond of national salvation, serial number 514971. The 33 interest coupons on the government bonds of national salvation have the same serial numbers, but the times of redemption are different. The first interest coupon can be redeemed since the 27th year of the Republic (year 1937), while the 33rd one can be redeemed in the 59th year of the Republic (year 1970). The timing of redemption increased year by year from the 1st coupon to the 33rd coupon. The coupons have a line "Use this interest coupon on the X year X month X day at any branches or authorized institutions of Central Bank to redeem the interest due, 2 dimes (jiao) of national currency".

All of the four government bonds of national salvation feature a Malayan tax stamp. On the five yuan bond, there are 10 cents (fen) stamps. On the one hundred yuan bond, there is a 25 cents (fen) stamp. These tax stamps have two common features. First, the designs on the tax stamps are the same: the scenic image of Malayan Klang Mosque architecture. Second, the stamps were all sealed with the words "Kuala Lumpur, 1938". According to the research, Kuala Lumpur is translated as "Ji long po" in Chinese, abbreviated as KL. It is located in the Selangor state of Malaya, and was the former capital of Malaysia. The words "Kuala Lumpur, 1938" means stamp tax was paid for the government bond of national salvation at Kuala Lumpur, Malaya, with the seal as a certificate of

（一）五元、十元等票，如临时收据，不由中国、华侨两银行经手可避免此税；（二）临时收据及汇款，均由各会馆、社团迳给并迳汇中行或总会，债票亦直接寄交之，即可免贴印税；（三）上两项乞通知总会及港中行，嗣后各社团迳汇之款详为登账，并注明地址，俾他日迳寄债券；（四）蒙承电示财部寄此间中国、华侨两银行五元至百元票各二百五十万元，迄未收到，是否系邮件梗阻之故？此项债券，既在重税之列，如未寄出，请止发。[1]

以上 4 条建议中提到，5 元、10 元等小额票据不经由中国银行、华侨银行汇回中国则可以避免缴纳印花税；临时收据、汇款及债票，如经由中行或南洋筹赈祖国难民总会转交回国内，也可免贴印花税。

华侨的每一笔汇款，认购的每一份救国公债，无论数额大小，都极为不易且珍贵。为了避税，当地的华侨

tax paid.

In order to avoid the expense of tax and to maximally transfer the donations back to homeland to support the War of Resistance, Chen Jiageng, the leader of Chinese immigrants, sent a telegraph to Song Ziwen to discuss about countermoves, and put forward four ways of tax avoidance, as recorded below:

1. The notes of five yuan and ten yuan, and such as temporary receipts, can avoid this tax when not being transferred through the Bank of China and the Bank of Overseas Chinese. 2. For the temporary receipts and money transfers, we should transfer all of them directly from clubs and associations and directly to the Central Bank or General Assembly, and also directly send the bond notes, then the stamp taxes are avoided. 3. For the above two suggestions, please inform the General Assembly and the Central Bank at Hong Kong, to register the funds directly transferred by the associations onto the account books with details, and write down the addresses, for the mailings of bond notes on later dates. 4. Please send a telegraph to the Department of Treasury to inform that we have not yet received the five yuan and one hundred yuan notes, 2.5 million yuan in total, from the Bank of China and Bank of Overseas Chinese by

[1] 中国第二历史档案馆：《宋子文与陈嘉庚为在新、马募集救国捐款事往来电函（1937 年 12 月—1939 年 7 月）》，《民国档案》2006 年第 3 期，第 28 页。

采取的一些对策，实属无奈之举。救国公债及印花税票是特殊历史时期的产物，同时也见证了南洋华侨不畏困难和阻挠，支援祖国抗战的历史。

罗佩玲

中国华侨历史博物馆

mail. Is that because of the delays in mails? Since this kind of bond notes were imposed with heavy taxes, if they are not mailed yet, please stop mailing.[1]

The above four lines suggested transferring the small denomination notes like five yuan and ten yuan back to China without going through the Bank of China and the Bank of Overseas Chinese, can avoid paying stamp taxes; and transferring the temporary receipts, money, and bond notes, through the Central Bank and the "South Ocean General Assembly of Fundraising and Relief for Homeland Refugee", can also avoid stamp taxes.

Every money transfer made and every government bond of national salvation purchased by the overseas Chinese, no matter large or small in amount, are all difficult and precious. In order to avoid the tax, the local Chinese immigrants had no choice but to make those countermoves. The government bonds of national salvation and the tax stamps were the products of a particular historical period. They witnessed the Southeast Asia overseas Chinese's brave and perseverance to support the homeland during the War of Resistance.

Luo Peiling, Chinese Historical Museum of Overseas Chinese

[1] Second Historical Archive of China: *Telegraphs between Song Ziwen and Chen Jiageng on fundraising in Singapore and Malaya*(1937.12 – 1939.7) *Republic Profile*, Issue 3, 2006, Page 28.

清刺绣《松藤绶带鸟图》与慈禧的六十寿庆

Qing Embroidery "Painting of A Ribbon Bird over the Pine Branch" (Song Teng Shou Dai Niao Tu) and the Sixtieth-year-old Birthday Ceremony for Empress Dowager Cixi

刺绣，古称"黹（zhǐ）"或"针黹"，是用绣针引彩线在织物上穿绕以线迹形成纹饰图案的一种工艺。

刺绣的起源可以上溯至远古时期，据《尚书·益稷》记载，早在舜帝时，统治者穿着的衣服上就带有以刺绣方法装饰的宗彝、藻、火、粉米、黼（fǔ）、黻（fú）纹样。在考古发现中，河南安阳出土的殷商时期的青铜器以及陕西宝鸡茹家庄西周墓中的泥块上都保存着刺绣的痕迹，是早期刺绣的实物例证。而后随着刺绣工艺的发展，其技法不断变化创新，以最基本的针法来说，就有直针、环针、齐针、套针、缠针、抢针、扎针、锁针、打籽针等几十种之多；在此基础上，各种针法有选择地组合起来，又形成

Embroidery, traditionally known as *zhi* or *zhenzhi*, is a handicraft of using the needle and colorful thread to weave and decorate fabrics.

The origin of embroidery could date back to ancient times. According to the Chapter Yishe in the *Book of Documents*, there were embroidery patterns like Zongyi (tiger and long-tail monkey), Zao (algae), Huo (fire), Fenmi, Fu (black and white), and Fu (blue and black) on the clothing for the ruling class during the time of Emperor Shun. Archaeological discoveries have found some embroidered fragments on the Shang bronze wares excavated in Anyang, Henan provence and in the dirt in a tomb of the Western Zhou Dynasty excavated in Rujiazhuang, Baoji, Shaanxi provence, which are the earliest material evidence for early China embroidery. With the further development

了多种绣法，如平绣、锁绣、纳绣、贴绣、打籽绣、钉线绣、钉金绣、串珠绣等，具有极强的艺术表现力。自宋代开始，刺绣中逐渐出现了仿摹文人绘画的欣赏性作品，这些作品以纸本绘画为蓝本，运用丰富多样的针法和绣法，配合以粗细不同、色彩各异的多种绣线，可以将绘画中的笔墨线条、色彩浓淡和风度气韵表现得极其传神，并且由于绣线独特的肌理质感，刺绣呈现出的艺术效果有时更甚于原作。这种艺术形式流传至清代，已发展得相当成熟，尤其是一些宫廷装饰用绣画，往往不惜工时成本，力图精益求精，由此产生了许多精美的作品，令人叹为观止。

北京艺术博物馆收藏的刺绣《松藤绶带鸟图》即是一幅清代光绪年间的绣画佳作。此绣画为国家二级文物，画心纵 136 厘米，横 67 厘米，在米黄色缎地上，以彩色绣线绣松树、藤萝和绶带鸟等图案。松树枝干挺劲，针叶繁茂，枝叶间有藤萝盘结缠绕，紫色的藤花成簇垂下，一片欣欣向荣的景象；松枝之上，一只红喙彩羽的绶带鸟正俯身向树下探看，神情专注生动，充满盎然意趣。松为常绿乔木，越寒不凋，四

of craftsmanship, new techniques were created. Based on more than ten basic stitching techniques that include straight stitch, circle stitch, aligned stitch, chain stitch, layering stitch, featherstitch, pricking stitch, locking stitch, couching and laid work, new techniques were developed via the combination of different stitches, such as plain stitch, chain stitch, gold and silver thread stitch, and beam stitch. Since the Song Dynasty, embroidery started to imitate the literati paintings and became artistic. Those works were mainly based on the painting on paper, adopted various stitches and embroidering techniques, and coordinated the threads with different thickness and of various colors to embody vividly the brushstrokes, colors and the aura of the paintings. But because of the texture of embroidery, its artistic effect sometimes emulated the original painting. This craftsmanship developed into quite a mature state in the Qing Dynasty. In order to make some embroidery paintings for the imperial court, the craftsmen would pursue the excellence at the expense of time and energy. This craftsman spirits have produced many masterpieces.

The embroidery work "Painting of A Ribbon Bird over the Pine Branch" (Song Teng Shou Dai Niao Tu) is such an excellent work made during the

清刺绣慈禧御笔《松藤绶带鸟图》

"Painting of A Ribbon Bird over the Pine Branch" with Empress Dowager Cixi's writings

reign of Emperor Guangxu, which is now a second-class cultural relic. The painting itself is 136 cm in length and 67 cm in width. The patterns such as the pine tree, wisteria and ribbon-bird were embroidered with color threads on the beige satin. The upright pine branch intertwining with wisterias and those purple flowers drooping down present a lively image. Over the pine branch, a ribbon-bird with its red beak and colorful feathers is lowering its body and looking down dedicatedly, which is vigorous and interesting. This is an auspicious picture with good wishes. The pine tree represents longevity and health because it is green year around even in the winter and known as the elderly among the trees; wisterias have the symbolic meaning of immortality, for they as large climbing vines like to twine with other plants such as pine trees; the pronunciation of the ribbon-bird (shoudai niao) sounds similar to the Chinese character longevity "shou".

The embroidery work juxtaposes various stitching techniques to represent. The shapes of the flowers, the bird and the pine tree were all rendered in a careful way. For example, chain stitches have been used to represent coiled curly wisterias; pine stitches are applied to show the exuberant tree; featherstitches are used to embody the texture of the

季常青，古代视其为百木之长，是长寿康健的象征；紫藤则是大型攀援缠绕性藤本植物，松藤相缠，寓意连绵不断、长生不老，再加上与"寿"谐音的绶带鸟，整幅绣画表达出鲜明的"益寿延年"的吉祥主题。

在物象的表现上，这幅绣画综合运用了多种针法技巧，将花、鸟、藤、树的样貌形态描摹得极为细致传神，如以缠针表现藤萝枝蔓的卷曲盘绕，以松针表现松树针叶的蓬松茂密，以施毛针表现绶带鸟的翎羽质感等，具有很强的写实性，其绣工精致细腻，设色淡雅柔和，显示出十分典型的"平、光、齐、匀、和、顺、细、密"的苏绣特点。尤为难得的是，绣画在物象细节的表现上，如松皮的鳞节、藤叶的脉络、鸟足上的爪钩等处，也毫不含糊，尽以绣线细致描摹，而并未采用晚清时期刺绣中常用的以笔墨着色代绣的简便做法，足见绣工之精细用心。

由于刺绣《松藤绶带鸟图》完全仿照纸本绘画原稿内容进行摹绣，因此也保持了清代绘画集诗、书、画、印于一体的形式。在绣画顶部的正中位置，一枚"慈禧皇太后之宝"的方形朱红绣印极为醒目，右侧则绣有"光绪甲午孟春上浣御笔"及"颐神养性""瀛海仙班""海涵春育"等多方慈禧的闲章印鉴，由此可以推知，这幅绣画是以慈禧御笔画作为底稿刺绣而成的。除此之外，在绣画的侧边

bird feathers, which is realistic. The chosen colors are mild and elegant, which displays the classical characteristics of Suzhou embroidery: flat, bright, neat, even, harmonious, smooth, thin and intensive. More importantly, the details are excellently done such as the scales on the pine branches, the veins of the wisteria leaves and the claws of the bird's feet. Instead of applying the inks to paint as an easier alternative largely used in the late Qing period, this work chose to use thin threads to embroider details, which shows the efforts of the embroiderers.

Because the embroidery is a completely copy of the original painting, it keeps the forms of Qing painting which combines poems, calligraphy, painting and seals. On the upper part of the work, there is an eye-catching red square seal which writes "The Treasure of Empress Dowager Cixi". On the right side are embroidered seals of Cixi such as "Guangxu Jiawu Mengchun Shanghuan, Empress Handwriting," "Cultivating Spirits," "Yinghai Immortals," and "Generosity and Tolerance," which could evidence that this embroidery is based on the painting with Cixi's handwriting. Besides that, on the sides of the work there are three poems: "Falling down are the green vines and purple wisterias/ Ribbons high into the clouds/Preferring

和底边处还绣有"宝络纷垂荫碧萝/凌云干耸缩乔诃/飘缨更喜招仙羽/春满华林瑞气多/吴树梅题","彩纳丹霞金凤舞/涛翻银浪玉龙蟠/琼楼缥缈排云出/锦羽翩跹湛露欢/陆润庠题","五色文禽藤采敷/今朝报喜集蓬壶/万年不老松长寿/正是天家瑞应图/陆宝忠题"3首臣官的祝颂题诗,其笔法各异,应该也是仿摹纸本画作上的原有墨书而绣制的。

从绣画上的落款来看,这幅《松藤绶带鸟图》作于光绪甲午孟春上浣,也即光绪二十年(1894)农历正月上旬。据史料记载,慈禧生于道光十五年(1835)十月初十,按照中国的传统记岁方法,光绪二十年正逢其六十寿辰。慈禧自登上清朝政治舞台以来,长期把持朝政,独断专行,俨然一代女皇,其生活铺张靡费,极尽奢华。随着岁龄渐长,她深感年华消逝,祈望长命百岁、永享荣华的心情也日益强烈起来。在其晚年的书画作品中,有相当一部分是表达与"寿"有关的主题,如这幅北京艺术博物馆收藏的刺绣《松藤绶带鸟图》,除此之外,还有她的御笔纸本墨书"寿"字、绢本水墨《松图》等。受到这

the fairy birds to falling flowers/Spring and trees showing, full of prosperity" by Wu Shumei; "Rainbows, clouds and golden phoenix dancing/rolling waves, silver swells and jade dragon entwined/ Beautiful building producing clouds mistily/Flying feathers flying over the dews happily" by Lu Runyang; "Five color bird covered with wisterias/Bring the good news to the prosperous land/ Immortality and longevity like pines/ This is exactly an auspicious painting" by Lu Baozhong. These three poems are embroidered in different styles, which should be copying the original painting.

Based on the inscriptions, this painting was made in the first half of January 1894. According to the historical sources, Empress Dowager Cixi was born on the tenth of the tenth lunar year, 1835 and she would have been sixty years old on the 22nd year of Emperor Guangxu based on the traditional Chinese counting method. Since she participated in politics, she grabbed the power, made the decision without consulting others, and became a female emperor who lived an extremely luxury life. With the growing age, she became worried about the passing time and hoped for longevity and eternal wealth. Therefore, many calligraphies and paintings made in her advanced years are related to longevity, such as

种祈寿心态的驱使，慈禧对于自己60岁的"花甲大寿"自然是极为重视，打定主意要好好操办一番。早在光绪十八年（1892），朝廷即开始着手为慈禧六十寿辰做准备，光绪皇帝颁下圣谕："甲午年，欣逢（慈禧太后）花甲昌期，寿宇宏开，朕当率天下臣民胪欢祝嘏。所有应备仪文典礼，必应专派大臣敬谨办理，以昭慎重。著派礼亲王世铎、庆亲王奕劻，大学士额勒和布、张之万、福锟，户部尚书熙敬、翁同龢，礼部尚书崑冈、李鸿藻，兵部尚书许庚身，工部尚书松溎、孙家鼐，总办万寿庆典。该王大臣等其会同户部、礼部、工部、内务府，恪恭将事，博稽旧典，详议隆议，随时请旨遵行。"为了展现"圣寿"的豪华隆重，清政府计划拨出3000万两银子的专款，除了对皇宫及颐和园进行修整建设，作为庆寿典礼的举办场所外，还依照慈禧下令设计的"万寿点景画稿"，预备在从西华门至颐和园的几十里道路上，沿途搭建经坛、戏台、彩殿、牌楼，组织僧道诵经祈福、戏班演戏庆贺，以供她在途中观览，即所谓的庆寿"点景"工程。现在矗立在西四十字路口西北和东北角

this ribbon-bird painting, calligraphy work of the character "Shou (longevity)", and silk painting with ink titled Pine Trees Painting. In the hope of longevity, Empress Dowager Cixi paid great attention to her sixtieth-year-old birthday ceremony and decided to plan something good and grand.

清慈禧御笔"寿"字
the character "Shou (Longevity)" written by Qing Empress Dowager Cixi

的两座曲尺形二层转角楼，就是在这次"点景"工程中建造的。面对如此"盛事"，各路官僚臣属也不敢怠慢，纷纷挖空心思争相为皇太后准备精美寿礼以博其欢心。刺绣《松藤绶带鸟图》的绣工堪称一流，蕴意喜庆吉祥，又是依慈禧御笔原画所作，很可能就是当时官员为慈禧六十寿辰而进献的贺礼。

然而彼时的大清帝国已是国势衰败，内忧外患，国库空虚几至入不敷出的地步，还要再拨付巨资举办这样规模宏大、豪华铺张的庆寿大典，实在是举步维艰。事实上，由于国际局势紧张，为了军备需要，清政府不得不举借外贷以应付军费开支。就是在这种情形下，慈禧仍旧一意孤行，为自己的寿典大肆挥霍，时有大臣上书进谏，请求停止颐和园工程，却惹得慈禧勃然大怒，悍然放话曰："今日令吾不欢者，吾亦将令彼终身不欢！"光绪二十年六月（1894 年 7 月），正当庆典筹备工作如火如荼进行之时，中日甲午战争爆发，清军虽奋力抗敌，却因军备、战略等原因节节败退，到九月寿典前夕，日军已渡过鸭绿江，大举侵入辽南，向大连、旅顺进犯。

Early in 1892, the court started to prepare for her birthday ceremony. Emperor Guangxu issued a decree to gather a group of officials from each department to plan a grand ceremony for Empress Dowager Cixi. In order to show its importance and grandness, the Qing government specifically appropriated 300 million ounces of silver. Apart form the refurbishment of the Palace and the Summer Palace, the empress dowager ordered people to design "Millions of Scenic Spots Illustrations of Longevity" for the ceremonial venues, which included a plan to build the temples, theatres, decorated palace, and decorated archway, and incorporated monks reciting the sutras and praying for happiness and actors giving performances so that she could enjoy on her way from the Xihua Gate to the Summer Palace. That was so-called the "Scenic Spots" project.

Now the two L-shaped two-story buildings on the northwestern corner and the northeastern corner of the Xisi Road were built for the project. Facing the "grand thing", each official did not dare to neglect; rather they exhausted their ideas to prepare gifts to please the empress dowager. The embroidery "Painting of A Ribbon Bird over the Pine Branch" was excellent in its craftsmanship and full of auspicious and pleasant meanings; the

清慈禧御笔《松图》

Pine Tree Painting painted by
Qing Empress Dowager Cixi

design was also from Empress Dowager Cixi's own painting. It is very possible that this work was a gift prepared by some official as a gift for her birthday ceremony.

However, the Qing Empire at that time was on the decline, beset by troubles from both at home and abroad. The national treasury was depleted and could not make ends meet. But even in such a terrible situation, the country had to allocate money to hold such a huge and luxury ceremony, which made the situation even worse. In fact, the Qing government had to make a loan in order to prepare the army for such an intensive international circumstances. Even so, Empress Dowager Cixi insisted in spending a lot of money on her birthday ceremony. Sometimes some officials paid their visit and asked about stopping the construction of the Summer Palace, which immediately irritated her. She even said, "For the people who do not make me happy today, I will make them miserable for the rest of their life!"

In July 1894, Sino-Japanese War broke out during the preparation of her ceremony. Even though the Qing army fought against the enemies, they were defeated because of the lack of armaments and strategies. In September of the same

文物背后的故事
stories behind cultural relics

慈禧迫于无奈，最终下旨取消了在颐和园的庆典以及沿途的"点景"工程，而将寿庆改在紫禁城内的宁寿宫举行。即便如此，从十月初一到十七为期半个多月的庆典，也花掉了白银540余万两，相当于当时拨付给前线战争用款的两倍多，其奢侈豪华和铺张浪费程度仍然令人瞠目。

刘远洋
北京艺术博物馆

year, right before the ceremony, the Japanese army already crossed the Yalv River, invaded the south part of Liaoning and marched towards Dalian and Lvshun. Empress Dowager Cixi was forced to stop the construction of the Summer Palace and the Scenic Spots project; instead, the venue for the ceremony was changed to Ningshou Palace. Even though, the preparation work lasting for seventeen months since October 1st had cost over 5.4 million ounces of silver, twice the money used for preparing the frontline warfare. It is astonishing to know how luxurious and extravagant this ceremony was.

Liu Yuanyang, Beijing Art Museum

中国人民大学博物馆藏徽州冥契文书浅析

Brief Analysis on Huizhou Funerary Contract Documents Collected in the Museum of Renmin University of China

中国人民大学博物馆 2009 年入藏一批徽州文书，在已结束的全国可移动文物普查工作中，我们对这批徽州文书的情况有了较为准确的掌握。在数量上，这批文书共计 21860 组 27400 件左右；在年代上，文书所属年代从明代后期一直横跨到 20 世纪 80 年代，其中最早的为明正德六年（1511）土地买卖契约；在类别上，这批文书涉及契约、赋役、宗族、法律、婚丧、会社、商业、民俗等，种类齐全；在地域上，文书大多来自徽州地区的歙县。经过整理，我们在这批文书中也发现了 7 件冥契文书，其中清末时期冥契 4 件，民国时期冥契 3 件。就目前笔者的了解，徽州地区冥契的材料只有黄山学院的 7 件文书有详细录文刊布，本次可移动文物普查中发现的

In 2009, a batch of Huizhou documents were collected by the museum of Renmin University of China. After the national census on movable cultural relics, we have formulated a relatively correct understanding of the details of these documents. We have 27,400 copies of documents in total which could be divided into 21,860 groups. These documents originated from the middle and late Ming Dynasty and had been carried out until 1980s, and the earliest copy is a land sale contract in the 6th year of Zhengde, Ming Dynasty. In terms of categories, this batch of documents are of various types including contract documents, tax documents, ethnic documents, law, marriage and funeral documents, community documents, commercial documents, folk custom documents, etc. And most of them were discovered in She County in Huizhou area. After collating, we also found 7

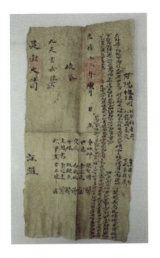

契一 清光绪十二年（1886）张坚
固卖地冥契

contract 1. Zhang Jiangu's funerary contract
documents
on land sale in the 12th year of Emperor
Guangxu, Qing Dynasty

契二 清光绪十八年（1892）吴氏买阴地冥契

contract 2. Wu's funerary contract documents on land
purchasement in the 18th year of Emperor Guangxu, Qing
Dynasty;

契三 清光绪三十二年（1906）东王公西
王母卖灵屋冥契

contract 3. Dong Wanggong (literal: East Duke) and
Xi Wangmu's (literal: West Qeen) funerary contract
documents on house sale in the 23th year of Emperor
Guangxu, Qing Dynasty

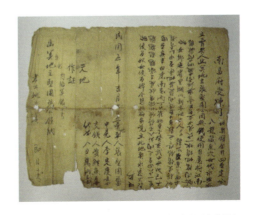

契四 民国五年（1916）张坚固卖地冥契

contract 4. Zhang Jiangu's funerary contract documents
on land sale in the 5th year of the Republic of China (1912-1949)

契五 民国十四年（1925）张坚固卖地冥契

contract 5. Zhang Jiangu's funerary contract documents
on land sale in the 14th year of the Republic of China
(1912-1949)

中国人民大学博物馆的这批冥契文书，将为徽州文书研究及古代买地券研究增添新的材料。

在形式上，契一、契二为赤契，一般来讲，赤契是买主报经县衙查理缴纳过契税、钤盖了官印的契书，官印是土地和财产在官府正式注册的依据。这两份冥契的印文虽已漫漶不清

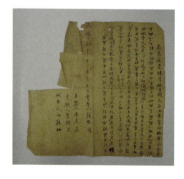

契六 民国十七年（1928）张坚固卖阴地冥契

contract 6. Zhang Jiangu's funerary contract documents on
land sale in the 17th year of the Republic of China (1912-1949)

copies of funerary contract documents, among which 4 originated from the end of Qing Dynasty and 3 originated from the Republic of China (1912 - 1949). As far as the author concerns, published details of this kind of funerary contract documents could only be found in Huangshan College, which had collected 7 copies of funerary contract documents. Therefore, the funerary contract documents in the Museum of Renmin University of China would add new materials to the research of Huizhou documents and land-purchase certificates.

Contract 1 and 2 are Red Contracts which generally refer to those approved and authorized by the government after submitting the contract tax. The official seals on the Red Contracts are evidence of official registration of land or other assets. The seals on the above two contracts could hardly be recognized. However, they couldn't be official seals but ones with divine color created by the folks. Therefore, these funerary contract documents would be even more effective and powerful than other contracts as they were authorized by the divine power. Contract 3, 4 and 5 are ordinary White Contracts (contracts without any official seals). In Contract 6 and 7, burial places, orientation, and the name of the dead are △ , therefore these two contracts

难以识别，但是从常识来讲它上面的"官印"不可能是真正的官印，而是民间拟造的象征神明的印章，以证明此份冥契得到了天地神明的认证，比一般冥契更具效力。契三、契四、契五为普通白契。契六、契七中土名、墓穴朝向、亡人姓名等具体信息均以△代替，应是契约范本。除契三外，其余6份契约采取一行顺书一行逆书形式书写，顺书逆书交叉的形式是冥契中独有的，区别于普通契约。

7份冥契的内容模式与当时徽州地区土地买卖契约基本相似，契约中明确了买卖双方姓名、买卖原因、土名、四至、金额、买卖双方权利义务、时间、中见人及代书人姓名等。但由于冥契的特殊性质，这些格式化的内容又有不同的表述：买卖原因上，将神仙卖地的原因解释为无钱使用，如契三东王公西王母"今因正用"、契四及契六幽冥地主张坚固"无钱使用"，照搬了现实社会中大多数土地交易的原因；土地四至无一例外均用"东至甲乙青龙，西至庚辛白虎，南至丙丁朱雀，北至壬癸玄武，中央戊己大地"或"东至青龙，西至白虎，南至朱雀，北至玄武，上至青天，

should be samples. Except Contract 3, other 6 funerary contract documents are written in a unique format different from ordinary contracts. In these contracts, the first line was written from up to the bottom but the next line was written from the opposite direction.

The format of the seven contracts are similar with other common land sale contracts in Huizhou area with ordinary contract items on them, including the name of the buyer and the seller, buying and selling reason, burial place, four reaches of the burial place, trade price, the rights and obligations between the seller and the buyer, time, intermediary and the name of allograph person. Due to the unique characteristics of funerary contract documents, the specific details of the above items are different from ordinary contracts. The reason of sale in funerary contract documents is generally that the immortals do not have enough money. For example, in Contract 3, the reason of sale is that the East Duke and West *Queen* " 今 因 正 用 " (need money for official purpose). In Contract 4 and 6, the reason is that *Zhang Jiangu*, the landlord in the afterword, " 无钱使用 " (has no money to spend). These could reflect the reasons of most land sales in the realistic world. And the four reaches are all "The east end is the habitation of Qinglong, the west end

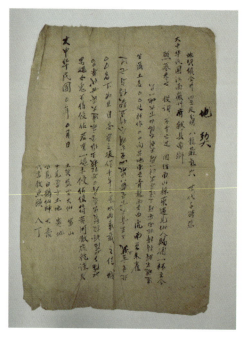

契七 民国某年买阴地冥契

contract 7. Funerary contract documents on
land sale during the Republic of China (1912 - 1949)

下至黄泉"表示；金额上用"金银
九万九千九百九十"表示，"9"这个
数字在古代意味着极限和圆满；卖主、
中见、交钱、代书等人物基本采用张
坚固、李定度、白鹤仙、双鲤鱼、蒿
李（里）父老、当方土地等道教神仙
形象。张坚固、李定度是在买地券中
经常一起出现的神仙，张坚固一般充
当卖地神仙，李定度则是中见神仙，
据已有的考古资料印证，至少在南朝
时期的买地券中就出现这二位神仙了，
此后二人逐渐成为了专职负责墓地交
易的神仙。而鲤鱼、仙鹤在道教思想

is the habitation of Baihu, the south end is the habitation of Zhuque, the north end is the habitation of Xuanwu and it covers the whole earth" (Note: Qinglong, Baihu, Zhuque, Xuanwu are gods of 4 directions worshipped by Taoism) or "The east end is the habitation of Qinglong, the west end is the habitation of Baihu, the south end is the habitation of Zhuque, the north end is the habitation of Xuanwu, and it reaches upper to heaven and down to hell." The price of the sale is normally "99,990" as "9" in the ancient China means extremism and completion. And the seller, intermediary and allograph person are generally immortals in Taoism including Zhang Jiangu, Li Dingdu, Faery of White Crane, Double Carps, folks in Haoli or local God of Land, etc. Zhang Jiangu and Li Dingdu could often been found in land-purchase certificates, in which Zhang Jiangu is the seller and Li Dingdu the intermediary. According to existing archaeological profiles, the two immortals appeared in the land-purchase certificate as early as in the Southern Dynasties. And later on, these two immortals became Gods in charge of funeral land sales. Carps and cranes could release souls from purgatory in Taoism. Therefore, in funerary contract documents, they could also lead the dead into the Pure Land. Haoli is home to the dead, and it refers to the afterworld

中均有超度、引领的含义，出现在冥契中也意味着一纸契约可将死者引渡到阴间极乐彼岸的含义。"蒿里"为人死后魂归之地，泛指阴间、墓地。这些神明形象都与人的生死有关。"地契镇（分）金井，四至定分明，八龙藏气穴（脉），万代子孙荣"是徽州冥契中的常用开首，出现在这7份冥契中的5份，另在黄山学院所藏的清代和民国冥契中也有类似的表达。就其字面意义来看，这样的语句反映了生者希望风水吉穴保佑死者后代人丁兴旺、世代荣昌的愿望。这样的词句在其他地方的买地券中还没有发现，即便徽州本地，清代以前的买地券也未出现此类词句，推测应是清代以后徽州纸质冥契特有的。

我们在关注冥契本身的内容和形式的同时，也试图探讨这种特殊文书蕴涵的诉求和意义，从内容和内涵上发掘清代、民国时期徽州冥契的独特价值。在中国传统社会中，土地是人们安身立命的根本，对生者来说，田地、房屋是安居乐业的前提，同样的，墓穴对死者也有同等重要的意义。要想在阴间安稳，有永久的居所，就要获得对墓地合法拥有权的承认，现实

and grave. And all of these immortals are related to life and death. In Huizhou area, funerary contract documents often start with a poem " The contract should based on a rich land, and the four reaches should be clearly identified. Eight dragons will fly freely under the ground and bless the future generations. " Five out of the seven copies all start with this beginning. And five copies of funerary contract documents of Qing Dynasty and the Republic of China (1912 - 1949) collected in the Huangshan College also start with similar expressions. Literally, this poem reflects the wish of the living that future generation will be blessed to boom and prosper. Such words have not been found in the land-purchase certificates in other areas. Even in Huizhou area, such words haven't appear until Qing Dynasty. Therefore, it is assumed that this expression is a unique feature of funerary contract documents in Huizhou during the Qing Dynasty.

We are attaching equal importance to the appeal and significance reflected in the documents when studying the content and format. We want to discover the unique value of funerary contract documents in Huizhou during Qing Dynasty and the Republic of China (1912 - 1949) from its content and meaning. In traditional Chinese society, land is the foundation

中墓穴坟水的买卖是原土地所有者与买主之间的协议，这与普通的田土、房屋交易没有差别。而冥契则是想象中的死者与阴府之间的协议，纯粹是人们对待死亡的心态表现。总的来说，人们希望通过设立买地券从而达到两方面的愿望：一是在阴间获得对墓地合法所有权的承认，使幽府各级官吏保护死者灵魂安稳，不受外鬼侵害，如契二、契五"毋许外人强占"，契三"倘有妖魔鬼怪魑魅魍魉不得争占"，契七"男魂女鬼不得侵占"等，倘若有鬼怪侵害了死者的安魂之所，后果也是很严重的，要么"奏到泰山门下女青案前发落"，要么"男侵者为仆女侵者为婢"，甚至"值符黄河澈底干"，这类诉求是冥契产生的初衷，自汉晋以来贯穿始终；二是祈求死者保佑后代家族兴旺，因此大多数冥契都以"地契镇（分）金井，四至定分明，八龙藏气穴（脉），万代子孙荣"为开首，契七说得更加直白，希望死者安葬于此风水佳穴后，能够保佑家族"荫子荫孙，招贤出贵，房房兴旺，积玉堆金，永远大发，世代荣昌"。

通过这次可移动文物普查，我

of people's life. For living people, land and house are the prerequisite of happiness. And similarly, tomb is of equal significance to the dead. If the dead want a stable and permanent residence in the afterworld, his legitimacy to own the residence (tomb) must be acknowledged. In the real world, the trade of tomb is an agreement between the buyer and the land owner. It is no difference from ordinary trade of land and houses. While funerary contract documents are agreements between the dead and the official of the afterworld, which could reflect people's spiritual appeal to deal with death. In a word, through land-purchase certificates, people wish to fulfill their desires in two aspects. Firstly, they want to get acknowledgement over their legitimate ownership of the grave, thus to have officials in the afterworld protect them from the threat of other ghosts. For example, in Contract 2 and 5, "The grave shall not be illegally occupied by others", and in Contract 3, "Ghosts shall not occupy this grave", in Contract 7 "All ghosts regardless of gender shall not occupy this grave". If any ghosts infringe the resting place of the dead, they would be harshly punished. For example, they might be sent to the Mountain Tai and being sentenced, or they might be punished to be slaves, or they might even be punished constantly until the water

们不仅发现了珍贵的徽州冥契，还了解到了古时冥契所反映出的人们对待死亡的心态，实在是普查工作的重大收获。

陈姝婕
中国人民大学博物馆

in Yellow River dries. This appeal was the original reason of the appearance of funerary contract documents and it has been carried out along the history since Han and Jin Dynasties. Secondly, people hope that the dead could bless the future generations of the family. Therefore, most of funerary contract documents all start with " The contract should be based on a rich land, and the four reaches should be clearly identified. Eight dragons will fly freely under the ground and bless the future generations". And in Contract 7, this appeal was put in an even blunter way, reading " Bless the future generation, so that they could be wise and powerful, prosperous and vital forever ".

Through the movable cultural relics census, we not only find the precious Huizhou Ming Qi, but also learn the ancient Ming Qi reflects people treat the attitude of death, which is really a great achievement of the census work.

Chen Shujie, Collection Department of the Museum of Renmin University of China

一张崔嵬使用过的渡航证明书

A Flight Certificate Used by Cui Wei

50多年前的一个冬日，中国一支由9人组成的代表团借道香港，乘坐一架英国客机踏上日本的国土，开始了为期28天的文化交流活动。

摆在大家面前的这张渡航证明书，

On a winter day more than 50 years ago, a group of nine Chinese people stopped in Hong Kong and took a British flight on their way to Japan, starting their 28-day cultural exchange.

The flight certificate below witnessed

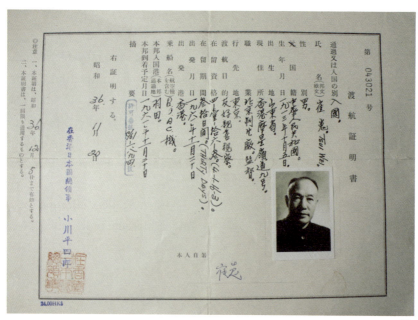

崔嵬渡航证明书正面[1]

the front side of Cui Wei's Flight Certificate[1]

---

[1] 渡航证明书上所填崔嵬的出生日期有误，应为"一九一二年十月四日"。

[1] The date of birth on the flight certificate was wrong. It should be October 4th, 1912.

就是当年这支代表团出访日本的重要见证。它的使用者是代表团中唯一一位电影界的代表——著名电影导演、演员崔嵬。

这支代表团的全称是中国文化友好代表团，团长为楚图南（时任中国人民对外文化协会会长），副团长为周巍峙（时任文化部艺术局局长，后曾任文化部党组书记、副部长、代部长）、孙平化（曾任中国人民对外友好协会副会长，中日友好协会副会长、会长），成员包括崔嵬、王守觉、常沙娜、崔泰山、吴应健等。

当时，崔嵬是在拍摄电影《北大荒人》接近尾声的时候接到这个任务的。分析他被安排访日的原因，大致有两个，一是因为他导演的电影《青春之歌》在日本上映后引起了轰动，1960 年 5 月 26 日至 7 月 31 日，《青春之歌》在日本东京、仙台、札幌、大阪、京都、广岛、福冈、名古屋等地共放映 36 场，受到观众的热烈欢迎。一些报刊撰文予以好评，许多进步团体还举办了有关这部影片的座谈会，日本青年纷纷将林道静作为自己选择生活道路和未来事业的榜样。1960 年 8 月 24 日，《人民日报》刊登

the delegation's visit to Japan. The owner of the certificate was Cui Wei, a famous film director and actor, as well as the only representative from the film industry.

This full name of the delegation was Chinese Delegation of Culture and Friendship. The group leader was Chu Tunan (President of the Chinese People's Institute of Foreign Culture) and the deputy leaders were Zhou Weizhi (He was the director of the Arts Bureau under the Ministry of Culture and later became the secretary, deputy minister and acting minister of the Ministry of Culture) and Sun Pinghua (Vice president of the Chinese People's Association for Friendship with Foreign Countries; Vice president and president of the China-Japan Friendship Association). Team members included Cui Wei, Wang Shoujue, Chang Shana, Cui Taishan, and Wu Yingjian.

Cui Wei got the mission when the shooting of his movie Beidahuang Ren (North Wildness) came to an end. There might be two reasons why he was appointed to visit Japan. Firstly, his movie Qingchun Zhi Ge (The Song of Youth) caused a great sensation after it was released in Japan. From May 26th to July 31st 1960, the movie was shown in Tokyo, Sendai, Sapporo, Osaka, Kyoto, Hiroshima, Fukuoka, Nagoya and other places for 36 times, which received a warm welcome from Japanese audience. Some newspapers gave positive reviews and many progressive groups organized some symposiums on the movie. Japanese

了一篇文章《〈青春之歌〉在日本》，专门介绍了这部影片在日本受欢迎的情况。二是适值日中友好协会举办中国电影周，崔嵬主演的电影《红旗谱》当时正好在上映之列，因此，崔嵬在日本已具有较高的知名度，派他去日本访问，会引起较大的反响，从而发挥较大的作用。

因为当时中日之间尚未建立外交关系，没有通航，所以代表团需经香港转机飞往日本。

代表团是提前两三天到达香港的，被安排住在新华社香港分社位于摩星岭的招待所，其具体地址就是摩星岭道9号。当时由于台湾国民党特务分子在香港活动频繁，特别是在新华社香港分社及其招待所周边，就布置有不少特务分子。为保证代表团成员的安全，接待方负责人专门向大家讲了注意事项：（1）尽量不外出；（2）外出时，如果看到有人过来握手，并拉家常套近乎，一定不要轻信对方所说的话，他有可能是特务……

据崔敏回忆，崔嵬回国后曾与夫人何延谈论过，说是当时只有一次外出购物的机会，而且有很多人一路陪同，在皇后大道上的皇后戏院（当时

young people regarded Lin Daojing as their life model to choose their lifestyles and future careers. On August 24th 1960, an article titled *The Song of Youth in Japan* was published on the *People's Daily* which introduced the popularity of the movie in Japan. Secondly, it happened to be the time the China-Japan Friendship Association had a Chinese film week and the movie Hongqi Pu (*Melody of the Red Flag*) which Cui Wei starred was on show. Therefore, in consideration of Cui Wei's reputation in Japan, his visit would cause wide attention and play an important role.

But the diplomatic relation between China and Japan was not established yet, and there was no flight to Japan directly and thus the delegation needed to transit in Hong Kong.

The delegation arrived in Hong Kong a few days earlier and was arranged to live in the hotel of Xinhua News Agency at 9th Mount Davis, Hong Kong. At that time, Taiwan Kuomintang secret agents and spies were active in Hong Kong, especially around the hotel. To ensure the safety of the delegation, the people responsible for reception reminded them of two tips: (1) Try not to go out; (2) If you must go out, do not easily believe the people who approached you, held your hands or chatted with you; do not believe what people said; it was possible that the person was a KMT spy.

According to Cui Min, he once talked about Hong Kong with his wife He Yan

香港中环最大的戏院）门口还看到了他执导的戏曲电影《杨门女将》的海报。常沙娜则只记得当时曾在山上（即摩星岭）游览过。

　　同时也是为了安全，代表团选择了英国的航空公司，即在渡航证明书上"航空公司名称"一项中所填的"BOAC 机"。BOAC 是英国海外航空公司（The British Overseas Airways Corporation）的简称，它成立于 1939 年 11 月 24 日。根据 1971 年通过的英国国会法，英国海外航空公司在 1974 年 3 月 31 日与英国欧洲航空公司（British European Airways）正式合并成为现在的英国航空公司（British Airways）。

　　代表团从日本回国时也途经香港并逗留了几日，恰遇成立不久的上海青年京昆剧团首次携两台大戏《白蛇传》《杨门女将》在香港演出。经新华社香港分社联系，上海青年京昆剧团在团长俞振飞的带领下专门到分社招待所进行了慰问演出，崔嵬还与俞振飞等人拍摄了合影。

　　还有一件事也给崔嵬留下了深刻的印象：当时代表团所坐的商务舱给每位乘客发了一个绿色的书包，崔嵬

after he came back from Japan. He said he only got one chance to go shopping and a lot of people accompanied them. On the door of the Queen Theatre on the Queen's Road (the largest theatre at that time in Central, Hong Kong), he saw the poster of his drama movie Yangmen Nvjiang (Female Generals of the Yang Family). But Chang Shana remembered that they only visited Mount Davis.

For the sake of security, the delegation chose the British airline, which was the "BOAC" in the blank for Airline on the certificate. BOAC was the abbreviation of the British Overseas Airways Corporation. It was founded in November 24th, 1939. Then according to the *British Act of Parliament* in 1971, the British Overseas Airways formally merged with British European Airways and became the present British Airways on March 31st, 1974.

The delegation stayed in Hong Kong for a few days before they visited Japan. There happened to be two plays namely *White Snake* and *Generals of the Yang Family* performed by a newly founded theatre troupe Shanghai Youth Jing Kun Troupe on show. Through the contact made by Xinhua News Agency in Hong Kong, the leader Yu Zhenfei took the troupe to the hotel and give a performance there. Cui Wei also took a photo with Yu Zhenfei and other people.

Another thing also left deep impression on Cui Wei. A green bag given

觉得很适用，又请翻译崔泰山到经济舱买了一个质量稍差一点的包，后来崔嵬在拍电影的过程中常用它们来装一些拍摄用资料和物品，只可惜最后没能保存下来。

1961 年 11 月 20 日，中国文化友好代表团抵达日本东京羽田机场，开始了友好访问。在日期间，代表团成员参观了电影厂，观看了戏剧团体的演出，参加了座谈会和酒会等，并访问了东京、大阪、横滨、箱根、名古屋、兵库、高知等 13 个城市，所到之处，均得到当地的热情接待。代表团下榻在东京当时条件最好的新大谷饭店，并举行隆重酒会。在此期间，适值日中友好协会主办的中国电影周上映《红旗谱》（改名为《燃烧的大地》）。崔嵬应邀与观众见面，受到观众的欢迎。代表团于 12 月 18 日结束访问，再次途经香港返回北京。这次中国文化友好代表团访日取得了良好的效果，加深了两国科学文化界的相互了解，增进了两国人民的友谊，为两国关系的改善起到了促进作用。后来，日本电影界友好人士还专门寄来一大箱电影资料，由当时的中国电影工作者协会接收并保存。

to each Business-class guests. Cui Wei thought it was a functional bag and thus he asked the translator Cui Taishan to buy a bag of worse quality from the economic class. Later Cui Wei used these two bags to store some filming materials and personal items. But unfortunately, these bags had not been preserved till today.

On November 20th 1961, Chinese Delegation of Culture and Friendship arrived at Tokyo Haneda Airport, and started a friendly visit. During their stay, the delegation visited the film studios, watched the theater performance, participated in seminars and parties, and visited 13 cities such as Tokyo, Osaka, Yokohama, Hakone, Nagoya, Hyogo and Kochi. Wherever they went, they received warm welcome and reception. The delegation stayed in New Otani, the best hotel in Tokyo at that time. Chairman of Japanese Communist Party Sanzo Nosaka met with all the members, and held a grand reception for them. But because the Taiwan secret agencies were active in Japan, Japanese leftists must make every effort to protect the delegation. During this period, China Film Week hosted by Friendship Association was showing *Hongqi Pu* (*later renamed as Burning Earth*). Cui Wei was invited to meet with the audience and received their welcome. The visit ended on December 18th and they flied back to Beijing via Hong Kong. This visit achieved good results, deepening mutual understanding of two countries, enhancing the friendship between two peoples, and playing a

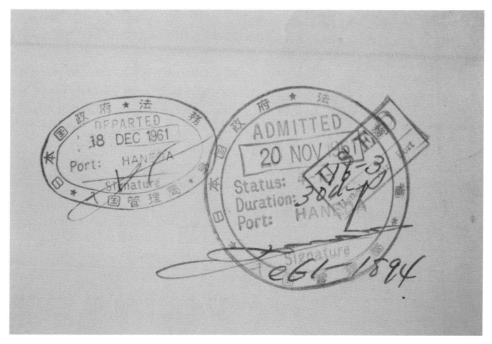

这张渡航证明书的珍贵之处还在于，在它的文字内容的正下方贴有1张崔嵬1寸黑白照片，照片左下方有崔嵬的亲笔签名。照片上右下角还盖有"在香港日本国总领事"的钢印，清晰可辨。在渡航证明书正文的最左侧，盖有蓝色文字戳"在香港日本国总领事 小川平四郎"，并且压着最后两个字盖有"在香港日本国总领事"的红色方形篆书印章。

在这份渡航证明书的背面，还清晰地盖有两枚蓝色印章，真实地记录

positive role in improving the bilateral relations. After that, the Japanese film industry sent a large box of materials on filming, received and stored by the then Chinese Film Workers Association.

The flight certificate was valuable also because of a 1-inch black and white photo of Cui Wei on the lower side and his signature below the photo. On the lower right corner stamped clearly "the Consul General of Japan in Hong Kong." On the left side of the text, there is a blue stamp that reads "the Consul General of Japan in Hong Kong Ogawa Heishiro". There is a red seal on the stamp that reads "Consul General of Japan in Hong Kong."

了代表团到达和离开日本的时间、地点。右边的是一枚接近圆形的入境章，标有入境日期、护照号码、停留时间、入境口岸及签名等；左边的是一枚接近椭圆形的离境章，标有离境日期、离境口岸及签名。

这张珍贵的渡航证明书由崔敏女士于 2009 年 10 月 8 日捐赠给中国电影博物馆。经历了 50 余年的风风雨雨，它依然保存完好，并将被永久地珍藏下去，同时它所见证的中日两国人民的友谊也将万古常青！

孙建民

中国电影博物馆

On the backside of the flight certificate, there are two blue seals, which record the time and the place the delegation arrived in and left Japan. On the right is an oval customs stamp that marked the date of entry, passport number, the duration of stay, the port of entry and signature. On the right is a similar stamp that marked the date of departure, the port of departure and signature.

The precious flight certificate was donated by Ms. Cui Min to China Film Museum on October 8, 2009. After over fifty years of ups and downs, the certificate is still in a good condition and will be preserved and treasured forever. At the same time, the friendship between China and Japan it witnessed will last forever!

Sun Jianmin, China Film Museum

宋庆龄的爱书情结

Sonng Chingling's Love for Books

此次可移动文物普查工作中，我馆两万余件藏品涉及各种项目分类，真所谓"麻雀虽小，五脏俱全"。此次普查通过深入接触文物、挖掘文物藏品的细节，占据总数近1/5的宋庆龄藏书显得十分突出。

我馆作为名人故居，为了呈献给观众宋庆龄生前的生活原状，她所有的藏书依然大部分陈列于她的书房。出于便利的角度考虑，宋庆龄书房与卧室相通，可见书籍在宋庆龄生活中的重要性。在馆藏的珍贵照片中，也经常可以看到宋庆龄工作期间，书桌案头上堆着的大小各类书籍报刊。

书房内共藏有书籍杂志3000多册。宋庆龄14岁就赴美国求学，后随孙中山先生居住于日本为共同的革命理想奋斗，孙中山去世后她又曾奔赴苏联、旅居欧洲。宋庆龄知识渊博，

During this national census of movable artifacts on the more than 20,000 collected items, our museum has involved a variety of categories. Indeed, our place is small but comprehensive. During the scrutinized studies of the artifacts, Soong Chingling's book collection, which accounts for nearly one-fifth of the total collections, has stood out.

As a museum of former residence, we choose to exhibit most of her books in the study next to her bedroom, trying to present visiters the original state of Soong's daily life. This convenient connection suggests the importance of books in the life of Soong Chingling. In the precious photos collected in museum, there are also many images of various books, newspapers, files, and documents piling up on the working desk of Soong Chingling.

The study stores more than 3,000 books and magazines. Soong Chingling

博览群书，书房内的藏书涉及英文、日文、法文、德文、俄文等多国文字。宋庆龄本人精通英文，她的绝大多数信件和文章都是用英文起草，后由秘书翻译成中文。

　　在整理宋庆龄藏书期间，通过书籍可以感受到宋庆龄本人良好的阅读习惯。但凡她阅读过的书籍，扉页都有亲笔签名"宋庆龄""Soong Chingling""SCL"等字样；但凡书是由友人赠送、赠予友人，或与书有关的重要事件，都附有年份签署。此次普查工作中让我印象最为深刻的一本书，就是埃德加·斯诺（Edgar Snow）于 1937 年出版的 *Red Star Over China* 一书，当时将它拿在手里的时候我眼前一亮，这就是在中国广为人知的《西行漫记》的英文原版，封面下方印记"LEFT BOOKCLUB EDITION NOT FOR SALE TO THE PUBLIC"，书内扉页上有宋庆龄友人李炳之印章。众所周知，此书是埃德加·斯诺记录自己 1936 年 6 月至 10 月在以延安为中心的陕甘宁边区进行实地采访的所见所闻的书，此书向全世界真实报道了当时的中国、中国红军以及红军领袖等

began to study in the United States at the age of 14. Later on, she lived with Mr. Sun Yat-Sen in Japan, fighting for their shared revolutionary ideal. After Sun passed away, she moved to Soviet Union and later lived in Europe. Soong Chingling is erudite and knowledgeable, as she read various books. The books in her study were written in English, Japanese, French, German, Russian, etc. Soong Chingling herself is very fluent in English. Most of her letters and articles were written in English, which were then translated back to Chinese by her secretary.

During the census, I and the other staffs at the residence museum all got to know the good reading habits of Soong Chingling. On the title page of the books she read, there are always her autographs " 宋 庆 龄 ", "Soong Chingling", and "SCL". The gift books from friends or to friends, or related with some important affairs, are all signed with years. For me the most impressive book during the census is Edgar Snow's *Red Star Over China*, published in 1937. Because this is the original English edition for the book popularly known in China as Xixing Manji (literally Roaming Record of a Journey to West). At the lower part of the cover, there is a line "LEFT BOOK CLUB EDITION NOT FOR SALE TO

的情况，直观体现了当时的中国革命历程。书籍是 1937 年发行的非公开版本，可以算该书最为原始的版本了，宋庆龄这本藏书的来源显示是友人的馈赠，书已明显陈旧，显然被阅读多次，可见宋庆龄一直关心着中国革命的进展与走向，同样关心着它在国际上的影响力。

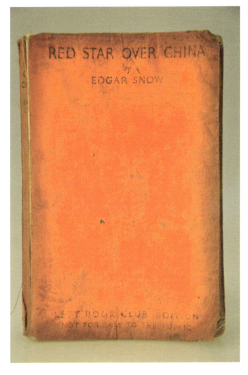

Red Star Over China 封面
cover of *Red Star Over China*

通过这次普查，宋庆龄藏书的书页内容上可见她阅读期间随手的标注和批写痕迹，书内还夹放有书签等。

THE PUBLIC". On the title page, there is a seal of Soong Chingling's friend Li Bing. As is widely known in China, this book compiled Edgar Snow's field reports on his journey in the Shaan-Gan-Ning Border Region with Yan'an at its center. This book trustfully introduced the condition of China, Chinese Red Army, and Red Army leaders at that time to the whole world. It directly presented the history of the Chinese revolution at that time. The book is a non-public edition published in 1937, which was the most original edition. It was a gift from Soong's friend. The book is obviously worn, apparently had been read for many times. It suggested Soong Chingling had been continuously concerning about the progress and direction of the Chinese revolution, and also concerning about its international influence.

Through this census, we found the annotations and comments made by Soong Chingling on the book pages, along with bookmarks. She arranged the books in different locations, with favorite books put on bedside shelves for convenience; the books, newspapers, and magazines related to work were put on her desk; the collected books, categorized by the frequency of use, were put on a giant bookshelf covering a whole side of wall; the other newspapers and magazines

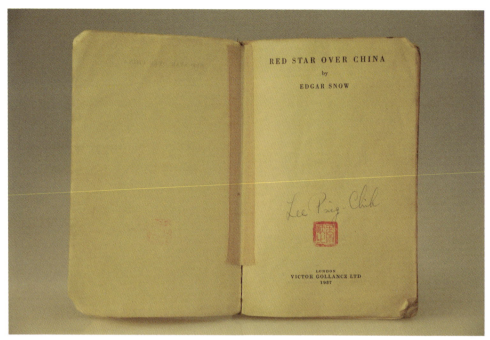

Red Star Over China 扉页

title page of *Red Star Over China*

书籍码放也很有规律，珍爱书籍都放置于床头书架便于随手翻阅，工作类书籍报刊置于书桌案头，藏书类根据使用率予以区分，放于面积占了整面墙的大书柜中，报刊杂志类放于搁架。同时从文物图书的保存状况来看，也体现出宋庆龄对书籍的热爱程度，哪怕是明显翻阅多次的一本书，呈现在读者面前的也只是阅读痕迹以及整齐严谨的笔记字体，泛黄增厚的纸张除了显示出年代感以外，一点不会让人觉得破旧不堪。普查过程中，我们每一位工作人员都被这份气息感染，不

were put on the stands. Furthermore, her enthusiasm for books was also reflected in the conditions of the books. Even with a frequently flipped book, we only saw marks of reading and her neat writings. Besides the yellowed and thickened pages that implicate the passing of years, and the books do not appear to be worn out at all. During the census, every one of us was moved by her love for books, and also started to have a sense of cherishment toward every collected book.

The book collections of Soong Chingling trustfully demonstrate her life of reading and learning. She had committed all of her talent and wisdom

由自主地也对每一本藏书产生珍视的情怀。

宋庆龄的藏书，真实地反映出宋庆龄这一生酷爱读书的特点，她将自己一生的才华和智慧都献给了中国革命和新中国成立后的福利事业。藏书的书籍类目大体能体现出宋庆龄与孙中山为之奋斗一生的革命理想和思想，包含各国名人著作；还有一部分图书能体现出新中国成立后宋庆龄对妇女、儿童等福利事业的心血倾注，藏书内容涉及妇女解放、妇幼身心健康、青少年儿童教育等。

另外，宋庆龄的一生跨越中国的近现代史，她如此庞大的图书阅读量，内容涉及多国文化及思想，宋庆龄不愧为博学多才的伟大女性之一。而且在新中国成立前后，各国之间的信息互通远不像如今网络化的信息时代，宋庆龄藏书的获得全凭与各国友人之间书信往来、跨海洋邮寄、探访捎赠等原始方式，庞大的藏书也鲜明地体现出宋庆龄本人交友广泛、友人之间情谊深厚。可见她的一生都在持之以恒的学习与努力开拓奋斗当中。我想，伟人之所以称之为伟人，就在于有异

to the Chinese revolution and the welfare development in the early period of the People's Republic of China. Most books demonstrate the revolutionary ideal and idea fought together by Soong Chingling and Sun Yat-sen throughout their life, as many of them are the works written by the great people who shared the same ideals in various nations. Another part of books showed Soong's great effort for female and children welfare after the founding of the New China, for the books were highly related to the liberation of female, the physical and mental health of female and children, and the education in early childhood and adolescence.

Furthermore, as Soong Chingling's life crossed the early modern and modern history of China, with her vast amount of reading and her understanding of many nations, cultures, and ideas, she was indeed one of the great females who were erudite and talented. During the periods of revolution and the founding of the New China, the communication between the countries was in no way to be compared with our contemporary age of information and Internet. Soong's communication with her international friends all went through the old ways of transoceanic mails or passed by the travelling friends. The gigantic collection of books impressively demonstrated the

于常人的眼界、思路以及良好的生活方式，值得后人去敬仰、去学习。

杨　帅
宋庆龄故居管理中心

wide social circle of Soong Chingling and her strong friendship with her friends. Her whole life was devoted to the continuous learning and persistent fighting. I believe the reason why a leader was called "leader" was because she had extraordinary vision and thought, along with a healthy living style, which are all examples to be admired and modeled by the future generations.

Yang Shuai, Song Chingling
Residence Management Center

走近老舍经典《四世同堂》

Approaching Lao She's *Si Shi Tong Tang* (Four Generations under One Roof)

在老舍纪念馆的第二展厅中，有这样 3 本书摆放在同一展柜，它们分别是《惶惑》《偷生》《饥荒》，它们都是老舍纪念馆的藏书，前两部是 20 世纪 40 年代出版的，《饥荒》是

In the second gallery of Lao She Memorial Hall are exhibited three books in one window case, *Huanghuo* (Flummoxed), *Tousheng* (A Wretched Existence) and *Jihuang* (Starvation), which are all in the collection of the

位于老舍纪念馆第二展厅展柜中的《四世同堂》三部曲：《惶惑》《偷生》《饥荒》

the three volumes of *Si Shi Tong Tang* in the second gallery of Lao She Memorial Hall: *Huanghuo*, *Tousheng*, and *Jihuang*

1975年出版，因保存条件有限，已经出现了发黄和霉点的迹象。作为普通的参观者，如果你只看这3本书的书名，一般很少有人会把它们和《四世同堂》联系在一起。众人皆知，《四世同堂》是老舍先生的百万字长篇小说，这样一部长篇巨著自然不会是一气呵成寥寥数日完成的。这部老舍先生最经典的作品是分3部写作完成的，即我们在展厅里所看到的这3本书。老舍先生于1944年初开始写作《四世同堂》第一部，最终完成于1949年左右，时间跨度5年多。

看到《四世同堂》这3部书，似乎把我带回到老舍先生写作的那个年代，可以料想到老舍先生在当时恶劣严峻的社会环境下能够完成这么杰出的作品，一定付出了常人难以想象的精力和经受了常人难以忍受的磨难。于是，我不禁对《四世同堂》这部伟作的创作过程和老舍先生当时创作时投入的状态产生了兴趣。

老舍先生的女儿舒济先生曾写文章《抗战苦痛孕育出的〈四世同堂〉——父亲是如何写作〈四世同堂〉的》，里面详细描述了老舍先生当时写作《四世同堂》时的真实情形，从中可以看

memorial hall. The previous two were published in 1940s while the last one *Jihuang* was published in 1975. Due to the limited preservation condition, three books all turned yellow and went moldy. As a visitor, if you only read the titles of the books, few people would associate them with the book *Si Shi Tong Tang* (Four Generations Under One Roof). As is known, this long novel written by Lao She, which consists of millions of words, was not finished in one or two days. This classical work actually combines three different volumes, namely the three books we have seen in the gallery. Lao She began to write the first part in 1944 and he finished the collection after five years around 1949.

The three volumes seem to bring me back to the hard times when Lao She wrote the book. I could imagine how many obstacles he had went through and how many efforts he had paid in order to finish his work under that social circumstances. Therefore, I got great interest in the process of writing the novel and Lao She's mindset during that process.

Lao She's daughter Shu Ji once wrote an article *Producing the Four Generation Under One Roof during the Wartime: How My Father Wrote the book Si Shi Tong Tang*. The article describes the real contexts and details of how Lao She wrote the book, which helps people to

到老舍先生缘何萌发写作《四世同堂》的想法，以及在写作中遇到的各种苦难。

1943 年 9 月，老舍的夫人胡絜青带着两个女儿和 8 岁的儿子，从日军占领了 6 年的北平逃了出来，11 月到了重庆北碚，与老舍团聚。抵达北碚后，每当客人来看望老舍夫妇时，夫人胡絜青都会向朋友们讲述北平人们在日本铁蹄下受的罪，此时的老舍会默默地在一旁倾听。例如，日军让每家焚烧西洋书；中小学派驻日本教官，日本教官全副武装，挎着日本军刀，在校园内巡视，吓得同学们不敢大声说话、玩耍；强制小学从三年级开始学日语；音乐课教唱日本歌曲和日本军歌等；因缺粮缺煤，北平百姓饥寒交迫，活活冻、饿而死的人，屡见不鲜。北平在日军占领下，成了人间地狱。老舍从家人口中听说到北平沦陷后的情况，怀着一颗沉痛的爱国之心开始创作长篇巨著《四世同堂》，这就是老舍先生写作《四世同堂》的缘起。那么老舍先生动笔写作后是否顺利，又遇到了哪些困难呢？

老舍先生全家在北碚团聚后，正值抗日战争的后期，国民党独裁专制

understand where the idea of writing the book came from and all kinds of obstacles he went through.

In September 1943, his wife Hu Xieqing escaped with their two daughters and eight-year-old son from Peking, which had been under Japanese occupation for six years. They arrived in Beipei, Chongqing in November and had their reunion with Lao She. Every time when any guests came to visit the couple, his wife would tell their friends the great sufferings in Peking while Lao She would listened to her in silence. For example, Japanese soldiers asked each family to burn down Western books; each elementary school and secondary school had fully armed resident Japanese instructors who carried Japanese swords and inspected on campus. Children were too frightened to talk aloud or play with each other. It became a mandatory rule for elementary students above Grade 3 to learn Japanese. Japanese songs including military songs were taught in the music class. Due to the dearth of food and coal, it was common that Chinese people were cold or starving to death. Peking under Japanese occupation turned into a livng hell on the earth. It was what happened to Peking that motivated Lao She to compose the work of *Si Shi Tong Tang* with a deep heart of love and sorrow. This is the story how Lao She started to write the book. But what kinds of difficulties

统治越发严厉，文人不仅写作自由受到限制，言行也受到特务的监视。老舍有时出门，就会有特务盯梢跟踪。这时，重庆的物资匮乏，货币不断贬值，物价飞涨，百姓怨声载道。老舍一家靠老舍卖文的稿费和胡絜青在国立编译馆当编辑的微薄工资维持生计。1943年10月，老舍在北碚动手术割治盲肠，出院后身体一直虚弱，他还常患疟疾、贫血、头晕，肠胃不好，有时多日头晕得不能起床。

陪都重庆，人口剧增，很不容易找到住处。老舍家人逃到北碚后，全家人就挤进了林语堂赴美前他一家人住过的小楼，与在国立编译馆工作的王向辰、萧伯青、萧亦五3位先生，一共十几口人一起共住。老舍夫妇住在小楼西南角上一间屋，是卧室、书房兼客厅；小孩们挤在一间像过道似的小西屋。夏天西晒，屋内热得似火炉，老舍形容西墙烫得能烤面包，夜晚热得难以入睡。到了冬天，全家人都穿着家里做的棉袄和棉鞋，可是孩子们的手脚还是冻得长冻疮。这里没有电，夜晚老舍夫妇点煤油灯，小孩们点灯芯草的小油灯；也没有自来水，用水靠挑江水。这里的老鼠多，很厉

did he go through during his writing?

With the Anti-Japanese War coming to its last period after their reunion in Beipei, Kuomintang Party strengthened its dictatorship in the occupied areas. Writers were restricted to write freely and their behaviors were under serious surveillance. Sometimes when Lao She went out, the spy followed him. Chongqing at that point was lacking all kinds of resources, and the currency was devalued continuously while the price soared which caused people's great discontent and grumbles. The entire family depended on the money Lao She earned from his writing and his wife Hu Xieqing's humble income by working as an editor at the National Institution for Compilation and Translation. In September 1943, Lao She had an operation on the cecum and did not recover very well after he came out of the hospital. He suffered from malaria, anemia, stomachache and headache which made him too dizzy to get up.

Population increased tremendously and it became harder even to find a place to live in Chongqing, the provincial capital of China during that time. After their arrival in Beipei, they lived in a small house that Lin Yutang used to live before he moved to the United States. The house was packed with over ten people including Wang Xiangchen, Xiao Boqing and Xiao Yi who also worked at the National Institution of Compilation

文物背后的**故事**
stories behind cultural relics

害，家中闹耗子，吃的穿的、书本纸张、日用东西什么都咬，老舍称自己的屋子是"多鼠斋"或"鼠肥斋"。

这样黑暗的时局，以及老舍忧虑的心情，严重影响了他写《四世同堂》的效率。据老舍自述："本想用两年的工夫把《四世同堂》写完，可是到（民国）三十四年年底，只写了三分之二。这简直不是写东西，而是玩命！"

时局的动荡，物资的匮乏，经济的窘困，加上糟糕的写作环境，以及极度不适的身体，在如此艰难的困境下，老舍先生虽然效率放慢，但没有停笔，依然执笔前行！

《四世同堂》的第一部《惶惑》、第二部《偷生》写作完成后不久，老舍先生应美国国务院的邀请赴美讲学，此时，《四世同堂》的第三部又是如何写作的呢？

1947年第二季度，老舍先生开始创作长篇小说《四世同堂》第三部《饥荒》。《饥荒》的写作过程也不是一帆风顺的。

在1947年11月给纽约友人的信中，老舍先生这样写道："在此一年半了。去年同曹禺到各处跑跑，开开

and Translation. Lao She and his wife lived in a room on the south-east corner which functioncd as their bedroom, study room and living room while their kids lived in a small room as narrow as an aisle on the east side. In the summer, the eastern room faced directly with the sun was extremely hot just like a stove. Lao She even described that the eastern wall was hot enough to bake the bread. It was impossible for them to fall asleep in the evening. Once the winter came, though all the family wore the self-made cotton-padded jackets and shoes, the kids still had frostbite on their hands and toes. Because there was no electricity in the house, the couple used the kerosene lamp for lighting while the kids could only use a tiny oil lamp. And water was not supplied, so they had to get water from the river by themselves. Besides, there housed a huge number of rats which bit daily necessities such as food, clothes, books and paper. Therefore, Lao She even named his room as "Duo Shu Zhai (Room with Many Rats)" or "Shu Fei Zhai (Room with Fat Rats)".

The dark, unstable political situation and Lao She's anxious emotions impacted significantly on his efficiency in writing. According to Lao She's own words, "I had planned to finish the book in two years but by the end of 1945, I only finished two thirds of it. It was not writing but risking my life!"

However, even in such a poor political,

眼界。今年，剩下我一个人，打不起精神再去乱跑，于是就闷坐斗室，天天多吧少吧写一点——《四世同堂》的第三部。洋饭吃不惯，每日三餐只当做吃药似的去吞咽。住处难找，而且我又不肯多出租钱，于是又住在大杂院里——不，似应说大杂'楼'里。不过，一想起抗战中所受的苦处，一想起国内友人们现在的窘迫，也就不肯再呼冤；有个床能睡觉，还不好吗？最坏的是心情。假如我是个翩翩少年，而且袋中有冤孽钱，我大可去天天吃点喝点好的，而后汽车兜风，舞场扭腚，乐不思蜀。但是，我是我，我讨厌广播的嘈杂，大腿细的恶劣，与霓虹灯爵士乐的刺目灼耳。没有享受，没有朋友闲谈，没有茶喝。于是也就没有诗兴与文思。写了半年多，'四世'的三部只成了10万字！这是地道受洋罪！"

老舍先生是在如此不利的环境下继续着《饥荒》的写作，写作末期，老舍开始着手将这部作品翻译成英文。1948年3月，他与美国作家浦爱德一起翻译《四世同堂》，至当年8月完稿。1949年8月，老舍与浦爱德在费城她哥哥的家里度周末，老舍和

economic and physical condition, Lao She never stopped writing.

Shortly after the first two volumes Huanghuo and Tousheng were finished, Lao She was invited to give lectures in the U.S.A. by the U.S. State Department. What about the third part of the book?

In the second quarter of 1947, Lao She started to write the third part Jihuang. But the process of writing did not go smoothly as well .

In his letter written on November 1947 to a friend in New York, he wrote, "I have been here for one year and a half. I traveled here and there with Cao Yu last year and I opened my eyesight. But this year I am alone by myself and thus, I have no spirit to travel around. So I sit in the small room and tell myself that no matter how much I could write, keep writing something every day—the third part of *Si Shi Tong Tang*. I am not accustomed to the food here and for me they are just like swallowing pills. It is difficult to find a place to live in and I am not willing to spend more money on it. Therefore, I keep staying in a crowded courtyard house; more appropriately, it is a 'building'. But compared to the difficulties during the war and the situations of friends who still suffer in China, I won't complain any more. Isn't it good to have a bed to sleep on? But the worst thing is my emotion. If

I were a young slacker with some pocket money from parents, I could eat and drink something good every day, and then drive and catch the wind, dance in the ballroom and forget what is happening at home. But I am not the like of him. I hate the noise of the radio and the terribly slim legs dancing under the neon lamps and jazz music which would merely make me feel dizzy and uncomfortable. No enjoyment, no friends to chat with and no tea to drink. Therefore, I lost the interest in making poems and writing articles. I have been writing for over half a year, but I only finished 100, 000 words for the third part! These are the foreign tortures I have gone through!"

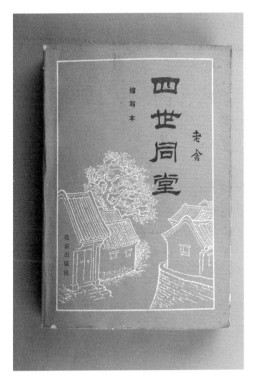

1982 年 7 月出版的缩写本《四世同堂》
the abbreviated version of *Si Shi Tong Tang* published
by Beijing Publishing House in July, 1982

她一起在树林里散步时，突然给《四世同堂》的英文版想到了一个很好的书名——*The Yellow Storm*（《黄色风暴》）。浦爱德后来在 1977 年给友人的信中提到："《黄色风暴》并不是由《四世同堂》逐字翻译过来的，甚至不是逐句的。老舍念给我听，我则用英文把它在打字机上打出来。他有时省略两三句，有时则省略相当大的段。最后一部的中文版当时还没有印刷，他给我念的是手稿。"

Even under such unpleasant circumstances, Lao She continued his writing of *Jihuang*. Right before he finished the entire book, he started to translate the work into English. In March 1948, he translated *Si Shi Tong Tang* together with American writer Ida Pruitt and later the translation was finished in August of the same year. In August 1948, when they spent the weekend together at Ida's brother's place in Philadelphia, they came up with a good English title for the book: *The Yellow Storm*. Later in 1977, Ida mentioned in a letter to her friend that, "*The Yellow Storm* was not a literal translation of *Si Shi Tong Tang*. Lao She read the text for me while I typed it down in English. Sometimes he would

老舍先生于 1966 年去世。在老舍生前,《四世同堂》从未出版过全书的单行本,这不能不说是老舍先生人生的一件憾事!如同这部百万字巨著创作完成的曲折不易,这部全书单行本的出版也历经曲折。第三部《饥荒》中后 13 段(88~100)中文原稿被毁,由马小弥据《四世同堂》的英文本 *The Yellow Storm* 再译为中文。北京出版社 1982 年 7 月出版《四世同堂》缩写本,将原著前 87 段做了删节,补进马小弥从英文本转译的后 13 段文字,才有了完整的 100 段的单行本。

知其书,更思其人。从《四世同堂》创作背后的过程,我们走近了这部老舍先生的经典名著,从而更加亲近了老舍先生的精神世界,增进了对老舍先生的敬仰和钦佩之情!

郑小惠

老舍纪念馆

omit some sentences or even an entire paragraph. At that time, the last part of the Chinese book was not even published. So he read his manuscript."

In 1966, Lao She jumped into the lake and committed suicide because of persecution. When he was still alive, *Si Shi Tong Tang* had never been published in one single volume, which was a pity for Lao She. Comparable to the twists and turns when Lao She wrote the book, to publish this single volume edition was also full of difficulties. Thirteen paragraphs (88-100) in the manuscript were destroyed and thus they were translated back from the English version *The Yellow Storm* by Ma Xiaomi. The abbreviated version of *Si Shi Tong Tang* was not published until July 1982 by Beijing Publishing House. This 100-paragraph work was the outcome of a deletion of some previous paragraphs and an addition of later translated thirteen paragraphs.

After we know the difficult writing process of the book, we miss the writer even more. The stories of the writing draw us into Lao She's classical work as well as his spiritual world, which enhanced our respect and admiration.

Zheng Xiaohui, Lao She Memorial Hall

最后一件工作
——巴金关于现代文学资料馆的手稿

Last Work in Life
—Ba Jin's Manuscript on the Archive of Chinese Modern Literature

在巴金晚年的工作中，有一件重要的事情便是筹备兴建一个现代化的文学资料馆，用来"搜集、收藏和供应一切我国文学的资料，'五四'以来所有作家的作品，以及和他们有关的书刊、图片、手稿、信函、报道……等等，等等"。巴金曾说："倘若我能够在北京看到这样一所资料馆，这将是我晚年的莫大的幸福，我愿意尽最大的努力促成它的出现，这个工作比写五本、十本《创作回忆录》更有意义。"巴金称这件事情为生前"最后一件工作"。

巴金最初萌生创办一所现代文学资料馆的想法是在 1979 年，这一想法的出现与他自身的经历有关，当时巴金在局势之下烧掉了许多珍贵的资料，

In his older years, Ba Jin had an important idea to plan and prepare for an archive for Chinese modern literature which would be employed to "acquire and collect all the materials about Chinese literature, including all the works by the active writers since the May 4th Movement, their publications, photos, manuscripts, letters, and reports". Ba Jin once said, "If I were able to witness the establishment of such an archive in Beijing, it would be the happiest thing for me in the rest of my life and I am willing to try my best to make it come true. It is even more meaningful than writing another five or ten volumes of *Chuangzuo Huiyi Lu (Thinking Back on Writing)*." Therefore, Ba Jin took this plan as "his last thing to do in his life".

Ba Jin first came up with the idea of building an archive in 1979, which was also relevant to his life experience

包括他与大哥李尧枚的一百多封通信。巴金作品《家》中的高觉新即是以大哥李尧枚为原型创作的，在创作的过程中巴金多次参阅同大哥的这些信件，从中寻找写作的灵感，但这些珍贵的资料永远地消失了。巴金在后来的日子里，每每想到这些资料就感到十分痛心和惋惜，于是产生了收集和保存这些资料的念头。

1981年，巴金在为香港《文汇报》开设的专栏《创作回忆录》中首次提出创办中国现代文学馆的倡议，同年3月12日这一倡议在《人民日报》刊载并引发强烈关注。一些老作家纷纷响应，表示愿意捐赠自己的手稿、书信等珍贵资料，老作家们的积极响应给了巴金莫大的鼓舞。但摆在他面前的一个迫切任务是寻找一个馆舍，因为不管是资料保管还是工作办公都需要一个稳定的场所。经过巴金的多方呼吁和中国作协工作人员的积极努力，中国现代文学馆终于在北京西郊古朴的万寿寺落成了。

1985年3月26日，中国现代文学馆举行了隆重的开馆典礼，著名作家夏衍、林默涵、沙汀、胡风、臧克家、林林、陈白尘、姚雪垠、骆宾基、

at that time. He was forced to burn many valuable resources in that political milieu, including over 100 letters between him and his elder brother Li Yaomei. The main character Gao Juexin in his work *Jia (The Family)* was created based on his brother. He referred to those letters for inspiration when he was writing the book. But those valuable materials had disappeared forever. Later when Ba Jin thought of these letters, he felt heartbreaking and extremely pitiful. Thus, he had this idea of collecting and preserving these materials.

In 1981, Ba Jin first proposed his idea of building an archive for China's modern literature in his column *Thinking Back on Writing* in the Hong Kong newspaper *Wenwei Po (Wenhui Bao)*. On December 3rd, the serial articles were published in *People's Daily* and attracted great attention. A lot of elderly writers gave positive response and showed their willingness to donate their manuscripts and letters, which gave Ba Jin great encouragement. But the most urgent task ahead of him was to find a place to preserve these materials and provide a working space for staff to keep these materials. With his efforts and the help of the colleagues in China Writers' Association, Modern Literature Archive was eventually established at the Wanshou Temple, a historical and quiet temple in Beijing suburb.

文物背后的故事
stories behind cultural relics

巴金手稿

Ba Jin's manuscript

周而复等应邀出席，81 岁高龄的巴金亲自到场主持并发表讲话，巴金动情地说："我相信中国现代文学是一股强大的力量，文学馆的存在和发展就将证明这个事实。我又病又老，可以工作的日子也不多了，但是只要我一息尚存，我愿意为文学馆的发展出力。我想，这个文学馆是整个集体的事业，所以是人人都有份的，也希望大家出力，把这个文学馆办得更好。"开馆之后，中国现代文学馆充分贯彻巴金先生对这一机构的设计理念，征集保存了一大批珍贵的文学资料，成

On March 26th ,1985, a huge opening ceremony of the archive was held and many famous writers such as Xia Yan, Chen Baichen, Yao Xueyin, Luo Bingji, and Zhou Erfu were invited. Ba Jin, already at his 81 years old, attended in person and addressed this ceremony. He was excited, "I believe China's modern literature would be a strong power and the establishment and development of the archive is an evidence. Although I am ill and old with a few time left for me to work, I am still willing to devote myself to the archive as long as I could breathe. The literature archive is a public treasure which should belong to everyone. And therefore, I hope everyone could do a bit to make it better." After its opening, The Modern Literature Archive followed the initial idea of Ba Jin and collected a large number of precious materials, which became an important archive for Chinese literature research. Later, under the initiative of Ba Jin, the archive was moved to a new place which can supply better preservation facilities for the materials.

The two manuscripts attached at the end of this passage are the two articles in which Ba Jin expressed his idea of building an archive, namely *Modern Literature Archive* and *Another Talk on China's Modern Literature Archive.*

为了国内文学研究的资料重镇。此后，在巴金的呼吁下，中国现代文学馆在2000年迁入保存条件更好的新址，使这些珍贵的文物资料得到了更好的保存。

本文图片中的两份手稿即是巴金关于创办中国现代文学馆的两篇文章：《现代文学资料馆》和《再说中国现代文学馆》，这两篇文章分别写于1981年4月4日和1982年8月17日，后收入《随想录》中的《真话集》和《病中集》。巴金在两篇文章中详述创办中国现代文学馆的由来以及艰辛的筹建历程，巴金为中国文学尽心尽力的拳拳之心充溢其间，令人动容。巴金虽已离我们而去，但他倾尽心力创办的这所中国现代文学馆将传承其精神，继续为中国文学的繁荣发展默默奉献。

崔庆蕾

中国现代文学馆

These two articles were written on April 4th, 1981 and August 17th, 1982, and later, they were respectively compiled into *Zhenhua Ji (Truth Collection)* and *Bingzhong Ji (In Sickness Collection)* of *Suixiang Lu* (Random Thoughts). In these two articles, Ba Jin outlined where his ideas came and the detailed plan to build the archive. His passion and devotion to Chinese literature still exude between the lines. Though Ba Jin passed away, his spirits are embedded in the archive will continue to contribute to Chinese literature.

Cui QingLei, China's Modern Literature Archive

校史纪念馆中的贝满之宝
——院士校友的作业

Bridgman's Treasure in the School History Museum
—Academician Alumna Xiexi De's Homework

学校发展的 152 个岁月间，从贝满女中到女十二中，再到一六六中学及附属小学，不断前行，我们骄傲于

Beijing No.166 Middle School has a history of 152 years, developing from original Bridgman Girls' School, to Beijing 12th Girls' School, then Beijing No. 166 Middle School with primary school attached. We are proud of the new model of basic education of Modern China that we have created, and we also admire the remarkable people graduated from our school, so we are always striving hard to inherit the essence and strength of our culture, and yearning for the secret of successful education therein.

At the beginning of 2014, our school called on the teachers and alumnae to collect the materials that could record the development of our school, and received up to 300 kinds of items, including homework compositions, exercise books, notebooks, certificates of merit, diplomas, the teachers' lesson

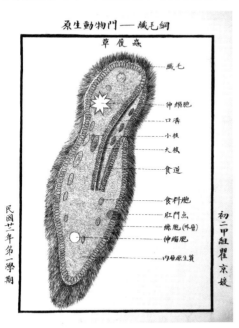

民国二十二年（1933）初二年级甲组生物作业：原生动物门，纤毛纲，草履虫

biological homework in 1933: protozoa, rhizopodea, paramecium, the second grade of junior middle school, group I

学校开创的中国近代基础教育的新模式，仰慕这里走出的一批批杰出人才，不懈努力传承学校文化的精髓与力量，渴望探究这里深藏的成功教育的秘密。

自2014年初，学校向师生校友募集能够记载学校发展历史的各类材料，我们接收了老校友赠予的作文、作业本、笔记本、奖状和证书、老师的备课本、亲手制作的教具等300余件物品。同时，我们将收集与整理相结合，在近1年半的时间里，调阅校史档案11000余卷次，协助编辑、录制了校史纪录片，协助完成了在校生对学校历史上3个主要时期校友的联系采访和回忆录的编制，协助完成校庆纪念册的编制。我校从收集、整理的实物和电子材料中选出200余件首批展出。

2014年10月12日，在我校博雅教育汇报暨庆祝建校150周年大会上，校园内历史最久的建筑物——曾经的学生宿舍楼——被赋予了新的使命，重新布置后成为了校史纪念馆，它的建成给大家开启了一扇门，无论是在校学生，还是满头银发的老校友，都仿佛畅游在百年教育求索与创新的历史长河中，振奋追逐梦想与塑造博雅的激情。在这其中，回忆美好的中学

plan books and handmade teaching aids as well. We did gathering and clearing up at the same time, consulted the school history document over 11000 times and made satisfying achievements. We helped with recording and editing school history documentaries, and students contacting, interviewing the alumnae of the three historical periods, then compiling their memoirs. We also finish compiling the School Anniversary Commemorative Album. We picked out 200 items from all the material objects and electronic materials and put them on display.

On October 12th 2014, the oldest building in our campus, the former student dormitory, received its new mission— to be the School History Musem at the our meeting of liberal education report and 150th school anniversary, which opens a new door to everyone. Both the students at school, white-headed alumnae could indulge their passion of dreams in the long history of seeking the truth of education and innovation, and recalling beautiful school time memories, experiencing the life-shaping middle school education.

We feel honored to introduce our treasure of museum here. It is far more than expensive in price. Instead, it presents the characteristic of our school in early period, and more importantly, it reflects the concept of education of our

时代，感受中学教育对于塑造人生的重要意义。

特别要给大家介绍的是我们的镇馆之宝，说它是宝，不是因为价格的昂贵，而是因为它不仅展现了建校初期学校的办学特色，更反映出学校始终秉持的严谨的治学理念。

校史馆中一本民国二十二年（1933）贝满女中初二甲组的"动物学"作业分外抢眼，变形虫、草履虫、水螅、水母、珊瑚、海葵、海胆、海参、鱼、蝗虫、蟾蜍、公鸡、兔子……一幅幅写实的动物图案跃然纸上，每种动物的各部分身体结构都清晰呈现，并以工整楷体字标注，严谨的学风不言自明。看到精美的作业，不禁令人联想到，20世纪30年代，当周围的学堂、私塾在吟诵四书五经时，在贝满的校园中，女同学们正在科学世界中探秘。在这其中，凸显的是学校"最早文理分科的班级授课制"的特点。

就在这本作业中，可以清晰地看到每位同学的名字，其中，"海葵"的作者之一，就是后来成为中国科学院院士、著名物理学家、原上海复旦大学校长的谢希德。

1933年，谢希德12岁那年，"凭

school—to be serious and rigorous.

In the school museum, one of the exercise books is very eye catching— the homework by students from Group Jia in Grade Eight from Bridgman Girls' School in Twenty-two years of the Republic of China. You can enjoy the fine brushworks of amoebae, paramecia, hydrae, jellyfish, corals and sea anemones, sea urchins, sea cucumbers, fish, locusts, toads, roosters, rabbits in the exercise books. Every work shows precisely the every parts of the body structure of each animal, with careful and neat regular

民国二十二年（1933）生物作业：目录页

biological homework in 1933: contents page

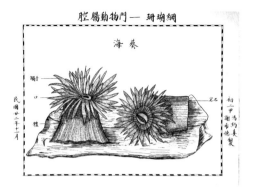

民国二十二（1933）生物作业，腔肠动物门，珊瑚纲，海葵
biological homework in 1933:coelenterata, anthozoa, actinian

着自己扎实的基础和优异的成绩，顺利地通过入学考试，转学到有着70多年历史、在北平颇有名气的贝满女中。这所学校校规很严，环境优美，‘敬业乐群’的校训给她以深刻的教育，对她品格的塑造产生了重大影响。她晚年回忆起在贝满女中的学习生活，不仅记忆清晰，而且显得那么激动和快乐。她说：‘我对于母校贝满给予我的教育，永远铭记在心。我常怀念那些对我既严格要求，又和蔼可信的师长们。频繁的突击式的小测验，督促我养成了经常复习功课的好习惯，所学到的知识，对后来的成长起了很大的作用。’”这段载于上海现代文化名人画传之《敬业乐群——谢希德画传》的文字，足以看出在贝满女中的学习生活经历令这位新中国第一位

script caption under them. That is self-evident for the rigorous style of study. It brings the visitors to the time of 1930s. At that time, the girl students in Bridgman were exploring in the world of science, while students in other schools around were reciting the Four Books. That was because our school was the among the first to implement subject curriculum class-teaching system.

There were clear writing of the name of each student in the exercise books, among which we found Xie Xide who became the academician of Chinese academy of sciences, celebrated physicist, a former president of Fudan University in Shanghai later.

According to illustrated Biographies of Shanghai Modern Culture Celebrities: *Commitment and Team Working---- Xie Xide's Biography-in-photo*: In the year 1933, the twelve-year-old Xie Xide, with her solid foundation knowledge and excellent performance, passed the entrance examination of Bridgman Girls' School which has a history of over seventy years and was also a quite famous school in Peking(former name for Beijing) at that time. This school had strict regulations and beautiful environment. The school motto " commitment and team working" affects her deeply and had great effect on shaping her personality. When

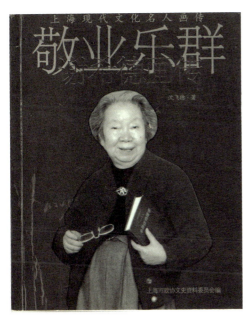

上海现代文化名人画传之《敬业乐群——谢希德画传》封面
the cover of *commitment and team working: biography of Xie Xide*

女大学校长深深怀念，也不难理解谢希德为什么要以"敬业乐群"命名自己的画传。

校史馆精心设计和展出的件件展品，让师生深深感受到，"敬业乐群"是贝满女中留给我们的巨大财富！学生"敬业"，必须要敬重自己的学业，这才是学业有成的保证。校史馆中的院士校友作业，引发了师生对于学科作业书写的重视，学校微信平台还就此展开了在校生与校友作业、笔记的竞赛。

十年树木，百年树人。从院士校

she recalled her memories of school life in Bridgman in her later years, she could remember things clearly, and even excitedly and happily. She said, "I always bear in mind the lessons Bridgman Girls' School gave to me. I often think of the teachers who were strict and friendly to me. Frequent drop quiz urged me to develop the good habit of going over my lessons often. The knowledge I gained are of great help in my growth." The above words clearly indicate that Xie Xide, the first woman university president in China, cherished the learning experience in Bridgman Girls' School deeply, and that also explains why she named her illustrated biography with Commitment and Team Working, the school motto of Bridgman.

The carefully designed display and each exhibit in our school history museum impresses both the teachers and students deeply that, "commitment and team working" is great wealth that passed down from the Bridgman Girls' School. The students should commit to their school work, which will lead to their academic success. Our academician alumna's homework causes the teachers and students attach more importance to the writing of homework. Our school also started a contest of homework and notes between at-school students and the

友的成就和她所讲述的体会中，我们感到，教育是一项用生命影响生命、用生命塑造生命的神圣事业，良好的教育带给人的影响是可受益终身的。

学校发展历史的脉络，学校文化传承的精神，都珍藏于一件件文档和实物当中，珍藏在它们身上曾经发生的故事当中。校史馆中的珍宝——这些珍贵的档案还有它们背后的故事，珍藏着学校发展的文化密码，这些故事需要我们去不断地挖掘和整理，引导我们思考教育的真谛。

毛学慧

北京第一六六中学

alumnae on our Wechat media publicity.

As the saying goes, it takes ten years to grow trees, but a hundred years to rear people. Academician alumna Xiexi De tells us that education is a sacred career in which one life influences another and one life shapes another. Good education brings life-long influence and benefits the whole society.

The history development and spirit of cultural inheritance of our school are kept in each document and archival object, and in their past stories. Both the documents and their stories are the treasures in our school history museum, in which the cultural code lies. They call for our constant excavation, and only in this way can we get more thinking of the true meaning of education.

Mao Xuehui, Beijing 166 Middle School

文普工作的一个小发现
——记北京人民艺术剧院戏剧博物馆藏梁思成手稿

A Discovery during the Census
—on the Manuscript of Liang Sicheng Kept in the Beijing Museum of People's Art and Drama

　　第一次全国可移动文物普查对于全国所有博物馆来说都是一件大事，于北京人民艺术剧院戏剧博物馆来说，更是一个摸清家底、明确账目、做好藏品档案与制定一套更合乎馆情的藏品管理方案的大好契机。

　　在参与此次可移动文物普查的过程中，笔者就发现了一些以前未曾关注却很有意义的藏品，这里想与大家分享一件北京人民艺术剧院戏剧博物馆收藏的著名建筑史学家梁思成的手稿。这份手稿并非梁思成先生那精彩绝伦的古建筑手绘图，或是关于建筑学的文稿讲义，而是其写下的关于一出话剧的一点建议。是关于哪部话剧的，又是如何收藏到北京人民艺术剧

The first national census on movable cultural relics was of great significance for all museums nationwide. For the Drama Museum of Beijing People's Art Theatre, it was a good opportunity for us to sort out and register all the collections, clear up our accounts and set up a new management scheme of collections better in accordance with our condition.

During the process of the movable cultural relics census, the author has discovered some meaningful collection which had failed to be noticed in the past. And here I would like to share with you the manuscript of Liang Sicheng, a great architectural historian. The manuscript is not about the magnificent diagrams and draft of architectures or other relevant literary notes, but Mr. Liang's advice on a drama. Which drama is it? How did we

院戏剧博物馆里的呢？

先来看看这件手稿。手稿为纸质，因年代久远，纸张已开始泛黄，但仍保存完好。手稿分为两页，第一页长 19.5 厘米，宽 27 厘米，第一行居中写有"关于布景的意见"，下面分为 3 部分，分别用一条横线隔开：

Ⅰ-2
管清波客厅的两幅画框的玻璃纸又皱又反光。

酒柜上的圆镜子是一块无光的灰色板。

酒柜上红灯在全部绿色环境中十分突出，除非特为引人注意而设，可否改用和缓一点的颜色。

对子下茶几上的白台布跳出很厉害，建议用极淡咖啡色染一下，在效果上仍是白色，但可避免跳出来。

Ⅰ-2 经理室的墙壁，卷窗纸都太新。

Ⅱ-1 工会办公室很好。只是墙皮脱落处可以加上一条比较明确的线，并显出墙皮的厚度。如下：

最后一段为了使表述更加形象，还在文字下面画图说明，落款是"梁

get this manuscript?

Let's take a look at the manuscript first. The paper manuseript started to show yellow discolouration due to the long history. But generally it is still well preserved. The manuscript could be divided into two pages, the first page is 19.5 cm long and 27 cm wide. The first line is in the center and it reads: Opinions on the sets. The advice below could be divided into three parts, separated by a horizontal line respectively.

I-2
The glassine paper in the two frames of the sitting room of Guan Qingbo wrinkles and glistens.

The round mirror on the wine cabinet should be a lightless grey board.

The red light on the wine cabinet is very outstanding in the all green environment. If there is no special intention for this sets, could you change a more plain color?

The white tablecloth under the tea table is dazzling, so I suggest to paint the cloth with slight brown. It looks still white on the stage, but less dazzling.

思成，53 年 1 月 10 日"。

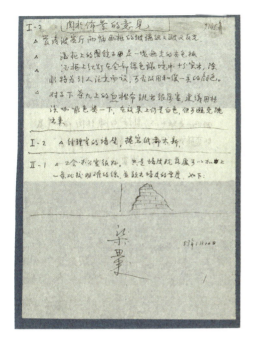

梁思成关于《春华秋实》布景的意见手稿

另一张手稿仅 19.5 厘米长，6.1 厘米宽，小小的一张方块纸上这样写着：

尾声以前，关于剧的"韵律"，似乎缺少一两个"高峰"。因此稍觉"太平坦"。我稍有对一些"起伏"的要求。

根据北京人民艺术剧院的演出年表，1953 年 1 月间演出的剧目为《麦收之前》《夫妻之间》《赵小兰》《喜事》四小戏，排练的剧目为《春华秋

I-2

The window paper and wall paper in the manager's office are overly new.

II-1

The office of Union is very good. And you can add a clear line at the edge of the peeling wall to represent the thickness of the wall.

In order to put it more vividly, he even drew a picture to illustrate his idea. And the inscribe is Liang Sicheng, 1953.1.10.

The other manuscript is only 19.5 cm long and 19.5 cm wide. It is a small square paper. Before the end, viewing from the rhymes of a drama, I think there is a lack of one or two "peaks" in the drama. The development is too flat. I slightly prefer some "ups and downs".

According to the *Timeline of Drama* in the theatre, we could see that the drama performed during January 1953 were *"Before the Harvest"* (《麦收之前》), *"Between husband and wife"*(《夫妻之间》), *"Zhao Xiaolan"* (《赵小兰》) and *"Good Things"*(《喜事》)". And at that time, they had the rehearsal of *"Fruit"*《春

实》，再根据手稿中提到的管清波为《春华秋实》的主人公，由此可以判断这件手稿是关于话剧《春华秋实》的。又据《北京人艺大事记》记载，1953 年 1 月 10 日 7 时半，《丁经理》[1]连排。周恩来等领导同志来审查，对戏予以肯定，并提出了中肯的修改意见。对照时间，想来当天来审查的领导里也有梁思成。梁思成不仅是清华大学建筑系主任，在新中国成立后还担任了北京市都市计划委员会副主任。都市计划委员会是在北京市委、市政府的直接领导下进行北京市的总体规划的机构，1949—1953 年正是北京城市总体规划初步形成阶段，在此期间梁思成为保护北京城的古建筑和古

华秋实》). And the manuscript mentioned Guan Qingbo, the hero of the "Fruit". So we could say that the manuscript is about Mr. Liang's advice on "Fruit". According to memorabilia records of Beijing People's Art Theatre, at 7:30 on January 10, 1953 , we had rehearsals of "*Manager Ding*" [1] (《丁经理》) Leaders including Zhou Enlai, Peng Zhen, Hu Qiaomu and Zhou Yang came to inspect it and made objective suggestions. And Liang Sicheng was also one of the leaders. Liang sicheng was not only the Dean of Architecture Department, Tsinghua University, but also the deputy director of the Beijing municipal commission of urban planning after liberation. City planning commission was planning the development of Beijing under the guidance and leadership of Beijing municipal party committee

---

[1] 即《春华秋实》，当时暂定名为《丁经理》。

[1] *Fruit* was then named as *Manager Ding*.

城墙提出了许多规划方案。此时梁思成一起参加《春华秋实》的审查也不足为奇。可为何会有这么多的领导来一起审查呢？这还得从《春华秋实》说起。

《春华秋实》是人民艺术家老舍先生1952年创作的一部三幕七场话剧，取材于当时正在进行的"五反"运动，描述了首都某一私营铁工厂的工人，在党和政府的领导下，与不法资本家之间的斗争故事。剧本的初稿是1952年2月后半月开始动笔的，初稿完成后，老舍先生将剧本交给了北京人民艺术剧院，此时老舍先生已与"老人艺"[1]成功合作了话剧《龙须沟》，彼此间已形成了默契。人艺的同志读过剧本后，觉得"内容欠充实，但有一两个人物。凭这一两个人物，值得再写"[2]。其后老舍先生三易其稿，暂定名《打虎》。随着"五反"运动的进一步发展，加之北京人民艺术剧院的演员剧组下到私营铁工厂体

and municipal government. 1949-1953 marks the preliminary stage of the plan formulation. During that period, Liang came up with many suggestions to protect the ancient buildings and ancient city walls. So it was not a surprise for him to inspect the drama with other leaders. But why did so many leaders go to inspect the drama together? We should look at the drama *"Fruit"* itself first.

Fruit was written by Lao She, "people's artist" in1952, which had 3 scenes and 7 acts based on the ongoing "five antis movement". The drama described the struggle between factory workers and illegal capitalists in a private iron factory under the leadership of the Party and the government. The first draft of the script was written in the latter half of February, 1952. After the first draft was completed, Mr Lao She gave it to the Beijing People's Art Theatre. Previously, Lao She had already cooperated with the old Beijing People's Art Theatre[1] in *"Dragon Beard Ditch"* (《龙须沟》). Hence there was the tacit understanding between each other. After reading the

---

[1] "老人艺"指北京人民艺术剧院的前身，是1950年元旦成立的包括歌剧、话剧、舞蹈、管弦乐团等的综合性艺术院团。1952年6月12日"老人艺"话剧团与原中央戏剧学院话剧团合并组成一个新的专业话剧院，仍称北京人民艺术剧院。
[2] 老舍：《我怎么写的〈春华秋实〉剧本》，《剧本》，1953年5月号。

---

[1] Old Beijing People's Art Theatre refers to a comprehensive theatre established in the New Year's day in 1950, including opera, drama, dance, orchestra and other types of arts.
On June 12, 1952, a new professional drama institute combined by the old Beijing People's Art Theatre and the Drama Troupe of Central Drama Academy in Peking, and it is still called Beijing People's Art Theatre.

验生活，反馈了许多真实的意见，老舍先生先后又改了6次稿子，每次基本都是从头至尾再写过一遍，直至第十稿才基本定稿。周总理等领导对北京人民艺术剧院和老舍先生一向是非常爱护和关照的，北京人艺从建立起就深受周总理及其他领导的关怀和指导，《春华秋实》是1952年新建院的北京人艺与老舍先生合作的第一个戏，也是北京人艺成立后的第一个大戏，领导们也给予了更多的帮助。老舍先生在《我怎么写的〈春华秋实〉剧本》中写道："首长们不仅提供有关政策的意见，他们也注意到服装、布景、灯光、造型上的等等问题。"由此可见，《春华秋实》无论是从剧本上还是演出效果上都得到了许多宝贵的意见。

1953年1月10日这天，领导看完彩排后，都谈了对《春华秋实》的意见，从北京人民艺术剧院戏剧博物馆保存的《春华秋实》艺术档案中仍能找到当时由工作人员整理记录下来的谈话记录。梁思成先生的这件手稿便是在1953年1月10日这天写下的。手稿中一针见血地指出了剧中一幕二场中客厅、经理室和二幕一场中工会

script, staff from the theatre believed that *"the content is not enriched enough, but the characters are good. And it worths revising."*[1] Premier Zhou always cared about the theatre and Lao She. All of Lao She's drama would be reviewed by Premier zhou personally and he would also give many important instructions. Since the establishment, Beijing people's Art Theatre had been developing with Premier Zhou's care and guidance. *"Fruit"* was the first cooperation between Lao She and the new Beijing People's Art Theatre which was newly established in 1952. And it was also the first big performance for the theatre. Therefore, leaders also offered a lot of support. Mr Lao She wrote in *"How do I write Fruit?"*: Leaders provided not only the opinions of the relevant policies, but also advice on the costumes, scenery sets, lighting, modeling and so on. Thus, *Fruit* had received many precious opinions both on the script and performance effect.

On January 10, 1953 after the leaders watched the rehearsal, all talked about the opinions about this drama. We could still find the conversation record arranged by staffs at that time from the art files of *Fruit* kept by the Bejing Museum of People's Art and Drama. Liang Sicheng wrote this manuscript on January 10,

---

[1] Lao She, *How do I write Fruit? Script*, 1953.5.

文物背后的故事
stories behind cultural relics

办公室布景上的细节问题，并细致地附上了解决方法，特别是文稿最后怕剧组的舞美人员不能完全理解他的意思，还在下面详细地绘出了效果图。手稿中所指出的虽然不是很严重的舞台问题，然于细微处见真章，梁思成用他建筑学家的眼光敏锐地发现了这些有碍观众观感、影响舞台整体形象的缺憾，并像每一位热爱着北京人艺的观众一样热心指出剧中所存在的问题，这些问题的解决必然让舞台效果更加真实，观众的视觉效果也更为舒适。这两张手稿质地一致，都是用很薄的草稿纸写下，其中一张的两侧有裁剪后的毛边痕迹，另一张仅6.1厘米宽，明显是从别的纸上裁下来的一段。如此"不修边幅"的两张纸，不禁让人推测应不是梁思成先生回家后写下再寄来的。仔细对比这件手稿与当天剧院工作人员整理的谈话记录，果然纸张的质地、规格完全一致，应是梁思成先生看完话剧便急急找工作人员要来了两张纸，细细地记录下自己看戏的意见，并交给了剧院。这两张薄薄的手稿就这样与其他的艺术资料一同完整地保存了下来，历经数十载，最终移交到2007年成立的北京人民艺

1953. He hit the nail on the head in the manuscript, pointing out the detail problems about the sets in the sitting room, the manager's office and in office of union in Act 1, Scene 2. Besides, he also attached a detailed solution. He was afraid that he could not get himself across, so he even drew a picture to illustrate his ideas. Problems pointed out in this manuscript were not very serious stage problems. But details should still be paid attention to. Liang Sicheng found these trivial blemishes of the play with his acute sensitivity as an architect, and pointed out all the problems like an ordinary audience. If all of these problems could be addressed, then the stage effect must be better, thus better comforting the audience. The two manuscripts were of the same quality. Both were written on a very thin scratch paper. There was traces of cuttings on either side of one piece of paper, and another was only 6.1 cm wide, apparently cut from a larger piece. These two pieces of paper were so "slovenly". Therefore, we guess that these manuscripts should be written at scene. Comparing this manuscript carefully with the conversation records arranged by the theatre staff, these two files were of the same quality and scale. Therefore, at the day of rehearsal, Liang must hurry to the staff and asked for two pieces of paper and wrote down his ideas immediately

术剧院戏剧博物馆。

《春华秋实》是一出历史性很强的戏，老舍先生对于剧中的主人公，不论是资本家还是工人都不十分熟悉，虽说这是他花费时间和精力最多的一部话剧，但并不能算是其最成功的一部作品，北京人民艺术剧院也仅在1953年演出过3轮共65场。然而，北京人民艺术剧院戏剧博物馆藏的这件梁思成手稿却成为《春华秋实》群策群力的一个见证，也是领导对于北京人民艺术剧院和剧作家爱护的历史见证，没有他们，就没有最后的《春华秋实》，更没有舞台上的人艺。

杨　琳
北京人民艺术剧院戏剧博物馆

after he watched the play. And so the two thin manuscripts have been kept well together with other materials. Several years later, these manuscripts were transferred to the Bejing Museum of People's Art and Drama established in 2007.

"Fruit" is a historic play. However, Mr Lao She, although spent most of his time and energy on it, did not know the characters, be it the workers or the capitalists, very well. So it was not a very successful drama. And it was only performed for 65 times in the theatre in 1953. While the manuscipt kept in the Drama Museum of Beijing People's Art Theatre is an embodiment of the pooled wisdom, and it also highlights the attention and care paid by leaders to drama writers and the theater. It is also a historical testimony of the theatre's bond with people's flesh and blood. Without them, there would be no *"Fruit"* on the stage. Without them, there would be no Beijing People's Art Theatre.

Yang Lin, Bejing Museum of
People's Art and Drama

小说架桥梁，文学无国界
——老舍小说的日本追随者

Literature without Borders as Novels Bridge the Gap
— Lao She's Novels Have Got Japanese followers

　　樱花虽然已经凋谢，芬芳却依然弥漫在空气里，徜徉其间，香馨陶醉，心旷神怡。位于日本东京文京区深处的小石川后乐园，是一座典型的中国苏式园林。走在其中犹如在油画里，那山那水那树那草，那天人合一构建的祥和妙曼的风景美不胜收，令人流连忘返。有人说，日本的小石川后乐园所形成的人文氛围，就是赫然写在园围墙上中国宋朝大文学家范仲淹的名句："先天下之忧而忧，后天下之乐而乐。"我们在这里，深切感受到中华文化的博大精深和强大的融合力。

　　如是，我们的日本之行，不仅见证了中华文化的强大感染力，也真切地感受到中日文化的不可分割的联系与深藏于两国人民间的情谊。

　　此次，我们肩负重托，赴东京参加由日本中国友好协会日本老舍研究会主办的"日本友人中山高志樣老舍作品翻译手稿捐赠交流会"。日本友人手抄翻译中国作家的作品，并把这样珍贵的文

Cherry blossoms have withered, but their fragrant aroma still hangs in the air. Roaming in this fragrance, one will feel relaxed and happy. Koishikawa Korakuen Garden, located deep in Bunkyo District in Tokyo, Japan, is a typical Chinese Suzhou garden. Wandering in the park and enjoying oil painting-like landscape, one would see an eyeful of mountains, waters, trees and grass constructing a beautiful picture, and nature and people coexisting with each other in harmony. The scenery is so fascinating that one would linger on and forget to return. Someone says that the humanistic atmosphere in Japan's Koishikawa Korakuen Garden can be described by the famous sentence written by Fan Zhongyan, a great writer in Song Dynasty, and inscribed on the wall of the park: "be the first to feel concern about state affairs and the last to enjoy yourself." Great fusion powerful of profound Chinese culture is palpable here.

Therefore, during our trip to Japan,

《骆驼祥子》日文译本手稿

the manuscript of the Japanese translation of *Rickshaw Boy*

物捐赠给中国人民，这个事件本身就令人感动和振奋，它再清楚不过地体现了中日两国人民之间的友好情谊，也体现了日本人民对老舍先生作品的喜爱，对他的深厚感情以及仰慕追随。在为中山高志先生的壮举感动之余，我们意外地被与会的日本老舍研究者和追随者的故事打动。在小石川后乐园大门口，我们采访了日本友人、日本老舍研究会会长杉本达夫先生。他把一本自己珍藏的手抄本打开，告诉我们，这是他80高龄时书写的中文版老舍小说《骆驼祥子》。他指着那些清秀而隽永的钢笔字说，抄写老舍先生的作品一直是他的心愿，因为就像伊藤敬一名誉会长说的，老舍笔下的社会风貌及世间百态，与战后日本社会的状况惊人的相似，那个洋车夫祥

we not only witnessed powerful appeal of Chinese culture, but we also deeply felt that Chinese and Japanese cultures are connected with each other and that people of the two countries separated only by a strip of water have developed firm friendship.

This time, we were entrusted to attend the Donation Exchange of Manuscripts of Japanese Friend Takashi Uchiyama's Translation of Lao She's Works held in Tokyo by Society of Lao She Studies of Japan in Japan-China Friendship Association. Japanese friends wrote by hand and translated works of a Chinese writer, and donated these precious cultural relics to Chinese people. The event itself is a touching and inspiring story. It has clearly demonstrated the friendship between Chinese and Japanese people, and it has also reflected Japanese people's love for Mr. Lao She's works, and their admiration for and attachment to Mr. Lao She. In addition to the great efforts made by Takashi Uchiyama, the touching story of Japanese researchers of Lao She studies and Japanese followers of Lao She in attendance was an unexpected surprise. At the gate of Koishikawa Korakuen Garden, we interviewed a Japanese friend Hiroo Sugimoto, chairman of Society of Lao She Studies of Japan. He opened a treasured manuscript, telling us that it was the Chinese version of Lao

中山高志后人与译稿
descendants of Takashi Uchiyama and translation works

子就是众多艰难困苦的劳动人民的写照，老舍写出了祥子的性格特征，也写出了那个时代日中两国劳动人民的共同特点。老舍的《骆驼祥子》让日本人民认识了中国，了解了中国人民的历史，也拉近了两国人民的距离。杉本达夫说，他用了20天就抄写完老舍先生的这部小说。这让我们很惊讶和震撼。要知道，他是日本人，对中文的把握也不是很好。特别是老舍先生这部作品里，基本上用的都是北京方言土话，主人公的一些口头语连今天土生土长的北京人都已经很少了解。他如何驾驭呢？杉本达夫告诉我们，他为了解决这个问题，翻阅了大量的资料，读了很多关于老北京语言研究的书和故事，一个一个记下，一个一个词地比对注释。抄写的时候一边抄一边记，稍微有些勉强的都要重

She's novel, Rickshaw Boy, and that the manuscript was written by himself at the age of eighty. He said, pointing to those well written characters, that it had always been his long-cherished wish to copy Mr. Lao She's works. Because just as what Keii Ito, honorary chairman once said, the society described in Lao She's work shares striking similarities with the post-war Japanese society. The life of rickshaw boy Xiangzi reflects the hardship suffered by working people. Lao She managed to describe the characteristics of Xiangzi's personality which were also shared by Chinese and Japanese working people at that time. The rickshaw boy Xiangzi in Lao She's novel enables Japanese people to know about China and to understand the history of the Chinese people, making

杉本达夫先生和他手抄的《骆驼祥子》

Mr. Hiroo Sugimoto and his manuscript of *Rickshaw Boy*

新查证，直到答案确认为止。我们有些惊诧，一个日本人，一个80多岁的外国老人，能有这样的精神，这样的精力，这样的热情，这样的毅力，这是为什么？杉本达夫说："我崇拜老舍先生，崇拜老舍先生的作品，崇拜中国，崇拜中国博大精深的文化。文学没有国界，我们这代日本人是读着老舍先生的作品长大的，是老舍先生的学生和追随者。希望日中两国人民永远友好，加强交流，促进人类文明文化的传承和发展，造福于两国人民。"

杉本达夫的话撞击着我们的心，他的故事感染了我们每一个在场的中国人。这种感动激励我们为弘扬老舍精神、继承老舍先生的事业继续努力。相信此番日本之行，必将产生巨大的影响，带来巨大的挑战，我们要充分发挥这种感动

people of the two countries closer to each other. Hiroo Sugimoto said that it took only 20 days for him to finish copying this novel of Lao She, which was surprising and impressive for us. This is because that he is a Japanese without mastery of Chinese. Particularly, in this work of Lao She, there are many Beijing dialects, and some of the colloquial expressions used by those protagonists are rarely known even to today's native Beijingers. Then how did he manage to understand those expressions? Hiroo Sugimoto told us that in order to solve this problem, he read a large amount of materials as well as books and stories about local Beijing language studies. He wrote down those expressions one by one, and made explanary notes for every of them. While copying those

产生的动力，百尺竿头，更进一步，为传承和发扬老舍的文学精神做出实实在在的贡献。

王红英

老舍纪念馆

words, he also tried to memorize them, and anything that he did not understand perfectly would be verified again until the answer was confirmed. We were somewhat surprised, and we wondered why an 80-yea -old foreigner like him was full of such spirit, energy, enthusiasm and perseverance. Hiroo Sugimoto said, " I admire Lao She and his works. I admire China and her profound culture. Literature has no national boundary, and Japanese of our generation grow up reading Lao She's works. We are his students as well as followers. I hope that Chinese and Japanese people can always enhance our friendly exchanges, contributing to the inheritance and development of human civilizations and cultures, thus benefiting people of the two countries."

His words generated great impact on our minds and hearts, and his story touched every one of us Chinese people in presence. Such feelings has inspired us to spare no effort to carry forward the spirit of Lao She and to continue studies on Lao She. I believe that this trip to Japan is bound to create greater impacts and challenges. We should make full use of the driving force generated by those touching stories, and work harder to contribute through our practical works to inheriting and carrying forward the spirit in Lao She's works.

Wang Hongying,

Lao She Memorial Hall

民国"萌"书，开心明智

Books with Lovely Stories in the Republic of China: Entertaining and Enlightening

中国妇女儿童博物馆近代儿童馆的展柜中陈列着几本小书，是商务印书馆发行的"幼童文库"丛书中的几本散件，民国二十三年（1934）出版，32 开本，彩色封面。

《王二的元宝》

Wanger's Ingot

In the showcases of Hall of Children in Modern China in China National Museum of Women and Children, there are several small books. They are components of Children's Literatures series issued by the Commercial Press. They were published in the 23rd year of the Republic of China, of 32 cuttings and with colorful covers. Titles of these small books are very simple——"*Cat*", "*Dog*", "*A Little Piggy Searching for a Job*", "*Bees and Sheep*", "*Good Boy*" and "*Wanger's Ingot*", and illustrations in them are also simple. With only a few pages, these books' appearance is by no means comparable to that of the modern books which are well bind and decorated, but they still caught my attention. Cultural relics census has finally offered me a good opportunity to know about the content of Children's literature in the Republic of China. Opening the book and reading page by page, I have to say this is really a marvelous set of children's literature. Though more than half of a century has

《猫》
Cat

past, this set of books are still with strong appeal and readability for both adults and children.

For example, on the upper part of the cover of the book "*Cat*", there is a Chinese character "cat" written in regular script against a white background, and there is an illustration below the character where a yellow and white cat is sniffing a fish on a dish. Inside the book there are black and white pictures, with texts put above the pictures or pictures above texts. The content of texts completely corresponds with that of illustrations. On the second page, for example, it is introduced in the text that "a cat has very sharp claws, hidden in its toes, and its thick foot pads enable it to walk without making any noise", and there were two pictures presenting sharp claws and thick foot pads of a cat respectively corresponding with the texts. Then when it comes to the cat's eyes, the introduction was that "at noon, its pupils will contract, while at dusk, its pupils will dilate", and the two corresponding pictures contain images of a cat's head, emphatically presenting the contracted and dilated pupils.

In addition to the realistic and detailed pictures which can well demonstrate the content of the texts, the texts are also with rich content written in

这几本小书书名很简单——《猫》《狗》《小猪找工作》《蜜蜂和羊》《好孩子》《王二的元宝》，插图朴实。几本小书均只有薄薄几页，其外观远非现代装帧精美的图书所能比，我的注意力却一直牢牢地被它们所吸引。民国的儿童读物到底会编写什么样的内容呢？借文物普查的机会，终于能够一探究竟。打开书页，逐篇翻过，我不禁惊叹，不得不说这实在是一套极好的儿童读物，即使大半个世纪过去，这套书无论对成人还是儿童来说，都具有很强的吸引力和极高的可读性。

　　以其中的一本《猫》为例，封面上方的白底上书一个楷体的"猫"字，下方配图一只黄白相间的猫正在嗅闻碟子上的一条鱼。书页内采用黑白配图，上文下图或上图下文的布局，文字内容与插图完全对应。比如第二页，文字内容介绍说"猫有很利的爪，藏在足趾里，足底又有一块厚皮，走路时没有声音"，就分别搭配了猫的利爪和足底厚垫的特写插图；接下来讲到猫的眼睛，"日中时候，瞳子会缩小；傍晚时候，瞳子会放大"，配图是两幅猫头部的特写，着重显示了瞳子放大和缩小时的样子。

　　除了配图写实详尽，能充分表现文字内容外，整个文本的信息量也非常充实，并且用语简洁，仿佛和小孩子面对面讲话，易于理解。仍以《猫》为例，文本首先说猫的形态特征，利爪、足垫、走路无声、瞳子变化，紧接着说猫的生活习性"猫喜欢捉老鼠"，最有趣的是下面两句"我们养猫，是要他捉老鼠"，"猫和狗是时常打架的"。这两句话带着浓浓的民国气息，是典型的

concise and simple language, the kind of language one would use when talking to kids face to face. Also in the book "Cat", for example, the text first introduces characteristics of a cat's appearance including its sharp claws, foot pads, silent walking, and changes of its pupils, and then it introduces living habits of the cat, "cats like to catch mice". The following two sentences are the most interesting ones: "we keep a cat to catch mice", "Cats and a Dogs often fight with each other". The two sentences carrying distinct characteristics of the Republic of China belong to typical languages used in that period. In the following texts, different kinds of cats are introduced, including "British cat" born in Britain, and "wild cat" and so on. The book is ended by a summary that "lions, tigers and leopards are of the same kind with cats". Though the book does not contain many words, its content is well structured with appropriate extension. For "children", I think it is just perfect.

　　The Republic of China is a period of social and cultural upheaval when a new era began and when Chinese and western cultures were blended. At that time, the imperial civil service examination system used for over a thousand years was abolished, and the modern education emerged. On the

民国式语言。之后介绍了不同种类的猫，生在英国的"英猫""野猫"等，最后是归纳总结"狮、虎、豹是猫的同类"。全书文字不多，内容层次分明，适当拓展，对"幼童"而言，我认为其知识量恰到好处。

民国是我国社会和文化急剧变革的时期，时期新旧交替，中西交融。沿袭了上千年的科举制被废除，现代教育兴起，一方面《三字经》《百家姓》这样的传统童蒙教材仍在沿用，另一方面，以现代教育理念，按照现代教育知识体系和结构编排的童蒙书籍被更广泛地需要和接受。新的国家、新的社会需要培养新的国民。这一时期，也是"儿童"被发现的时期，儿童不再被认为是缩小的成人，而是有自身的身心发展规律和特点，"儿童本位"的观点被文学和教育领域所接受，并得到大力主张，符合儿童认知特点的教材和书籍被开发出来。另一个不能被忽略的重要事件就是白话文运动，白话文取代了文言文的地位，这一运动的结果在文学和教育领域影响尤大。而这几本小书，编录在商务

one hand, traditional enlightenment textbooks for children including the Three Character Classic and the Book of Family Names were still in use. On the other hand, modern enlightenment textbooks for children edited according to the modern education knowledge system and structure are accepted and needed on a wider scale. New country and new society need to develop new people. This is also a period when the concept of "children" was identified. Children were no longer regarded as miniatures of adults, but a group with its own regularities and characteristics of body and mind development. The "children-centered" ideas were accepted and upheld by fields of literature and education, and textbooks and other kinds of books catering to children's cognitive characteristics were also developed. Another important event that should not be ignored is the Vernacular Movement during which modern Chinese replaced classical Chinese to become the orthodox language, and the results of this movement generated great impact especially on fields of literature and education. These small books belong to Children's Literatures series issued by the Commercial Press. Though only over a hundred words and dozens of pictures, these books have comprehensively reflected ideological, cultural and social

印书馆发行的"幼童文库"丛书系列中，虽字仅百余，配图十余幅，却综合折射出当时的时代思想、文化和社会的变革，是民国时期文化和教育发展的杰出成果。

吕梦雅

中国妇女儿童博物馆

changes at that time. They are remarkable achievements made in educational and cultural development during the period of the Republic of China.

Lv Mengya, China National Museum
of Women and Children

与赵孟頫并称于世的书法
——鲜于枢行草书《进学解》卷

Xian Yushu's Running-hand Calligraghy Style of "Explanation of Studies"

— His Masterpiece of Calligraphy is as Famous as Zhao Mengfu's

"我生大江南，君长淮水北。忆昨闻令名，官舍始相识。我方二十余，君发黑如漆。契合无间言，一见同宿昔。春游每拏舟，夜坐常促席……奇文既同赏，疑义或共析……刻意学古书，池水欲尽黑……"是谁与大书法家赵孟頫如此亲密切磋，惺惺相惜？鲜于枢是也。

在元代，能脱离赵孟頫的藩篱而独树一帜的书法家极少，而能与之分庭抗礼、并称于世者，仅鲜于枢一人。

鲜于枢，字伯机（又作伯几），世居扬州，后迁杭州，因居住在西湖虎林，故号"虎林隐吏"，又因为喜欢闭门读书写字，其书斋叫"困学

"... I was born to the south of Yangtse River, while you were born to the north of Huai River. I could still recall the day when I first met you in the feudal office. Back then, I was over 20 years old and you had beautiful black hair. We felt close to each other at the first sight and then we spent a night together chatting with each other. During the spring, we often went boating, and in the evening, we often chatted for a whole night... We would always appreciate good proses together and discussed about them... We learned calligraphy of ancient style together and the lake nearly turned black because we would wash our brush in it..."

The man described in this poem is definitely in close relationship with Zhao Mengfu, a famous Chinese calligrapher. Who is it? The answer is, Xian Yushu.

In Yuan Dynasty, nearly no single

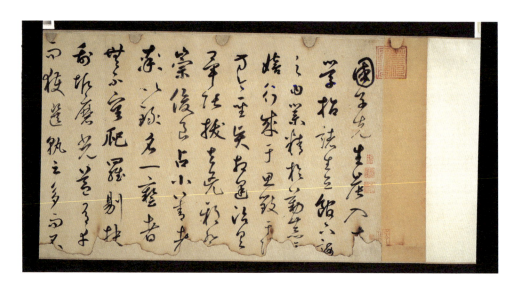

斋",自封别号"困学民"。

从各种记载中看,鲜于枢是个慷慨豪爽、多才多艺之人。他擅弹琴,精诗文,还是个书画、古器物的鉴定高手;"开轩弄玉琴,临池书练裙"(《松雪斋文集》),"每酒酣骜放,吟诗作字奇态横生"(《柳待制文集》)。当然,最为后人称道的是他的书法,尤其是行草。

元代人认为,宋人书法去古已远,把王羲之、王献之父子为代表的魏晋风格完全改变了。因此,元代的书法家以赵孟頫为代表,力求恢复晋唐风貌,在复古中出新。鲜于枢也

calligrapher could be able to get rid of the influence of Zhao Mengfu, as Zhao's uniqueness in calligraphy paled all his counterparts, except Xian Yushu.

XianYushu, also known as Boji as his style name, or courtesy name. He lived in Yangzhou (today's Yangzhou, Jiangsu province) with his family and then moved to Hangzhou (today's Hangzhou, Zhejiang province). He settled in Hulin near the West Lake in Hangzhou. As a result, he called himself "Hermit in Hulin". He did not like to go out and preferred to stay indoor and practice calligraphy. Therefore, his study was called "Kunxue Study" (literally translated as "being trapped in studying"), and he called himself "Kun Xuemin" ("the trapped").

是这场复古运动的主要人物，同赵孟
頫一道，对元代书法的发展起了重要
作用。

首都博物馆收藏的鲜于枢行草
书《进学解》卷，全文共 108 行，
每行 2 至 10 字不等，不拘泥一体一
式，将行书、草书以及楷书糅合在一
起——前 20 行以规整的小草为主，以
后渐有行书出现，字的形体开始出现
大小参差的变化；中段有完全用行书
的，间有几字近于端楷，均匀的行书
出现几行之后，突然信笔作草；后面
的大字行书，犹如行云流水般的乐曲
中，打击乐器重锤数次，振聋发聩，
极具视觉冲击效果。接下来逐渐温和
而轻快，最后几个大字收尾，恰到好
处。纵观全卷，一气呵成，用笔中锋
直下，笔势飘逸而不狂怪，墨色枯润
相间而气势不断，点画所至皆有意
态；各种体式的变换信手拈来，自然
和谐，那种轻松、适意、自信和书卷
气跃然纸上，是鲜于枢墨迹作品中具
有个人笔势特点的一件精品，是"奇
态横生"的杰作。长卷上钤"鲜于枢
伯几父"白文印，"渔阳""虎林

Seen from various literature, XianYushu is a man of generosity and versatility. He was good at playing the Chinese zither and writing poem, and he was also an expert on the identification of painting and calligraphy. "He would play the Chinese zither in his study and then practiced calligraphy beside the lake" (Songxue Study Literature); "Every time when he was drunk, he would write poem and practice calligraphy wildly" (Liu Daizhi Literature). Of course, his calligraphy was the most acknowledged by people, especially his cursive.

People in the Yuan Dynasty believed that calligraphers in Song Dynasty had already transformed the tradition of calligraphy, changing the style of Wang Xizhi and Wang Xianzhi in Wei and Jin Period. As a result, in the Yuan Dynasty, calligraphers, such as Zhao Mengfu, made every effort to restoring the tradition of Jin Period and Tang Dynasty and improving the calligraphy style. Xian Yushu was also a representative during the Archaist Movement. He also played an equally important role as Zhao Mengfu to the development of calligraphy during Yuan Dynasty.

Xian Yushu's running-hand calligraphy of Explanation to Studies is now displayed in the Capital Museum. The full text altogether contains108 lines, with

隐吏"朱文印。全卷近 8 米长，可谓
巨制。

赵婷

北京日报

2 to 10 characters in each line. There are several different types of calligraphy in this masterpiece, including running script, cursive script and regular script together. The first 20 lines were mainly written in running script and then cursive script appeared. In some lines in the middle, regular script was adopted while at the end of this masterpiece, the calligrapher changed his style to cursive again. The whole piece is like a flowing music, with percussion and visual impact followed by mild regular script. Then the last few characters were written in cursive script, presenting a proper ending. The whole piece was written with extraordinary coherence. Every stroke is fluent and strong with special intention of the calligrapher. He could freely change the script style during practicing calligraphy. The harmony, ease, confidence and scholarliness of the calligrapher could be seen on the paper. It is among the most unique masterpiece of Xian Yushu. There were white print "Xian Yushu Bojifu", and red print "Yuyang" "Hermit in Hulin" etc. The paper roll is 8 meter's long. It is indeed a masterpiece.

Zhao Ting, Beijing Daily

第四编 Fourth series

文物背后的故事

杂玩汇通品古味
others

慧海拾遗珠
——记雍和宫第一次可移动文物普查

Seeking for the Lost Pearl
— On the First Movable Census on Cultural Relics in Yonghe Lama
Temple

2012 年 10 月，国务院启动全国第一次可移动文物普查工作，此次普查意义重大，工程浩繁，是摸清我国文物家底的好时机。我单位接到通知后高度重视，成立了以主管主任为组长的工作组，并根据我单位的实际情况结合北京市文物普查方案制订了我部门文物普查方案。通过对库房实地调查，我馆确定了边普查、边清理、边改造库房，分批、分库、分类逐步完成文物普查的方针。

一、克服困难确保文物普查顺利进行

我馆文物库房依托古建，保管条件较为简陋，有些库房不能保持恒温恒湿和防尘防灰的条件。库内环境受

In October 2012, the State Council launched the first movable census on cultural relics, which was of great significance to sort out and check all cultural relics in our country. The census took lots of efforts. My department attached great importance to the census after receiving the notification from the State Council. We set up a special task force led by our director, and made our census plan according to the actual condition of our department and the general census plan of Beijing municipal government. After the field survey in the warehouse, we decided to carry out the census when renovating the warehouse, dividing the cultural relics into several groups in several warehouses, and implementing our plan step by step.

Part One. Overcome the difficulties to ensure the smooth implementation of the

外部气候影响较大，夏季和冬季温度湿度变化较大，对普查人员的身体是很大的考验。我们集思广益，想尽各种办法，在不损坏文物的前提下用各种物理方法来调节库内环境。很多文物由于是原状陈列，表面覆盖尘土极厚，有时甚至分辨不清器形和颜色，我们用小毛刷像考古发掘一样，一点一点拨开尘土，清理出文物的原貌。一天清理下来，很多普查员头上、脸上、衣服裤子上、鼻子里全是灰尘，嗓子很不舒服，但是为了普查工作还是克服困难努力坚持了下来。

二、普查中的新发现

在此次文物普查中，我们贯彻普查无死角的原则，对各个殿堂、库房进行了细致的排查和登记，不放过每一个可疑点。在清理库房时，我们发现了乾隆时期制作的彩绘玻璃果供。这些器物刚被清理出来时并没有引起大家的注意，后来在一个木箱中又陆续清理出 11 件相同器物，普查员查找老账目时发现该器物名称记载的是"灯罩"，时代、款识等其他信息没有记载。后期在查找雍和宫相关档案时，发现乾隆时期制作过一批彩绘玻璃果

cultural relics census.

Our warehouse was constructed based on the ancient architecture, and the preservation was relatively simple. Some warehouse cannot keep constant temperature and humidity and cannot prevent dust. The ambient inside the warehouse was greatly influenced by external climate, and it would pose great challenges for us enumerators, as the temperature and humidity would vary greatly during summer and winter. Therefore, we pooled our wisdom and tried a variety of physical means to adjust the environment inside the warehouse under the premise of no damage to cultural relics. Many cultural relics in the warehouse were displayed without any protection and covered with thick dust, sometimes even making it hard to distinguish the shape and color of the relic. We used a small hair brush which was often employed in archaeological excavations, and cleared the dust bit by bit, thus to reproduce the beauty of cultural relics. After a day of hard working, our faces, clothes pants and noses were full of dust, and our throat became very uncomfortable. Despite all these difficulties, we still spared no efforts in the census and finally successfully finished it.

供，并且明确记载为雍和宫供奉，由此才知这批所谓的"灯罩"实际上就是档案中记载的果供。这些玻璃果供是作为供佛鲜果的替代品供奉在雍和宫的。

清乾隆彩绘玻璃果供

colored glass vessel with glass fruits
carved inside during Qianlong's reign, Qing Dynasty

果供胎体为白色透明玻璃，整体呈倒心形，上窄下宽，底部收口出底足，足墙垂直，边缘有制作时留下的切痕。果供表面凸出，呈各种水果样式。内壁在凸起部分以写实的手法彩绘相应的果实，有苹果、橘子、菠萝、桃、梨、石榴、枣、佛手等。果供颜色艳丽但胎壁较薄，可透光。由于年代久远，内画彩绘大多出现开片，部分果供颜料剥落严重。果供的造型比较奇特，表面凸出的水果堆积如山，给人很强的视觉震撼力。果供通体未

Part Two. New discoveries during the census

During the cultural relics census, we carried out our job comprehensively, checking and registering every corner of every hall, never letting go any details. When cleaning up the warehouse, we found a colored glass fruit pot made during Qianlong's reign in Qing Dynasty. We didn't pay much attention to these wares at first. But later, we found 11 more similar wares in another old wooden cabinet. The enumerator looked up the old accounts and found that these wares were recorded as "lampshade". But there were no more details about the time or other information of these wares. Later, when we looked up some related files in the Yonghe Lama Temple, we found that during Qianlong's reign, a batch of colored glass vessel with glass fruits carved inside had been made and kept in the temple as offerings. And we realized these so-called "lampshade" were actually those glass vessel registered in the files. They were the substitute of fresh fruit kept in Yonghe Lama Temple as offerings.

The body of the glass offering is white and transparent. The heart-shaped ware is like a bowl with its foot vertically standing on the table. There are traces of cutting and carving on the edge of the body. The surface of this

清乾隆彩绘玻璃果供（底部）

colored glass vessel with glass fruits carved
inside during Qianlong's reign, Qing Dynasty

ware is protruding with different types of glass fruits. And these fruits are all colored and carved in a realistic way, including apples, oranges, pineapples, peaches, pears, pomegranates, jujubes and bergamots, and the colored glaze is gorgeous but thin, and it could be penetrated by light. Due to the long history of the ware, the colored drawing or pattern inside the ware had been worn out mostly. And paint had flaked off from some of the carved glass fruits. The shape of the ware is unique. The glass fruit mountain impressed us a lot. There is no seam on the ware. Therefore, it should be blown as a whole. The 11 pieces of wares are almost in the same shape, and their sizes are also the same which is hard for manual production. These glass fruits must be produced with uniform models. The body in the sunken place of the fruits is thin and there are also sparse bubbles in it. The mouth of the bottom is quite large, facilitating the removal of the model. And there are carving traces at the bottom.

According to the file from the royal workshop in Qing Dynasty, in the 12th year of Qianlong, Qing Dynasty (1747), on 10th of the Lunar December, Sanhe from Imperial Household Department came to report that the Eunuch Hu Shijian submitted a glass fruit ware. And then Emperor Qianlong demanded "Replicate

见拼缝，应为整体吹制而成。这11件果供的形制几乎一样，测量后发现尺寸也相差无几，如此复杂的造型恐怕纯手工制作不太可能，应是吹制时有模具可以压出凸出的水果。在果供的内凹处玻璃胎体较薄，且有少量的稀疏的气泡。底部开口很大，应该是方便模具的撤出。在底口处有制作完成后切下的痕迹。

据清宫造办处活计档的记载，乾隆十二年（1747）十二月初十日内务府大臣三和来说，太监胡世杰交玻璃果供一件，传旨："着照样烧造八件，钦此。"于乾隆十三年（1748）四月三十日由催总邓八格烧造得玻璃果供8件。乾隆十四年（1749）九月二十八日传旨："雍和宫万福阁着添做玻璃果供七件、玻璃五供二分，随苓芝花蜡，钦此。"十月初三日做得玻璃果供 7 件、五供上配得花蜡，安供在雍和宫。如今故宫也藏有玻璃果供，与雍和宫所藏果供形制完全一样，这与造办处档案所记载一致。

但有个细节需要注意，当今雍和宫所藏果供数量比记载略多，不知是乾隆时期又增添，还是后代又照样烧造，仅以外形无法区分，尚待研究考证。

如此众多的玻璃果供体现的是乾隆皇帝崇尚佛教的思想，也体现了乾隆对雍和宫的重视与关注。这些新清点出来的文物填补了相关馆藏的空白，对研究雍和宫的历史和宗教文化有了新的史料支撑。

三、及时总结经验教训

全国第一次可移动文物普查的历史意义可以说相当重大，无论是文化部、国家文物局还是各省市、区县都十分重视，多次召开相关会议，在人力、物力、财力上都给予政策支持。对于雍和宫来说，此次普查机会难得，是摸清文物家底的好时机。我们要牢牢把握此次机会，充分认识普查的重要性和紧迫性，以对国家、民族、宗

the ware and make another eight". Therefore, in the 13th year of Qianlong (1748), on 30th of the Lunar April, Deng Bage made another 8 wares. In the 14th year of Qianlong (1749), on 28th of the Lunar September, Emperor Qianlong announced the decree "Wanfu Pavilion of Yonghe Lama Temple shall make 7 glass fruit wares and 2 sets of five containers in which offerings are put in when offering sacrifices to ancestors with Lingzhi Flower (苓芝花) Wax." On the 3rd of the Lunar October, 7 glass fruit wares and 2 sets of five containers in which offerings are put in when offering sacrifices to ancestors with Lingzhi Flower Wax were finished and kept in Yonghe Lama Temple. Besides, Similar wares with exactly the same shape and format are also kept in the Forbidden City, which is in line with the archives in the royal workshop.

There is another detail we need to pay attention to. The amount of fruit wares kept in Yonghe Lama Temple today are more than those recorded in the archive. It still remains unknown whether they were made during Qianlong's reign, or replicated by the later generation. More details could be accessible along with the research. We cannot distinguish them merely from the appearance, thus we need more concrete evidence. So many

教，对历史和未来高度负责的态度，积极推进本次文物普查工作有序开展，为保护珍贵文化遗产贡献一份力量。

苏 昊

北京雍和宫管理处

glass fruit wares could reflect Emperor Qianlong's promotion of Buddhism, as well as his attention paid to the Lama Temple. These new discoveries made up for the shortage of similar collection in the museum, and provided new historical materials to study the history and religious culture of the lama temple.

Part Three. Summarize the experience and lessons

The first national census on movable cultural relics is significant. Ministry of Culture, bureaus and departments of culture and various provinces and cities, counties, all attached great importance to the census, having conference for many times and providing all kinds of policy support in manpower, material resources and financial resources. The census is also a good opportunity for us to check out and register all cultural relics kept in the Lama Temple. We should firmly seize this opportunity and be fully aware of the importance and urgency of the census, and we should actively promote the cultural relic census work orderly in an responsible attitude for the nation, ethnic groups, religions, history and future, contributing to the protection of these precious cultural heritage.

Su Hao, the Management Office of the Yonghe Lama Temple

"万世师表" 匾额背后的变迁

The Vicissitudes behind the Plaque of "the Teacher for all Ages"

北京孔庙作为元、明、清三朝皇家祭祀孔子的场所，始建于元代大德六年（1302），后经明永乐九年（1411）原址重建，历有清一代逐步增建，于光绪年间，形成目前的建筑规模和形制。

大成殿作为北京孔庙祭祀孔子的主殿，殿内供奉有孔子像及其神位，两侧分立颜回、孔伋、曾参、孟轲四大弟子的四配神位，东、西两侧还有闵损、端木赐、仲由、冉求、朱熹等十二哲人的牌位。现在的北京大成殿内悬挂有清朝历代皇帝及民国大总统黎元洪的御题匾额：雍正题写的"生民未有"、乾隆题写的"与天地参"、嘉庆题写的"圣集大成"、道光题写的"圣协时中"、咸丰题写的"德齐帱载"、同治题写的"圣神天纵"、光绪题写的"斯文在兹"、宣统题写的"中和位育"及黎元洪题写的"道

Beijing Confucian Temple, as a royal sacrificial site to Confucius in Yuan, Ming and Qing Dynasty, was originally built in the 6th year of Dade, Yuan Dynasty (1302), rebuilt at the same site in the 9th year of Yongle, Ming Dynasty (1411) and gradually expanded during Emperor Guangxu's reign in Qing Dynasty to the current scale and structure.

The Dacheng Hall is the main structure in the Confucian Temple, worshiping the statue of Confucius and his memorial tablet. And the tablets of Yan Hui, Kong Ji, Zeng Shen and Meng Ke, four proteges of Confucius, are on the either side of the tablet of Confucius. Another 12 philosophers' tablets are located on both sides too, including Min Sun, Duanmu Ci, Zhong You, Ran Qiu, Zhu Xi, etc. Now inside the Dacheng Hall in Beijing Confucian Temple, horizontally inscribed boards inscribed by emperors in Qing Dynasty and the President Li Yuanhong in the Republic of China (1912 - 1949) are hanged. Emperor Yongzheng inscribed "生民未有"(The only sage in the world); Emperor Qianlong inscribed "与天地参" (Equal to God); Emperor Jiaqing inscribed "圣集大成" (The essence of

洽大同"。

大成殿外檐下，悬挂一匾，分外显眼，这就是康熙皇帝御书"万世师表"匾。该匾金字蓝地，正中金字楷书右起"万世师表"4个大字，左侧一行小楷落款"康熙甲子孟冬敬书"八字。小字落款上半部分压款印章一枚，内容为阴文篆书"广运之宝"，满、汉文两种字体。匾额饰四周金漆，浮雕双龙戏珠图案。该匾总长449厘米，宽227厘米。然而，就是这块皇帝御题金匾，它本来悬挂的位置并不是大成殿外，是后来才被放置到大成殿门檐下的，这背后有着一段曲折的变迁故事。

有清一代，对孔子及儒家学说都

wisdom); Emperor Daoguang inscribed "圣协时中" (Saint of golden mean); Emperor Xianfeng inscribed "德齐帱载"(Representation of the highest morality and wisdom); Emperor Tongzhi inscribed "圣神天纵" (Saint in the world); Emperor Guangxu inscribed "斯文在兹" (The embodiment of morality and knowledge); Emperor Xuantong inscribed "中和位育" (Objectiveness and adaptation) and Li Yuanhong inscribed "道恰大同" (Morality and great harmony).

Outside of the Dacheng Hall, under the roof hanged an eye-catching plaque on which was inscribed "万世师表" (The teacher for all ages). It was inscribed by the Emperor Kangxi. The plaque is blue, and the inscription were golden. Four characters "万世师表"(The teacher for all ages) are in the middle of the plaque, under which there is a line of small characters "康熙甲子孟冬敬书"(Inscribed by Kangxi

极为推崇，皇帝本人也积极推行汉文化，尊崇孔子及儒家思想。正是在这样的统治思想下，皇帝祭孔成为一项常规性的活动，即使在康熙皇帝南巡过程中，他也不忘祭拜孔子，"万世师表"四字就是在这个过程中书写的。

康熙二十三年（1684）十一月十七日，康熙皇帝南巡经由泗水县到达曲阜，当天与国子生孔尚任等人交流儒学。次日，康熙皇帝銮驾由曲阜城南，进南门，至圣庙，由甬道旁步行至大成殿，行三跪九叩之礼，命大学士王熙宣谕衍圣公孔毓圻等曰："至圣之道与日月并行，与天地同运，万世帝王咸所师法，逮公卿士庶罔不率由。尔等远承圣泽，世守家传，务期型仁讲义，履中蹈和，存忠恕以立心，敦孝弟以修行，斯须弗去，以奉先训，以称朕怀，尔等其只遵毋替。特谕。"

在这段话中，详细阐释了"万世师表"四字的微言大义，即儒家思想的伟大可以与天地日月相提并举，为历代帝王的行为表率和师法对象。

衍圣公孔毓圻等跪听，谢恩完毕，康熙皇帝上大成殿瞻仰孔子圣像圣迹，后又回到大成殿前，命大学士明珠、王熙宣谕："至圣之德与天地日月同，

in lunar October in Jiazi (1684) on the right side. Above the small characters, there is a seal in which characters were cut in intaglio, both in Manchu and Chinese, reading "广运之宝"(a royal seal). The plaque is decorated with gold lacquer around the rim with anaglyph of two dragons playing with a bead. The total length is 449 cm, and the width is 227 cm. Originally, the gold plaque was not hanged outside the Dacheng Hall. Actually, it was moved there afterwards. Behind the plaque is a tortuous story.

In Qing Dynasty, Confucius and his philosophy were highly regarded and the emperor also took a proactive role to promote Han Culture and attached great importance to Confacianism. Therefore, guided by this reigning philosophy, the memorial ceremony for Confucius became a royal routine. Even when Emperor Kangxi was on a tour of inspection to the southern China, he never forgot to worship Confucius. And the plaque was inscribed during his inspectiontrip.

On Nov. 17th, the 23rd year of Kangxi (1684), during the south-bound tour of inspection, Kangxi arrived in Qufu through Sishui County, and exchanged ideas about Confusion with Kong Shangren, a student in Guozijian (the Imperial College in Qing Dynasty). The next day, namely Nov. 18th, the 23rd year of Kangxi, the emperor went to the southern part of Qufu and arrived at the temple. Then he walked through the paved path to the Dacheng Hall and implemented the grand kowtow, kneeling thrice and bowing for nine times. And

其高明广大，无可指称。朕向来研求经义，体思至道，欲加赞颂，莫能名言。特书'万世师表'四字，悬额殿中，非云阐扬圣教，亦以垂示将来。"

在这一段话中，康熙皇帝解释了题写"万世师表"四字的原因和目的，即以"万世师表"四字来表达对儒家思想哲理至道的敬仰和赞颂，其目的不仅是在当代弘扬儒家思想，同时，也希望能够对后世子孙起到启示作用。

衍圣公孔毓圻等跪接御书。从这时候起，康熙皇帝御笔的"万世师表"正式"悬额"大成殿中。

康熙二十四年（1685），北京孔庙获得康熙皇帝颁揭御书"万世师表"匾额，并悬挂在大成殿中，据乾隆本、道光本《钦定国子监志》记载："殿

"万世师表"匾额原先的悬挂位置——大成殿内

the original place where the plaque of "the teacher for all ages" hanged

then he commanded Wang Xi, the grand secretary to announce the imperial edict to Kong Yuqi, the descendent of Confucius: "The highest morality is equal to the heaven and all emperors shall follow the morality, so shall all subjects. Your family has always been under the grace of the God, and the morality has been followed and carried out generation by generation. You have attached great importance to benevolence and the golden mean. You are loyal, kind and filial. You should keep going and continue following this morality. You shall not change it.

This edict elaborated on the meaning of "The teacher for all ages", claiming that Confucian was equal to the heaven, and it was the guidance of all emperors.

Kong Yuqi kneeled on the ground and listened to the edict, and then he expressed his gratitude to the emperor. After that, Kangxi went into the Dacheg Hall to look at the sacred statue of Confucius with reverence and then commanded Ming Zhu and Wangxi, grand secretaries, to announce the edict: "The highest morality is equal to the heaven. Its sacredness is undeniable. I have always been leaning classics of Confucian and thinking about its philosophy. I want to appreciate it but I cannot find exact words. Therefore, I here inscribe 'the teacher for all ages' on the plaque and hang the plaque in the hall, not only to promote Confucian, but also enlighten the future generations."

And this piece of edict elaborated

中悬圣祖仁皇帝御书额一，曰'万世师表'。康熙二十四年颁揭。"

那么，这块代表了封建帝王对孔子无上褒奖的匾额怎么从殿中被转移到了殿外呢？

时间来到了 1912 年，中华民国成立，袁世凯窃取革命成果，成为大总统。袁世凯死后，黎元洪继任大总统，1916 年，当时的北京政府教育总长范源濂将北京孔庙大成殿内清代帝王所书匾额悉数取下，将黎元洪手书的"道冶大同"四字匾额悬挂于大成殿内。

从康熙二十四年（1685）到 1916 年，"万世师表"匾额在北京大成殿内悬挂了 231 年。

1983 年，贾文忠等先生们经过半年之努力，将康熙手书"万世师表"

the reason and goal that Kangxi inscribed "the teacher for all ages." He wanted to show his appreciation and respect to Confucian philosophy, not only in order to promote Confucian at that time, but also to enlighten the future generations.

Kong Yuqi and other proteges kneeled down on the ground and received the edict. Since then, the plaque of "the teacher for all ages" inscribed by Emperor Kangxi was officially hanged in the Dacheng Hall.

In the 24th year of Kangxi, Qing Dynasty (1685), Beijng Confucian Temple received the plaque of "the teacher for all ages" inscribed by Emperor Kangxi and hanged the plaque inside the Dacheng Hall. According to Note in Guozijian in Daoguang's reign and Qianlong's reign, "The plaque of 'the teacher for all ages' inscribed by Emperor Kangxi was received in the 24th year of Kangxi." However, as the representation of the highest appreciation in the feudal

"万世师表"现在悬挂位置——大成殿外檐下

the current place where the plaque of "the teacher for
all ages" hanged

匾额修复如旧，这次修复完毕后，"万世师表"匾额被妥善放置于北京孔庙大成殿神龛后面。

20世纪80年代中期，首都博物馆下辖的北京孔庙大成殿对外开放，大成殿内被范源濂下令取下的清代皇帝御书匾额除"万世师表"匾额外，均被重新悬挂到大成殿内，与黎元洪手书的"道洽大同"匾额共同构成了目前大成殿内的现有匾额布局。"万世师表"匾额作为历代皇帝御书匾额中的重要一员，如何将其安置却是令人颇为踌躇，因大成殿内正中已经悬挂有黎元洪的"道洽大同"匾额，为尊重历史真实起见，经由专家协定，最终决定保持黎氏"道洽大同"匾额位置不变，将修复好的"万世师表"

society, why would the plaque be moved from inside the hall to outside?

In 1912, the Republic of China (1912 - 1949) was founded. Yuan Shikai became president after stealing the fruit of revolution. After Yuan died, Li Yuanhong took over his position. In 1916, Fan Yuanliang, the chief director of education department of Beijing government removed all plaques in Dacheng Hall inscribed by emperors during Qing dynasty, and instead hanged the plaque of "morality and great harmony" inscribed by Li Yuanhong.

Therefore, the plaque of "the teacher for all ages" was hanged in the Dacheng Hall for 231 years from the 20th year of Kangxi, Qing Dynasty (1681) to 1916 A.D.

In 1983, after Mr. Jia Wenzhong and his colleagues' half-year endeavor, the plaque of "the teacher for all ages" was restored. And then this plaque was safely placed behind the shrine in the Dacheng Hall in Beijing Confucian Temple.

In the mid-term of 1980s, Beijing Confucian Temple governed by the Capital Museum started to open to the public. All plaques inscribed by emperors in Qing Dynasty were again hanged back in the Dacheng Hall except the plaque of "the teacher for all ages", forming today's layout of plaques inside the Dacheng Hall. The plaque of "the teacher for all ages" is an important royal plaque while the place to hang it was discussed for

匾额悬挂于北京大成殿外檐下。

1996 年，首都博物馆组织专家对大成殿内原来悬挂的"万世师表"等 10 方匾额进行重新整理完善，"万世师表"匾额也在此次修复、完善之列。

从 1916 年被范源濂取下，到 20 世纪 80 年代首都博物馆将"万世师表"匾额重新悬挂，康熙皇帝御书"万世师表"匾额在经历了数十年的尘封之后，终于重新焕发光辉，与其他匾额一起，共同构成了北京孔庙大成殿目前殿内外匾额的放置格局。

至此，北京孔庙"万世师表"匾额于大成殿外的悬挂位置成为全国孔庙"万世师表"匾额悬挂位置的一个唯一特例，正是这种位置的变迁，反映了一方御书匾额背后那段真实而又曲折的故事。

李瑞振
孔庙和国子监博物馆

many times. Since the plaque of "morality and great harmony" inscribed by Li Yuanhong had already been hanged inside the Dacheng Hall, experts finally decided to hang the plaque of "the teacher for all ages" under the roof outside the Dacheng Hall to respect the authenticity of history.

In 1996, the Capital Museum organized a batch of experts to renovate 10 plaques originally hanged inside the Dacheng Hall including the plaque of "the teacher for all ages".

From 1916 to 1980s, the dust-laden plaque of "the teacher for all ages" inscribed by Emperor Kangxi became alive again with other plaques, forming the current layout of plaques in the Dacheng Hall of Beijing Confucian Temple.

Until now, Beijing Confucian Temple is the only Confucian temple in China which hanged the plaque of "the teacher for all ages" outside the Dacheng Hall. And the changes of its position is exactly a reflection of a tortuous story behind it.

Li Ruizhen, Beijing Confucian Temple and the Imperial College

老照片背后的故事
——清华大学微型汽车研制

The Story behind an Old Photo
—the Development of Mini-Car in Tsinghua University

通过可移动文物普查工作，我们发现在北京汽车博物馆馆藏文献中，有这样一张拍摄于1959年国庆节当天的老照片，记录的是清华大学的学生

清华大学的学生们驾驶着他们制成的微型小汽车走向
天安门广场

Tsinghua students driving their self-made mini-car toward Tian'anmen
Square

In the national census of movable cultural relics, we discovered an old photo taken on October 1st, 1959. It is now kept in the documents of Beijing Automobile Museum. In this picture, we could see Tsinghua students cheerfully driving a self-made mini-car toward the Tian'anmen Square to celebrate the 10th anniversary of People's Republic of China. In order to self-develop automobile vehicles in China, the faculty and students in the Department of Automobile Engineering of Tsinghua University applied theory to real practice and combined learning and innovation in an attempt to develop the mini-car. They developed the first successful model in 1958, and then made further improvements through repeated tests, and achieved small-scale production at last. So what is the story behind this old photo? Let us review those years of "sparkling ideas and exciting developments" along the trajectory of history.

们驾驶着自制的微型小汽车欢快地走向天安门广场庆祝建国 10 周年的情景。微型汽车是我国为了开发自主汽车产品，由清华大学汽车工程系的师生们以理论联系实际，将学习与独创相结合尝试进行研制的产品。1958 年微型汽车首次研制成功，而后反复测试又进行了一些改进，最终实现了小批量生产。那么这张照片背后的故事是怎样的呢？让我们沿着历史的脉络回顾那段"思想火花碰撞，研制激情燃烧"的岁月。

1958 年初，我国第二个五年计划正式开始实施，计划中提出"相应发展运输业和商业，提高人民生活水平"。从运输业发展来看，1956 年解放牌 CA10 载货汽车的下线实现了我国汽车工业零的突破，但我国小型汽车的研制仍属空白，市内小型汽车基本以苏联吉斯、吉姆、华沙胜利 20 等进口车为主，使用也仅限于局级以上的干部。北京市内交通基本依靠人力客运，在街头接送客人的都是人力三轮车。为了改变这种落后面貌，提高人民生活水平，周恩来总理提出了制造微型车的想法。清华大学汽车工程系

In the beginning of 1958, the second Five-Year Plan of China was officially started. We proposed to "respectively develop the transportation industry and commerce to improve the livelihood of our people" in this plan. In terms of the transportation industry, the launch of Liberation CA10 Truck marked the groundbreaking moment of our nation's automobile industry. However, there was still no development in sedan production. Sedans on urban roads at that time were mainly dominated by imported cars such as Soviet ZIS, ZIM, and Warsaw Victory 20, which mainly served the interest of high-rank cadres. The in-city transportation of Beijing basically relied on manpower vehicles. Tricycles were the main passenger vehicles on streets. In order to change this underdeveloped condition and to improve people's standard of living, Premier Zhou Enlai proposed the idea of producing mini-car. The faculty and students in the Department of Automobile Engineering of Tsinghua University started to research and design a kind of mini-car featuring simple structure, convenient operation, and elegant appearance. They cooperated with the Beijing Automobile Repair and Assembly Factory to do test manufactures and productions.

The fist mini-car was the graduation

的师生开始着手研究设计一种结构简单、操作方便、美观大方的微型汽车，并与北京市汽车修配厂合作加工试制。

早期人力三轮车客运

the manpower tricycle passenger
transportation in early periods

第一辆微型汽车是清华大学汽车工程系的毕业设计课题，由清华大学余志生、徐大宏、黄实和蔡景泉等几位老师带领着学生们在汽车实验室内设计研制。当时采用了北京摩托车厂生产的单缸发动机，没有现成的车架，就按照图纸利用自行车车架钢管焊接了一个，经过多次试验制成了一辆前轮驱动、后轮转向的三轮微型汽车。1958年7月25日，这辆微型汽车在清华大学校园内试车，立即引起了全校师生的围观，大家都被这辆新颖的小车吸引住了。1958年8月，这辆微型汽车参加了清华大学毕业设计成果展，

design project of the Tsinghua Automobile Engineering Department, made in the automobile laboratory, designed and developed by the Tsinghua students led by several teachers including Yu Zhisheng, Xu Dahong, Huang Shi, and Cai Jingquan. It adopted a single-cylinder engine manufactured by Beijing Motorcycle Factory. Without any readymade car frames, they could only weld a frame made of bicycle frame steel pipes based on the blueprint. After repeated tests, they developed a three-wheel mini-car with front-wheel driving and rear-wheel steering. On July 25th, 1958, the mini-car had a test drive on the campus of Tsinghua University. In August 1958, this mini-car was demonstrated in the Tsinghua University Graduation Design Exhibition. On August 24th, Premier Zhou Enlai noticed the small car during his visit to the exhibition, and highly praised the work. He encouraged Tsinghua University to design a more advanced mini-car before the National Day, and to present it as a gift to the country.

When they heard the words of the Premier, the faculties and students of Tsinghua Automobile Engineering Department immediately started to work on the new design and development. This time they used the parts from a four-

8月24日，周恩来总理参观展览时看到了这辆小车，给予了很高的评价，并希望清华大学在国庆节之前再设计制造一台更好、更先进的微型汽车向国庆献礼。

听到这个消息后，清华大学汽车工程系的师生们立即投入新的设计试制工作，这次他们采用了北京汽车厂制造的四缸风冷发动机的配件设计了一台全新的单缸发动机，布置上采用后横置发动机的设计，选用皮带无级传动系统，取消了一般汽车所需的排挡，以便不会开车的三轮车师傅驾驶。经过40个昼夜的努力，清华大学汽车工程系终于在1958年国庆节前制成了一台更高级、更便利的全新微型小汽车。

国庆期间，这辆微型小汽车开进了中南海总理办公室大院。周恩来总理在技术人员的指导下试开了微型汽车，并鼓励大家将车子的噪音和震动再减少一些，将来还可以向社会推广，供家庭用。

回校后，清华大学的师生们改进了设计，将单缸发动机改成了卧式对置双缸风冷发动机以减少震动，完成

cylinder air-cooling engine, manufactured by Beijing Automobile Factory, to design a brand new single-cylinder engine. In the general design they used the layout of rear-engine transversely-mounted. They chose the belt continuously variable transmission (CVT) system, which did not need the driver to manually shift gears as in the common cars, so it could be conveniently driven by the tricyclists who did not know how to drive a car. After 40-day endeavor, they finally made a more advanced and more convenient brand new mini-car before the National Day of 1958.

During the National Day Festival period, this mini-car was driven into the Premier office compound in Zhongnanhai. Premier Zhou Enlai tested the mini-car under the instructions of technicians. He encouraged everyone present to further reduce the noise and vibration of the car, so in future it could be extensively promoted in society for the family use.

After returning to the campus, the Tsinghua faculties and students improved the design. They changed the single-cylinder engine to horizontally opposed double-cylinder air cooling engine, which reduced vibration. The test production of the three-wheel car model was completed. During this test production, Premier Zhou Enlai, for many times, brought

第一辆试制成功的微型汽车
the first successful model of mini-car

了三轮样车的试制。在此期间，周恩来总理多次带领外国元首来清华大学参观，并向外宾展示微型汽车。

1959 年建国 10 周年前夕，清华大学汽车工程系的师生们精心打造了 3 辆定型为 V 型的微型汽车，参加了国庆游行活动，并拍摄国庆 10 周年献礼片，本文开篇那张珍贵的老照片正是记录了这一刻。国庆之后，这辆微型汽车曾小批量生产了 100 多辆，组成了出租车队，在北京站和儿童医院之间运营，直至 1961 年年底。

清华大学汽车工程系试制的微型汽车不仅使学生在设计制造的实践中增长了知识和经验，还在一定程度上

visiting foreign leaders to visit Tsinghua University, and showed them the mini-car.

Just before the 10th anniversary of the People's Republic of China in 1959, the faculties and students in Tsinghua Automobile Engineering Department carefully produced three mini-cars defined as the V type. They took part in the National Day parades and in a film paying homage to the 10th anniversary. The precious old photo in the beginning of this article recorded this precious moment. After the National Day, more than a hundred mini-cars of this type were produced in a small scale. They formed a taxi fleet which served between Beijing Station and Children Hospital until the end of 1961.

改变了北京交通依靠人力客运的面貌，为北京交通运输业的发展做出了贡献。

王蓓蓓

北京汽车博物馆

During the design and production of these mini-cars, students from the Automobile Engineering Department in Tsinghua University did not only accumulate knowledge from real practices, but also in some degrees changed the condition of Beijing's passenger transportation that once relied heavily on manpower, thus making great contribution to the development of transportation in Beijing.

Wang Peipei, Beijing Automobile Museum

猫儿山二战美军轰炸机残骸

Wreckages of the US Bomber Discovered in Mao'er Mountain

2012 年 10 月，国家首次开展全国可移动文物普查工作，中国人民抗日战争纪念馆借助这次文物普查工作，摸清家底，深入挖掘藏品背后蕴藏的故事，让每件藏品承载的信息通过展览、网站、多媒体等多样化的手段传递给人们，让人们去感受那段岁月，去感悟那段历史。在展厅中，展出的猫儿山二战美军轰炸机残骸，正是中美人民并肩抗击日本法西斯的铁证。

在抗日战争期间，一支赫赫有名

广西猫儿山发现的 B-24 轰炸机氧气瓶

the oxygen tank of the B-24 bomber
discovered in Mao'er Mountain in Guangxi province

In October 2012, the government carried out the first national census on movable cultural relics. The Memorial Museum of Chinese People's Anti-Japanese War (hereinafter referred to as the Memorial Museum) took the opportunity to sort out all cultural relics kept there and discovered stories behind these relics, allowing everyone to feel and relive that period of time by multiple approaches such as exhibitions, websites and multi-media technologies. Wreckages of American bomber during World War II discovered in the Mao'er Mountain was exhibited in the Memorial Museum. They are unshakable evidence of the cooperation between Chinese and Americans to fight against Japanese fascism.

During the Anti-Japanese War, there was a famous American air force team which was better known by its name "flying tigers". The official name of these "flying tigers" was American

的美国空军队伍被中国人所熟知，它的名字叫"飞虎队"。飞虎队的正式名称为美国志愿援华航空队，由飞行教官陈纳德于1941年在缅甸仰光创建。1942年6月11日，陈纳德将军率领飞虎队的4架P-40E型和8架P-40B型"战鹰"式战斗机到达桂林。此后两年多时间里，英勇的飞虎队队员与顽强的中国军人和桂林人民在炮火纷飞的战争年代里并肩作战。1942年6月12日凌晨，飞虎队刚刚来到桂林第二天，秧塘基地便响起了空袭警报，敌机带着震耳的引擎声呼啸着空袭桂林。飞虎队立即起飞升空，与敌机在桂林上空激烈交火。最终，11架敌机被击落，其中有两架受了重伤逃遁后坠落。飞虎队虽损失两架飞机，但两位飞行员均返回基地，飞虎队到桂林后首战告捷（"六一二"大捷）。桂林民众群情振奋。进入1943年下半年后，飞虎队与中美空军混合部队并肩战斗，取得了桂阳空战、义宁空战、轰炸台湾新竹机场、支援常德会战中国军队地面作战等一系列战斗的胜利，威震长空，大大鼓舞了桂林民众抗战的决心。1944年夏秋间，日寇以12万

Volunteer Group (AVG), established by the flight instructor Claire Lee Chennault in Yangon, Myanmar in 1941. On June 11st, 1942, General Chennault led the AVG to fly four P-40E fighters and eight P-40B hawk fighters and arrived Guilin. And during more than two years since then, the brave "flying tigers" cooperated with strong Chinese soldiers and Guilin people to fight against common enemies in the war. At the midnight of June 12nd, 1942, the second day when "flying tigers" had just come to Guilin, the air alert was triggered, and the enemy planned to implement an air strike on Guilin. The "flying tigers" took off immediately, and fiercely fought against enemies over Guilin. Finally, 11 enemy aircrafts were shot down, among which two fell on the ground during escape. Although the "flying tigers" also lost two jets, both pilots returned to the base safely, and they had won the first battle after they came Guilin (Also known as the June 12nd Victory). Guilin people were excited. Especially during the second half of 1943, the "flying tigers" became even more famous after they won the air fight in Guiyang, Yining together with Chinese soldiers and supported to bomb the Xinzhu Airport in Taiwan and the Battle in Changde, greatly inspiring the Guilin people to fight against the invaders.

兵力发动所谓打通大陆交通线的湘桂战役，攻占了长沙，继而包围衡阳，再图南进广西。8月，衡阳反包围战正在激烈进行。1944年8月31日，美国陆军第14航空队375轰炸中队的一架B-24型轰炸机，奉命从柳州机场起飞，轰炸停在台湾某港口的日本军舰，返航时因柳州基地遭日本轰炸改飞桂林秧塘机场，由于机件失灵，在还未到达桂林上空时就偏离航线，途中因撞上猫儿山坠毁。猫儿山平均气温7摄氏度，整日里刮着七八级偏北大风，一年当中有3/4的时间是阴雨漫雾，常常是大雪封山，下雪结冰要持续四五个月之久，饥寒交迫，再加上有那闻腥即来的猛兽、毒蛇，很快10名机组人员全部遇难，机组人员中年纪最大的26岁，最小的只有19岁。也由于前述这些因素，52年来，这架被认为返航途中不明去向的机组的机骸和骨骸，得以在这里沉睡。52年后的1996年10月2日，该机残骸在猫儿山保护区仙愁崖地段，偶然被当地的采药农民所发现。为了寻找10名英雄的遗骨、遗物，中美双方开始了历时近3年、前后4次的联合搜寻行动，经过艰苦的清理、发掘，终于完成了

Between the summer and fall in 1944, the Japanese aggressors waged the Xiang-Gui Battle with 120,000 troops, expecting to open up transportation lines in central China. They occupied Changsha, besieged Hengyang and expected to penetrate into Guangxi province. In August, anti-siege battle in Hengyang was unfolding. On August 31st, 1944, a B-24 bomber of the Brigade 375, Flight Division 14 of the United States Army took off from Liuzhou airport after they received the order to bomb a Japanese warship in a port in Taiwan. When they returned, the Liuzhou base was bombed by the Japanese air force, so they had to fly to Yangtang airport in Guilin. However, due to the failure of the jet parts, the bomber deviated from the original route and crashed into the Mao'er Mountain on the way to Guilin. The average temperature there was only 7 ℃ , and the north wind was normally as strong as 7 to 8 grade. It was rainy or snowy in three-quarters of a year. The snow and ice could block the mountain for four to five months. There were also many beasts and snakes. Faced with multiple threats, starvation and coldness, all 10 crew members died, among whom the oldest was 26 years old and the youngest only 19 years old. Also due to these factors, the wreckage of the jet and the remnant of all crew members could rest here for 52 years.

失事遗骸的搜寻工作。兴安县文物部门，将清理、发掘的美国飞行员的骨骸，集中保管，并用考古技术对遗骸做了特殊处理，特制了骨盒，并将这些遗骸移交给美国。10名英雄得以魂归故里，永久安息在美利坚合众国的土地上。

为了纪念与中国人民并肩战斗、共同抗击日本法西斯不幸牺牲的美国空军英雄，广西壮族自治区人民政府建造了一座美军失事飞机记事碑，并将清理、发掘的飞机残骸入藏兴安县博物馆。中国人民抗日战争纪念馆目前展出的飞机残骸，是2005年由兴安县博物馆捐赠的。

任京培
中国人民抗日战争纪念馆

52 years later on October 2nd, 1996, the aircraft wreckages near the Chou Cliff in the Mao'er Mountain Reserve were found by a local herbalist by accident. In order to find the remnant of the ten heroes, the Chinese government and the American government spent three years on four joint search actions. Thanks to all the endeavors, we finally collected all the wreckages and remnant successfully. The cultural relics department in Xingan County kept the bones of all crew members and employed the archaeological craft to process these bones and made them into a special bone box before handing it over to the American government. The 10 heroic souls returned hometown finally, resting in peace forever in the land of the United States of America.

To commemorate the sacrificed American soldiers in the joint action to fight against the Japanese fascism, the people's government of Guangxi autonomous region built a monument to record the history of the crashing U.S. military jet. And wreckages of the jet were now kept in County Museum in Xingan. And the wreckage on display now in the Memorial Museum was donated by the County Museum in 2005.

Ren Jingpei , the Museum of the War of Chinese People's Resistance Against Japanese Aggression

广西猫儿山发现的 B-24 轰炸机机翼残骸

the debris of wings of the B-24 bomber
discovered in Mao'er Mountain in Guangxi province

中国同胞尸骨见证的抗战故事

A War Story Witnessed by Blood and Bones of Chinese Compatriots

在这次可移动文物普查中，我们整理出一箱累累白骨，望着这整整一箱白骨，我们的心情久久难以平静。

七七事变后不久，日本侵略者为了镇压中国人民的反抗，在长辛店建起了宪兵队、警务段和狗队。狗队的番号叫"加藤部队"，1938年成立，是驯养军犬和杀人的部队。为首的日军叫加藤，是受过专门训练的特务，手下有驯狗技师吉田和一大帮军犬手，平时这里驯养着四五百条狼狗，最多的时候有上千条。日军认定八路军都是穿便衣的，所以每天都要用穿便衣的人当狗队的训练对象，狗一见了穿便衣的就咬。加藤部队除了为其他部队提供军犬外，还成了处决"犯人"的机构。成批抗日军民和无辜群众被抓进去，都被狼狗活活吃掉，甭想活

In the national census on movable cultural relics, we sorted out a box of skeletons and bones. Looking at the remnant of our compatriots, we could hardly calm down.

Shortly after the July 7th Incident of 1937, the Japanese invaders in Changxindian, Fengtai District, Beijing, established military police, police station and a team of dogs in order to suppress the resistance of Chinese people at that time. The team of dogs was called "Kato Forces". Founded in 1938, it was a team where dogs were trained to kill innocent Chinese people. Led by Kato, a well trained spy, the team of dog consisted of a great many of dog walkers and a special dog trainer called Yoshida. In this boot camp for dogs, there were normally four or five hundred of dogs, and thousands of dogs at its height. The Japanese invaders believed that all members of the Eighth Route Army soldiers would wear plain clothes. As a result, every day, they would train their dogs to bite those people in plain clothes. Besides providing other military forces with dogs,

着出来。日本侵略者在长辛店驻扎军队，霸占长辛店铁路工厂，改名为"华北交通株式会社长辛店铁路工厂"。狗队的位置在长辛店铁路工厂的西部，由长辛店火车站往西，走不到一里地，从西北角往南的一大片院子及西边的大片空地（今长辛店二七机车厂东北部，长辛店公园北部山冈的西坡）就是"吃人狼狗队"的所在地。"吃人狼狗队"在此筑起高墙，墙上加电网，岗哨林立，戒备森严，还盖了上千间狗房，一条狗一间，由一个日本兵看管训练，而且还为这些狗盖有专门的狗厨房。大小狗分大小灶做饭，大狗吃的是牛羊肉、大米饭；小狗吃的是鸡子儿、牛奶；稍大一点的狗给增添肉和米饭。每条小狗配一套被褥，各有一名日本兵看管，日夜按时巡视，哪怕夜里小狗把被子蹬开了，也会有人给及时盖上。

训练好了的狼狗运送到各地，成为日军残害中国人的罪恶的工具。加藤是个心狠手辣、杀人不眨眼的魔鬼，他一天要化几次装在工厂内外转悠，唯恐工人从远处把他认出来。他看谁不顺眼立刻抓起来，进行严刑拷打，

Kato Forces also took responsibility for executing "criminals". Many soldiers in the Anti-Japanese Army and innocent people were captured and sent to that boot camp. They would be eaten up by those wolf dogs alive, never expecting to survive. The Japanese invaders stationed in Changxindian, occupied the local railway factory, and renamed it as "Changxindian Railway Factory of North China Transportation Joint-stock Company". The team of dog was situated in the west of the Changxindian railway factory. Walking for less than 1 li (500 meters) west-bound from the railway station of Changxindian, one could see the team of dogs in the yard and a large area of glade (now in the northeast of the Erqi Locomotive Manufacture Works, on the west slope of the hill in the north of Changxindian Park). The "cannibal team of dogs" set up a high wall and installed electricity net with high-level security. The team also established thousands of kennels. Every dog had one kennel and was taken care of by one soldier. There were even special kitchens for those dogs. Different dogs had different menus. Large dogs would eat beef, mutton and rice; while small ones would eat egg and drink milk. When the small ones became larger, meat and rice would be generally added into their menu. Every puppet would have a set of bedding and one Japanese soldier to look after it. Soldiers would patrol around these puppets. They would even blanket the puppets when puppet kicked the quit at night.

Those trained dogs would be sent to other places in China, becoming the

然后送到狗队，让狼狗进行撕咬。曾经有一个工人，因为穿了一双像八路军穿的鞋而被抓起来，最后活活地惨死在里面。日军还经常把狗带到外边去，让狗随意咬中国老百姓，住在附近的工人和农民，不知有多少人被狗咬死、咬伤。侵华日军把整个长辛店和周围一大片地区，变成了人间地狱。日军为了使中国人成为日本的亡国奴，对工人子弟进行奴化教育，只准说日语，不准说中国话。日军什么活都让工人子弟去干，包括为狗队定期清扫狗窝。

"吃人狼狗队"害人无数，1989年，长辛店二七机车厂建厂房时，在"吃人狼狗队"原驻地挖出了大量人骨，经考证都是当年被日军狼狗吃掉的中国军民的尸骨。1997年5月24日，北京第一批爱国主义教育纪念地暨国耻纪念地标志碑揭幕，其中就有"长辛店侵华日军吃人狼狗队遗址"标志碑，碑文如下：

一九三八年，日本侵略军在长辛店建立了驯养狼狗的基地，负责人叫加藤，基地的番号称为"加藤部队"。

evil tool which facilitated the Japanese invaders to kill Chinese cruelly. Kato was wicked and merciless, killing people without even blinking his eyes. He was the devil and he would make up for many times a day and patrol around the factory, lest workers working there recognized him from a distance. He would capture anyone whom he didn't like, torture them and then send them to the team of dog, making dogs bite them. There used to be a worker died horribly in the boot camp, merely because he worn a pair of shoes which looked like those worn by soldiers in Eighth Route Army. And the Japanese soldiers would also take those dogs out, letting them bite ordinary Chinese people. Many workers and farmers living around were bit to death. The Japanese invaders had turned Changxindian and its periphery into a living hell on earth. In order to make Chinese subservient to Japan, the Japanese invaders imposed the slavery education on workers' children, only allowing them to speak Japanese instead of Chinese. And they would make these children to do all the chores in the camp, including clearing the kennels for the team of dog.

The "cannibal team of dogs" had killed countless Chinese people. In 1989 when constructing the Changxindian Erqi Locomotive Manufacture Works, workers found many skeletons and bones of human beings in the premises where the team of dog originally stationed. And these bones had already been proved to be the remnant of Chinese soldiers and people who were eaten up by the wolf dogs trained by the Japanese

在这里驯养了四五百条狼狗，多时上千条。日军把它们训练为吃人成性的杀人工具，成批的抗日人民群众被送到狼狗队，活活让狗吃掉，不知有多少中国人惨死在狼狗口里。一九八九年，二七机车厂建厂房时，挖出大量人骨，经考证，均为当时叫狗咬死的中国军民遗骨，现在遗骨已被中国人民抗日战争纪念馆收存。

中共北京市委宣传部
北京市文物事业管理局
丰台区人民政府
一九九七年十月立

Army. On May 24th, 1997, the first batch of memorial monuments for patriotic education and national humiliation in Beijing were unveiled. And the "site of cannibal team of dog trained by Japanese invaders in Changxindian" was one of them. The inscription was as follows:

In 1938, the Japanese invaders established the team of dog in Changxindian, Fengtai Districe, Beijing, led by Kato. The team was called Kato Forces. There was four to five hundred of dogs in the camp, and at most thousands of dogs at its height. The Japanese army trained these dogs to be the killing machine. A great many Chinese people and soldiers were sent to the team and eaten up by

日军在长辛店建立"狗队"咬死的中国同胞的尸骨
the team of dog, killing machine of the Japanese invaders

长辛店二七机车厂将建厂房时挖出的累累白骨，于1997年7月捐赠给中国人民抗日战争纪念馆保存。

任京培
中国人民抗日战争纪念馆

the dogs. Countless people died. In 1989 when constructing the Erqi Locomotive Manufacture Works in Changxindian, lots of skeletons and bones of human beings were discovered, which later were proved to be the remnant of Chinese soldiers and people eaten up by those dogs. Now, these bones are kept in the Museum of the War of Chinese People's Resistance Against Japanese Aggression.

Propaganda Department of Beijing Municipal Party Committee of the Communist Party of China
Beijing Municipal Administration of Cultural Relics and Heritage
People's Government of Fengtai district
1997.10

Bones were discovered in Changxindian when workers were constructing the Erqi Locomotive Manufacture Works. And they were then donated to and now kept in the Museum of the War of Chinese People's Resistance Against Japanese Aggression.

Ren Jingpei ,the Museum of the War of Chinese People's Resistance Against Japanese Aggression

将军的挎包[1]

General's Bag [1]

2015 年，根据第一次全国可移动文物普查工作要求和北京市可移动文物普查工作部署，永定河文化博物馆开展了本馆第一次全国可移动文物普查工作，完成本馆上报藏品的数据采集、补录、登录等普查相关工作事项。

2015 年恰逢 "纪念中国人民抗日战争胜利暨世界反法西斯战争胜利 70 周年" 之际，在此次采集工作进行中有一件藏品显得极为珍贵。

永定河文化博物馆三层 "平西抗日斗争史陈列" 中展出的一个皮质挎包，是一件抗战文物，这是邓华将军生前使用过的物品。

1984 年初，门头沟区筹办 "门头沟区革命斗争史展" 时，向曾经战斗在门头沟地区的老战士、老将军征集

In 2015, according to the requirements of the first national census on movable cultural relics and the working deployment of Beijing movable cultural relics census, Yongding River Culture Museum carried out the census on movable cultural relics for the first time, finishing relevant work including collecting, sorting out, and registering the data of relics we have already reported.

This year marks the 70th anniversary of the victory of the Chinese People's War of Resistance against Japanese Aggression (the War of Resistance) and the victory of the Anti-Fascist War of the World. Hence, the museum would launch an exhibition showing the anti-Japanese endeavors in Western Beiping Resistance Base. Therefore, during the census, we mainly focused on the information of cultural relics representing the revolutionary history and we found two pieces of relics with great significance.

---

[1] 本篇故事中内容和数据参考罗印文著《邓华将军传》，中共中央党校出版社，1995 年。

抗战文物，邓华将军的夫人李玉芝收到信后亲自来到位于门头沟西峰寺的博物馆，将邓华将军在抗战中缴获敌人的战利品——跟随邓华40余年的挎包捐给博物馆，以教育后代。邓华夫人李玉芝讲述了挎包的由来。

1937年9月在平型关前线，邓华作为八路军第一一五师三四三旅六八五团政训处主任，深入连队进行战斗动员，以迎战猖狂一时的日军板垣师团第二十一旅的战斗。

当年9月25日零时，一一五师部队出发，战士们顶着狂风暴雨，涉过急湍山洪，在拂晓前到达指定地区，把全师主力布置在平型关到东河南镇10余里长的公路南侧山地边缘上。在这次伏击作战中，第六八五团预伏在灵丘至平型关公路上的关沟地区，担负切断辛庄子东跑池日军的联系、歼灭辛庄子及其以东地区日军的任务。

25日晨，雨后初晴，战区的能见度极好，一个约4000余人的日军联队，以100余辆汽车为前导，紧接着是200辆大车、九二式步兵炮以及少数骑兵殿后，由灵丘方向开来，进入从东河南镇到关沟10余里长的狭谷

There was a leather bag on display in the exhibition of Anti-Japanese War in Western Beiping Resistance Base on the third floor of Yongding River Culture Museum. It is a cultural relic of the war, a used items of General Deng Hua.

At the beginning of 1984, Mentougou District held a museum exhibition of "History of the revolution in Mentougou District", collecting cultural relics of the war from veterans and generals in Mentougou. Li Yuzhi, wife of General Deng Hua went to the museum located in the Xifeng Temple, Mentougou, and donated the trophy, a leather bag which has accompanied General Deng Hua for more than 4 decades, to the museum, thus to educate the future generations. Li Yuzhi told us the origin of the leather bag.

In September, 1937, in the front line of Pingxing Pass, Deng Hua, the director of political training in Regiment 658, Brigade 343, Division 115 of the Eight Route Army, mobilized the soldiers to fight against the rampant Brigade 21, Itagaki Forces.

At the midnight of September 25, Division 115 charged in the storm, waded the rapid flash floods, and reached the designated area before dawn, deploying the main forces in the edge of the hill south to the road from Pingxing Pass to Donghenan

之中。

卢沟桥事变后，入侵我国华北地区的 30 万日军，虽经国民党第二十九路军等爱国军人的奋起反击，但终因各部配合、指挥协调等方面失策，使进入平型关的日军大摇大摆如入无人之境，他们没想到此地竟有人布下天罗地网。

7 时许，日军全部进入预设伏击圈，第一一五师立即下达了攻击命令。顷刻间，全线部队像猛虎下山般向日军出击，步枪、机枪、手榴弹一齐开火，首先冲到马路上的第六八五团第二营五连，在第一波冲锋中炸毁日军汽车 20 多辆，被炸死、射杀、刺死的日军躺在马路上。同时，我方也付出了重大伤亡，受伤的连长拉响了手榴弹与日军同归于尽。连长牺牲了，指导员负责指挥；指导员负了重伤，排长接替指挥，两个排长先后阵亡。战至最后，五连百名壮士，凯旋时只剩 30 多人。

经过 5 个多小时的拼杀，辛庄及其以东的日军被六八五团歼灭，后又协助六八六团歼灭老爷庙附近敌人 300 余人。至 27 日，平型关战役结束后，

Town, which covered over 10 li. In the ambush warfare, Brigade 685 hid in the Guangou area along the road from Lingqiu to Pingxing Pass, responsible for cutting off the connection between the Japanese army stationed in Xinzhuangzi and Paochi Village, and annihilating all of them.

In the morning of 25th, September, the visibility in the war zone was really good thanks to the rain. A Japanese Brigade, consisting of about four thousand soldiers, were marching toward Lingqiu, led by over 100 vehicles and followed by 200 large vehicles and some cushions. They entered in the gorge stretching about 10 li connecting Donghenan Town and Guangou Area.

After the Lugou Bridge Incident in 1937, 300,000 Japanese invaders in northern China were resisted by the Route 29 Army of Kuomintang (KMT) and other patriotic soldiers. Due to ill cooperation and incoordination of commanding, those invaders swaggered into the Pingxing Pass area rampantly. But they didn't know what was waiting for them there.

At 7:00 pm, the Japanese force all entered into the preset ambush area, the Division 115 immediately gave the order to attack. Suddenly, all soldiers were like tigers, charging toward the Japanese invaders, attacking them with rifles,

据打扫战场统计，共歼敌板垣师团
1000多人，炸毁汽车百余辆，大车辆
百余辆，缴获枪支、弹药食品及其他
军用品无数，邓华的挎包就是这次战
役中缴获的战利品。由于平型关战役
是中国抗战开始后取得的第一次大胜
利，粉碎了日军不可战胜的神话，因
此此战役中的战利品有着不同寻常的
意义，邓华格外珍惜它，后来这个挎
包跟随他进入平西创建根据地。

根据党中央、毛泽东同志创建冀
热察地区抗日根据地的指示，1938年
3月初，邓华率部队进入平西斋堂地区
（现门头沟斋堂镇），在西斋堂村的
聂家大院设立了司令部。之后，首先
协助地方党组织筹建政权，3月下旬，
在东斋堂村公开成立了北京第一个抗
日民主政府——宛平县政府。1938年
3月31日至4月3日，邓华率支队打
进门头沟，占领了火车站，炸毁日军
碉堡，又攻打香山碧云寺等，给了日
伪军沉重的打击，使平西人民抗战热
情更加高涨。

1939年2月7日，八路军冀热察
挺进军正式成立，这一时期，邓华和
军政委员会的领导同志们一起负责领

machine guns, and grenades. Company 5, Regiment 2, Brigade 685 firstly rushed into the road and blew up over 20 vehicles, killing numerous enemies. At the same time, we also suffered a large death toll. The injured captain blew up the grenades to die with the enemies. And the instructor took the charge to command the fight. After the instructor got hurt, the platoon leader took over the commanding. And the two platoon leaders both sacrificed during this warfare. In the end, only 30 out of 100 soldiers in the Company 5 survived.

After more than five hours of fight, Brigade 685 annihilated all Japanese invaders in Xinzhuang and its eastern periphery. Then, they also helped Brigade 676 to eliminate around 300 enemies in Laoyemiao area. The Pingxing Pass Warfare ended on 27th, September. And we killed over 1,000 enemies in the Itagaki Forces, blew up over 100 vehicles and over 100 large vehicles, and seized numerous guns, ammunition, food and other military items. Deng Hua's bag was among the trophies. The battle of Pingxing Pass was the first large success achieved ever since the start of the war, crushing the Japanese army's myth of invincibility, hence the great significance of these trophies. Deng cherished the bag very much. Then General Deng took this bag with him to Western Beiping and established a resistance base there.

邓华曾用过的挎包

the bag used by Deng Hua

导平西、冀东、平北 3 个地区的军政
工作，指挥部队向日寇频频进攻。同
时，他还发动群众组织自卫队，广泛
开展游击战争，创建开辟了南至涞水、
涿州，北至昌平、延庆、怀柔等地在
内的冀热察抗日根据地，为形成和确
立"巩固平西、坚持冀东和开辟平北"
三位一体总任务、创建冀热察抗日根
据地做出了巨大贡献，直到 1940 年初
春时节，邓华离开平西到五分区，踏

1984 年初邓华夫人李玉芝将挎包送到门头沟博物馆

at the beginning of 1984, Li Yuzhi, Deng Hua's wife donated the

bag to the Mentougou Museum

Following the command of central committee of CPC and Comrade Mao Zedong to create Jirecha Anti- Japanese base, Deng Hua led his men to the Zhaitang area in Western Beiping (now Zhaitang Town in Mentougou District) in early March 1938, and established a headquarters in the family compound of Nie. Then he helped the local Party organization to build regime. In late March, the first anti-Japanese democratic government, Wanping government was established in Eastern Zhaitang Village in Beijing. From March 31st, 1938 to April 3rd, Deng led a team to penetrate into Mentougou and occupied the train station, blew up the Japanese bunker, and then attacked the Biyun temple in Xiang Mountain, etc., bringing a heavy blow to the enemies and stirring up the enthusiasm of common people in Western Beiping area to fight against Japanese invaders. On February 7th, 1939, the Eighth Route Army Jinchaji Devision was formally established. During this period, Deng Hua and other comrades from the administrative committee were responsible for the military and political work in Western Beiping, Eastern Hebei and Northern Beiping, leading forces to attack the Japanese aggressors frequently. Meanwhile, he also mobilized the common people to establish the self-defense forces and to implement extensive guerrilla warfare, paving the way for the Jinrecha Resistance Base

上了新的征程。

据邓华夫人回忆，此挎包一直跟随将军经历了抗日战争、解放战争以及抗美援朝战争。

谭 勇

永定河文化博物馆

stretching from Laishui, Zhuozhou in the south, to Changping, Yanqing, Huairou in the north. The establishment of this resistance base has made great contribution to the "consolidation of Western Beiping, the holding of Eastern Hebei and the penetration to Northern Beiping". In the early spring of 1940, Deng Hua left Western Beiping for Wufen, embarking on a new journey.

His wife recalled that the bag had accompanied the General during the Anti-Japanese War, Liberation War and the war to resist U.S. aggression and aid Korea.

Tan Yong ,Yongding River Culture Museum

"全能神" 大黑天

"Almighty God" Mahakala

如果您对藏传佛教有一定了解的话，就一定听说过大黑天。"大黑天"是梵语"玛哈嘎拉"的意译，也译为"救怙主"，藏语称"贡保"。他原是古印度的战神，后来被藏传佛教吸收为护法神，颇受密教崇奉，位居诸大护法神之首。常见的大黑天有两臂、四臂、六臂三种形象，身体呈青黑色，三目圆睁，毛发竖立，头戴五骷髅冠，左手托骷髅碗，右手拿月形刀（四臂、六臂像持更多法器），双腿站立，右腿屈，左腿伸，脚踩异教徒，身后有火焰背光。听起来这个形象似乎有点恐怖，其实大黑天所呈现的这种愤怒相，恰恰是为了震慑邪魔。

大黑天崇拜由来已久，在不同历史时期和不同地区，人们将他视为战神、财神、瘟神、福神……在今天中国的很多地区，不少民族仍然崇拜大黑天。其实早在很久以前，人们对这

If you know about Tibetan Buddhism, then you must have heard of Mahakala. Mahakala is a free translation of Sanskrit "Mahākāla", and it is also translated as "Saviour". In Tibetan language, it is called "Gonpo". Originally, he was the god of war in ancient India, and later he was absorbed by the Tibetan Buddhism as a guardian deity (Dharmapala), worshiped by Esoteric Buddhism, and listed as the leading guardian deity (Dharmapala). There are three kinds of images of Mahakala that are most commonly seen, with two, four, and six arms respectively. The body of Mahakala is in greenish black, and he has three big round eyes and erect mane, wearing a crown with five skeletons, holding in left hand a skeleton bowl, and right hand a crescent knife (those with four arms and six arms would hold more implements). He stands on its two legs, with a bending right leg and a stretched left leg, trampling on a heretic, and there is flame behind him. This image seems a little bit scary, but this image of anger presented by Mahakalas is used exactly for deterring evil spirit.

样威力无边的一尊"全能神"的崇拜就已经漂洋过海，传到了东南亚很多地区。但很多人不知道的是，大黑天其实早在 750 年前就已经来到北京安家落户了，他的落脚点就是今天位于西城区阜成门内大街的白塔寺。

妙应寺，俗称白塔寺，始建于辽寿昌二年（1096）。元至元八年（1271），元世祖忽必烈亲自勘察选址，敕令在辽代永安寺塔的旧址上重新修建一座藏式佛塔。8 年后，佛塔建成，他又下令以塔为中心，修建了一座占地约 16 万平方米的皇家寺院，时称"大圣寿

六臂大黑天

Mahakala with six arms

Worship for Mahakalas has a long history. In different historical periods and different regions, people regarded him as the god of war, wealth, plague, bliss, etc. Today in many parts of China, many ethnic groups still worship Mahakalas. In fact, a long time ago, worship for this "almighty god" with enormous power was spread across the ocean to many regions in the East Asia and South Asia. But what many people do not know is that as early as 750 years ago, Mahakalas had come to Beijing, and his statue was placed in White Pagoda Temple located in today's Fuchengmennei street in Xicheng district of Beijing.

Miaoying Temple, commonly known as White Pagoda Temple, was initially built in the second year of the reign of Shouchang in Liao Dynasty (1096 AD). In the eighth year of the reign of Zhiyuan of Yuan Dynasty (1271 AD), Kublai Khan surveyed and selected a location, and ordered that a Tibetan stupa be built on the site where Yongansi Pagoda once stood. Eight years later, when the stupa was completed, according to his order, a royal temple covering an area of around 160,000 square meters was built with the stupa standing at its center. The royal temple was then called Dashengshouwanan Temple (Temple of Monastery, Greatness, Sacredness, and Peace). Here you may ask, what are the realtions between the Tibetan white pagoda, the Dashengshouwanan Temple

万安寺"。说到这，您也许会问，这藏式白塔和大圣寿万安寺与大黑天又有什么关系呢？

其实，关于白塔和大圣寿万安寺的修建，还有一个鲜为人知的故事。元朝时，蒙古贵族普遍信奉藏传佛教，大黑天被视为蒙古军队的保护神。据说忽必烈征战时就常把他的画像带到军中，作战前必先祈祷。蒙宋战争全面开始后，蒙古骑兵凭借超强的战斗力，一路南下，所向披靡。但是他们万万没想到，一个长江边上的城市阻挡了自己前进的脚步，这一挡就是足足 6 年，期间忽必烈增兵 10 万，却始终没有攻克它。如果您看过金庸先生的小说《神雕侠侣》，那您一定猜到了这个城市的名字，它就是襄阳。襄阳之战是中国历史上宋元王朝更迭的关键一战。这次战役从 1267 年蒙将阿术进攻襄阳的安阳滩之战开始，到 1273 年吕文焕力竭降元结束，历时长达 6 年。战事的胶着让忽必烈非常苦恼，于是他向自己的帝师八思巴请教应对之策。八思巴给了忽必烈一个建议，让他在大都城的西北方修建一座藏式佛塔，塔里供奉战神大黑天，这样就能够保佑战事顺利推进。果然

and Mahakala?

In fact, in terms of the building of the White Pagoda Temple and the Dashengshouawnan Temple, there is a little-known story. In Yuan Dynasty, Mongolian aristocrats generally believed in Tibetan Buddhism, and Mahakala was regarded as the patron saint of the Mongolian army. It is said that Kublai Khan often took the portrait of Mahakala to the army during wars, praying before fighing with enermies. After the full start of the war between Song Dynasty and Mongolia, the Mongolian cavalries fighting southward with strong battle effectiveness were invincible. But it never came to them that they were stopped by a city along Yangtze river for 6 years. During this period, Kublai Khan deployed another 100,000 soldiers, but did not succeed in conquering it. If you have read Mr. Jin Yong's novel *Legend of Condor Hero*, then you must know that the name of this city is Xiangyang. The battle of Xiangyang is crucial to the change from the Song Dynasty to the Yuan Dynasty in China's history. The war started from the year of 1267 when Mongolia general Aju attacked Anyangtan of Xiangyang. It lasted for 6 years and was ended in 1273 when Lv Wenhuan who was defending the city got exhausted and surrendered to the Yuan army. The war stalemate upset Kublai Khan, so he turned to to his imperial tutor Pagba for solutions. Pagba suggested that Kublai Khan should

婆罗门大黑天
Brahmanical Mahakala

1271年白塔开始修建后不久，战事就渐渐变得顺利。1279年白塔落成之年，恰逢元灭南宋，彻底统一中国。于是这座神奇的白塔也被命名为"胜利三界大宝塔"。就在今天，襄阳当地依然流传着一些关于大黑天的传说，说蒙古军队在攻打这座坚城时，城中将士突然看到天兵天将布满天空，于是宋军不战而降，据说就是大黑天所显的威灵。元末1368年的一场天降雷火焚毁了整个寺院，两个月后，徐达带兵攻入北京，元朝灭亡。冥冥之中，这里似乎真的与元朝的运数有着千丝万缕的联系。

build a Tibetan stupa in the northwestern part of DaDouCheng city, enshrining Mahakala. He said that it could bless the army to win the battles. In 1271, shortly after the construction of White Pagoda began, their conquering gradually started to proceed smoothly. In 1279, the year of completion of the White Pagoda, the Yuan Dynasty managed to replace the Song Dynasty, and achieved the unification of China. And this magical White Pagoda was also named as "The Great Pagoda of Victory". Today, there are still some stories in Xiangyang about Mahakala. It is said that when Mongolian armies attacked this city, soldiers in the city suddenly saw a sky full of divine troops and then surrendered to their enemies without fighting. People believed that Mahakala made his presence. If you think this was just a coincidence, it should also be mentioned that one day in 1368 at the end of the Yuan dynasty, thunder and fire came from heaven and burned down the entire temple, and two months later, Xu Da invaded Beijing with his troops, which marked the end of the Yuan Dynasty. It seems that magical and strong connections do exist between this pagoda and the rise and fall of the Yuan Dynasty.

Worship for Mahakala also prevails in areas inhabited by ethnic minorities in China. In Yunnan province, he is regarded as the patron saint able to rid local people of illnesses. It is said that, once upon a time, a god was jealous of

大黑天信仰在我国少数民族地区也十分盛行，在云南，他就被视为能够祛病除疫、护持一方的保护神。传说曾经有一位天神由于嫉妒大理的人间美景，在玉帝面前进谗言，陷害白族人民，说他巡视苍山洱海时，见到这里的百姓男不耕，女不织，上不孝，下不养，既懒又坏。玉帝听了大为震怒，立即派他的心腹爱将大黑天带上一瓶瘟药，到大理去惩罚黎民百姓。大黑天驾着云朵来到大理时，只见男人们忙着犁田，女人们忙着栽秧，邻里和睦，人民生活非常幸福，与他听说的完全不一样。他被善良的人们所感动，不忍降下瘟疫，又担心完不成玉帝的命令无法交差。最终，他为了使当地的百姓免遭灾难，毅然打开瓶子，独自把瘟药全部吞下，瘟药毒性发作，大黑天被毒成了浑身青黑的模样。他以牺牲自己挽救了大理千千万万的无辜百姓，从此那里的白族人民都把他奉为保护神，世代尊奉。今天，如果您去大理的著名景点崇圣寺游玩，您一定别惊讶，为什么这里的第一个大殿天王殿中供奉的是大黑天，而不是我们通常会见到的弥勒佛。

更有意思的是，如果我告诉您，

the beautiful landscape in Dali, and thus slandered Bai people in front of the Jade Emperor, saying that when he visited Cangshan mountain and Erhai lake, he saw that people there were lazy and bad, for men were not plowing, women were not weaving, and that they did not support elderly family members or raise children. After hearing this, the Jade Emperor was very angry, immediately sending his favorite general Mahakala to punish Dali people with plague using a bottle of poisonous substance. When arriving at Dali by riding clouds, Mahakala saw that men were busy in plowing, and women planting seedlings. All the neighbors lived in harmony, and people were leading a happy life. All of this was totally different from what he was told. Struck by the kindness of people, he was not willing to make the plague spread among them, but he was afraid that he would not be able to complete the mission assigned by the Jade Emperor. Eventually, in order to spare local people suffering, he opened the bottle and swallowed all the poisonous substance by himself, and when toxicity attacked, the color of his skin turned into greenish black. He sacrificed himself to save tens of thousands of innocent Dali people, and from then on, the Bai people there regarded him as their patron saint, and the worship for him proceeded generation after generation. Today, if you visit Chongsheng Temple, a famous scenic spot in Dali, you'll see Mahakala that is worshiped in the Hall of Celestial

现在随处可见的招财猫也是源于大黑天，您一定觉得难以置信，这么萌的猫咪，居然和我们通常所见的怒目圆睁、凶神恶煞的形象是一个人。招财猫的造型源自日本。历史上随着佛教传入日本，大黑天的信仰也随之东渡。日本最为信仰的财神就是大黑天，加上日本本土文化认为猫有辟邪的功能，所以就以大黑天财神的形象为基础，把他的外表改成猫咪的样子，而设计出了招财猫。当然，除了招财，大黑天也被视为能给人们带来好运的福神。

说了这么多关于大黑天的故事，您是不是迫不及待地想亲眼目睹一下他的风采？欢迎您来白塔寺，近距离观赏"藏传金铜造像艺术精品展"，也可以趁绕塔的时候，在白塔下的西南角亭一睹他的真容。

康蕾

北京市白塔寺

King which is the first hall you will see in the temple, rather than Maitreya commonly seen in other temples.

What is more interesting is that fortune cats which are ubiquitous also originate from Mahakala. It may be hard for you to believe that the cute cat and the fierce-looking god glaring at us actually come from the person. The modelling of fortune cat originates from Japan. As Buddhism was introduced into East Asia, so was the worship for Mahakala. Mahakala is the god that Japaneses believe in the most, besides, it is believed in Japanese native culture that cats can ward off bad luck. Therefore, based on the image of the Mahakala, the god of wealth, Japanese people changed his appearance into that of a cat, and this is how the image of fortune cat was designed. In addition to fortune, of course, Mahakala is also regarded as the god of bliss who can bring people good luck.

After being told so many stories about Mahakala, are you eager to see the statue of him by yourself? Welcome to White Pogoda Temple to visit the "Fine Works of Art Exhibition of Tibetan Gold and Bronze Buddha Statues". You can also see his statue at the Xinanjiao pavilion under the white tower, while wandering around the pagoda.

Kang Lei, White Pagoda Temple in Beijing

守望花锦衣，细抚彩罗裙

Keep the Beauty of Ethnic Costumes

女孩们对花衣裳的迷恋绝对是天性，当可移动文物普查团队的 6 名女孩走进北京服装学院民族服饰博物馆的一刹那，她们再也按捺不住内心的激动与喜悦："好漂亮的衣服""原来衣服可以这样绚丽""这可是一份最幸福和快乐的工作啦"……

和漂亮的花衣裳相伴是令人开心的，但其意义却远不止此。但凡最近几年到访过少数民族地区的人，兴致勃勃地踏上行程，却总是怀着小小的失落归来，因为想象中身着七彩民族服饰载歌载舞的异域风情，并未如自己预期的那般到来。随着经济的发展，生活水平显著提高的少数民族地区，经历了一段"旧貌换新颜"的现代化进程，传统正在被现代文明慢慢替代。在少数民族地区已经很难看到纯粹的原生态场景，民族服饰也自然在这段进程中逐渐被取代、淘汰。幸好，北

Fascination with beautiful clothes is absolutely a part of girls' nature. The moment they entered the Ethnic Costume Museum of Beijing Institute Of Fashion Technology, the six girls from the Census Team on Movable Cultural Relics could no longer suppress their inner excitement and joy, cheering "So beautiful!", "I have never seen such beautiful clothes!" or "This is the greatest job in the world!"

Working with beautiful clothes sounds nice, but it is of much greater significance. In recent years, people who visited areas inhabited by ethnic minority group with high expectations always came back with slight disappointment, for they did not see the exotic scene where people dressed in colorful ethnic costumes sing and dance as what they had imagined before the trip. The ethnic minority areas with economic development and marked improvement of people's living standards, have experienced modernization which transforms their landscape, and their traditions are being eroded. Now in ethnic minority areas, it is very hard to find natural landscape without any human influence on it. Ethnic costumes, in this

京服装学院的老师们凭着敏锐的直觉和长远的眼光，在最紧要的关头留住了美丽。成立于 2000 年的北京服装学院民族服饰博物馆，其实早在 20 世纪 80 年代末就开始了对传统服饰的收集和保护。

民族服饰博物馆收集的每一件藏品背后，都有一连串的故事，酸甜苦辣，五味杂陈，但最后留下的往往是喜悦。博物馆老师们深知每一件衣服的来之不易，为了一件衣服，他们可能就要翻越几座山头，深入大山深处的村寨。他们要克服饮食上的不适，蚊虫的叮咬，甚至在云南遭遇过地震。

process, are also at stake. Fortunately, teachers at Beijing Institute of Fashion Technology, with their keen intuition and vision, kept the beauty at the most critical juncture. Founded in 2000, the Ethnic Costume Museum of Beijing Institute of Fashion Technology actually began to collect and protect traditional costumes at the end of 1980s.

Behind each costume in the museum's collection, there are always a series of stories which may contain ups and downs, but more than often, these stories are with happy endings. Staff at the museum know well that none of these costumes comes easily. To collect a single piece of clothes, they may have to go over a few mountains to visit a village located in remote mountainous areas.

为了获取这些衣服，老师们要博得老乡的信任，说服他们拿出压箱底的祖传衣物绝非易事，很多民族的风俗就不喜欢将自己的衣物送与别人，但最后他们总是为老师们的执着所感动。博物馆目前收藏的背扇，有很多缺一个小角，那是老乡们根据风俗剪下来的，这样他们才能安心地将它们递与博物馆考察的老师。

也许正是这些酸甜苦辣的记忆，让亲历这一过程的老师步入展厅时和普通观众的感觉截然不同。屹立在金

They had to overcome the discomfort caused by diet as well as the mosquito bitcs. Once they even encountered an earthquake in Yunnan. In order to obtain these clothes, they needed to win the trust of the villagers, but to persuade them to take out those precious clothes left by their ancestors was by no means an easy task. Influenced by their customs, people of many ethnic groups are reluctant to give their clothes away to others. But in the end, the villagers were always moved by the persistence of those staff. In the museum's collection, many "Beishan" (pieces of cloth used as baby carriers) are with small missing parts. This is because of the local customs according to which the villagers cut those parts off, and only

藏族八宝银法器

8 Tibetan silver implements

工首饰厅入口处的硕大的银器，是藏族寺庙里供奉的法器，为藏族八宝，之所以不是8件，其中也有着不为人知的秘密。这组银器是民族服饰博物馆邀请西藏日喀则地区的一位老银匠纯以手工打制而成，老人家在服装学院"叮叮当当"地整整敲了大半年，完成了其中的法螺、谷、桃、麦4件法器。但由于北京与青藏高原有海拔和气候上的差异，加上老银匠年事已高，这4件藏品成为老人最后的作品。位于少数民族厅的赫哲族鱼皮衣，是民族服饰博物馆最具特色的藏品之一，它曾经获得过"全国博物十大陈列精品——最佳制作奖"的殊荣。这件鱼皮衣的来历，也颇为曲折。1999年底，面对濒临失传的鱼皮衣文化，民族服饰博物馆的老师们前往赫哲族聚居区黑龙江省同江市街津口乡，找到掌握完整鱼皮衣制作工艺的尤翠玉老人，说明缘由，想完整记录下鱼皮衣的整个制作过程。由于是冬季不便捕鱼，直到第二年7月考察团队才再次奔赴街津口乡，在这期间团队一直和当地政府保持沟通，等待时机成熟；当时已经73岁高龄的尤翠玉老人大病一场，更是让博物馆的老师们甚是揪心。

in this way can they feel assured when giving their beloved items to those staff at the museum.

Perhaps it is these bittersweet memories that generate totally different feelings for those staff who have been a part of this process as well as for the general audience when they enter the hall. At the entrance of the Metalworking Jewelry Hall stand four giant silverwares which are ritual implements enshrined and worshiped in Tibetan temples, and they are called the "Eight Tibetan Treasures". One may wonder why they are made up of four instead of eight wares. The reason is unknown to many people. This set of silverwares were handmade by an old silversmith from Xigaze district in Tibet at the request of Ethnic Costume Museum. Staying more than half a year in the institute, the elderly craftsman completed four ritual implements in the images of triton, millet, peach and wheat respectively. However, due to differences in altitude and climate between Beijing and Tibet, and because of the old age of the silversmith, these four items became the final works of the old man. The Hezhe fish-skin garment, presented in Exhibition Hall of Ethnic Minority, is one of the most unique costumes in the museum's collection. It has won the "Ten Best Items on Display in China——the Best Craft Award". There were also many setbacks in the process of getting this fish-skin garment. At the end of 1999 when the fish-skin garment culture was about to die out, staff at the Ethnic Costume Museum

待捕鱼季节一到，考察团队的老师们亲自踏上渔船捕鱼，费尽周折才打捞上足够制作一件鱼皮衣的鱼。正是这种执着，让鱼皮衣最终走入民族服饰博物馆的展厅，呈现在全国各地观众和北京服装学院学子面前，整个制作过程也拍摄成纪实影视人类学影片《赫

赫哲族鱼皮衣，20世纪早期，黑龙江省同江市
Hezhe fish-skin garment, early 20th century, Tongjiang, Heilongjiang province

哲族的鱼皮衣》，并获得大奖。

民族服饰博物馆的藏品就这样在谱写故事的过程中从无到有，越来越丰富、齐全。目前民族服饰博物馆收藏有50多个少数民族的服饰，其中仅苗族就收藏有百余个支系的近两千套服饰。金工首饰厅里的凯棠苗银花冠

went to Jiejinkou township in Tongjiang city in Heilongjiang province, an area inhabited by Hezhe people and found You Cuiyu, and elderly craftsman mastering the complete process of making fish skin garments, explaining to her that they wanted to record the whole producing process of a fish-skin garment. Winter was not a season suitable for fishing, therefore they did not went to Jiejinkou township until July in the next year. In the meantime, the team kept in touch with the local government to wait for the right time to come. At that time, You Cuiyu who were seventy-three years old just went through a serious illness, which worried the staff at the museum. When fishing season came, the team members got onto fishing boats and fished by themselves. They made great efforts to get fish the amount of which was enough to make a fish-skin garment. It is this persistence that finally enabled the fish-skin garment to enter the exhibition hall of the Ethnic Costume Museum and to be presented in front of the visitors coming from all parts of China and students of Beijing Institute Of Fashion Technology. The whole production process was also recorded in an anthropology documentary film called *the Hezhen Fish-skin Garment* which won awards.

Story after story emerged in the process of collecting costumes, just in this way the Ethnic Costume Museum started from scratch and gradually became full-fledged. At present, the Ethnic Costume Museum has collected ethnic costumes

运用苗族錾花与花丝工艺制作，极其繁复精美；少数民族服饰厅里的藏族氆氇镶虎皮男袍，要用一整只大虎的皮来裁制，整件袍服威武气派；织染绣厅里中国八大织锦应有尽有，包括辫绣、锁绣、绞绣、堆绣、马尾绣、绉绣、数纱绣、十字绣、打籽绣、蹙金绣、锡绣、镂空绣、剪贴绣等各种绣法，都能在这里找到实物；汉族服饰厅里的竹衣，用一个个米粒大小的小竹管串起，精美别致；图片厅收藏有中国影像人类学的先驱、纪实摄影

of more than 50 ethnic minority groups, among which nearly two thousand sets of costumes come from over a hundred branches of Hmong. The KaiTang Hmong silver crown with flower pattern displayed in the Metalworking Jewelry Hall is extraordinarily complicated and delicate with filigree craft and carving craft adopted in the production process. Tibetan male gown made of tiger-skin and Tibet wool displayed in the Exhibition Hall of Ethnic Minority Costumes is in a majestic style, and its production requires a whole piece of skin of a big tiger. In the Painted Embroidery Hall one can find everything of China's eight major kinds of brocades, including works made with all kinds of techniques including stranded

四川石渠县藏族袍服

Tibetan clothes in Shiqu county，Sichuan province

大师庄学本先生于 1934 至 1942 年间，在四川、云南、甘肃、青海四省少数民族地区进行近 10 年考察所拍摄的珍贵照片；奥运服饰厅专门展示北京服装学院老师为 2008 年奥运会设计的服装作品及获得的相关荣誉。这些丰富的藏品，见证了民族服饰博物馆的发展历程，是创业者和守业者共同的功绩。

岁月酝酿出传统服饰的沧桑之感，但时间也给它们留下了不可磨灭的印记。即使安逸地躺在博物馆的展柜里，不饶人的时间也总会在这些宛若少女的藏品脸上刻下道道皱痕。尽管民族服饰博物馆为减少藏品的光照损伤，只在每周二、周四全天和周六下午对观众开放，这些藏品每年呈现出的性状也都会有所不同。大家总认为瓷器是最为娇贵的文物，精品元青花至今所剩无几，但殊不知还有一类文物更为娇贵，那就是纺织品，这也是我们看到的完整服饰多属明清及以后时期的原因。尽最大努力挽留这些藏品，成了一项艰巨的使命。

民族服饰博物馆为了留住历史，除了利用保护和修复等技术手段外，正在进行一场数字化革命。民族服饰

braided embroidery, lock embroidery, hank embroidery, piling embroidery, horsetail embroidery, crepe embroidery, symmetrical embroidery, cross-stitch, spot embroidery, gold embroidery, tin embroidery, hollow embroidery, clip embroidery and other embroidering techniques. The bamboo clothes displayed in the Hall of Han are made of strings of small grain-sized bamboo tubes, looking elegant and unique. The collection of Image Hall contains precious photos taken by documentary photography masters Zhuang Xueben, pioneer of China's images of anthropology, who spent nearly 10 years between 1934 and 1942 traveling around areas inhabited by ethnic minority groups in Sichuan, Yunnan, Gansu and Qinghai provinces. In the Olympic Apparel Hall clothes designed by teachers in Beijing Institute Of Fashion Technology for the 2008 Olympic Games and other related honors are demonstrated. These diverse collections have witnessed the development of the Ethnic Costume Museum, and they are also the great achievements created by founders and keepers.

Time has endowed the traditional costumes with a unique appeal as well as indelible marks. Even though these costumes are well preserved in the showcases, time will still leave undesirable folds on them, just like leaving wrinkles on a young girl's face. The collected costumes are displayed by the museum only on Tuesday, Thursday and Saturday afternoon in order to reduce

博物馆正在对每件藏品进行数字化处理：拍摄高清照片，运用电子显微镜拍摄织物组织结构，为每一件藏品建立电子档案数据库，定期记录其性状特征。如今，我们只要打开电脑，就能检索并查阅这些珍贵藏品的详细信息，人们跟馆藏的脆弱纺织品的直接接触将大大减少，它们的信息共享程度及使用价值却会得到大大提升。

邓翔鹏

北京服装学院民族服饰博物馆

damages on costumes caused by lights, but changes of them are still identifiable when they are presented every year. People tend to believe that chinas are the most delicate of cultural relics. Indeed, few fine Yuan blue and white porcelains are left, but textiles are even more delicate than them. This is also the reason why most of the well-preserved costumes are from the Ming and Qing Dynasties and the following periods. How to try our best to save the collection has become a difficult mission in front of us.

In order to keep the history, in addition to technical means such as protecting and repairing techniques, the Ethnic Costume Museum is also experiencing a digital revolution. The museum is carrying out digital processing over each item, taking high-definition pictures, using electron microscope to photograph the internal structure of the fabric, building digital file database for each item and recording the states and traits of the items on a regular basis. Now, simply opening a computer, we are able to retrieve and get access to the details of these precious collections. The direct contact of people with the fragile textile collected in museums will be sharply reduced, and the amount of information and utility value of these objects have been greatly improved.

Deng Xiangpeng, Ethnic Costume
Museum of Beijing Institute of
Fashion Technology

沧桑的守望者

The Witness Who Survived from Disasters

北京钟鼓楼，始建于元至元九年（1272），当时鼓楼名曰"齐政楼"。现存鼓楼重建于明永乐十八年（1420），钟楼再建于清乾隆十二年（1747），是新老北京城的一组地标性建筑，位于北京传统意义上南北中轴线最北端，也是北京城内最高的皇家建筑，由北至南，俯瞰京师，尽收眼底，登楼观山，无不壮丽。此外，这组巍峨的建筑在古时的北京，起着重要且必要的作用，那就是为全京城报送标准时间，百姓闻其声起，听其声息，城门也依据钟声进行启、闭，是北京城的司时中心，也是至高无上的皇权的象征。

北京钟鼓楼，顾名思义，钟楼悬钟，鼓楼置鼓。钟楼悬挂一口重约63吨、铸于明永乐年间的铜钟（中国古钟之最）；鼓楼置鼓25面，一面主鼓象征一年，24面群鼓代表24个节气。击鼓报时予铜钟，而后击钟告予全京

Beijing Bell and Drum Towers were constructed in 9th year of the reign of Emperor Zhi Yuan in Yuan Dynasty (AD 1272) originally. During that period, Beijing Drum Tower was called Qi Zheng Tower (Seven Elements Tower). The extant Drum Tower was rebuilt in 18th year of the reign of Emperor Yong Le in Ming Dynasty (AD 1420). The extant Bell Tower was reconstructed in 12th year of the reign of Emperor Qian Long in Qing Dynasty (AD 1747). They are the landmarks in the ancient and new Beijing City. They are situated at the north end of the axis line of Beijing. Besides, Beijing Bell and Drum Towers are the highest imperial buildings in Beijing. When you stand on them, you can have a bird's-eye view of the Beijing City from the north end of the axis. What's more, you can enjoy the magnificence of the mountains from the second floor of them. Besides, the two towers played important roles in Beijing. They told the correct time to everyone. The residents got up or went back home by the sound of them. Following them, the gates were opened or closed. They worked as the timing center of Beijing. They are also the symbolization of the supreme imperial power.

城。现铜钟保存完好，25 面更鼓仅存主鼓一面，且已残破。其余的 24 位"家人"呢？追溯到 1900 年，这是耻辱的一年，也是令国人警醒的一年。这年八国联军入侵北京，慈禧携光绪逃亡陕西西安，北京城沦陷，京城遭疯狂烧杀抢掠，众多国宝被抢或遭损毁。八国联军"光顾"了众多古迹，紫禁城、中南海、颐和园、古观象台无一幸免。八国联军大肆洗劫官府、衙门等，当然，北京钟鼓楼也未能逃脱此劫，钟楼墙体遭侵略者刺刀刻字；鼓楼损失较为惨重，二层报时群鼓 24

Beijing Bell and Drum Towers, as the name implies, a bell was hung up on the second floor of the Bell Tower and drums were set on the Drum Tower. A bronze bell which was cast during the reign of Emperor Yong Le in Ming Dynasty was hung up on the second floor of Bell Tower. The bell weighs 63 tons. It's the biggest and heaviest one in China. 25 drums were placed on the second floor of the Drum Tower. The main drum symbolizes a year. 24 mass drums represent 24 solar terms. The drummers beat drums to tell time to the watchmen on Bell Tower. And then the watchmen rang the bell to tell the time to the Beijing city. At present, the bell is preserved well. However, only the main drum which was damaged badly has survived. What about the 24 mass drums? Back in 1900, this

鼓楼报时主鼓

the main time drum in the drum tower

面被破坏殆尽，只有报时主鼓存留，且已被损毁至面目全非，鼓面可见刀痕处处。该报时主鼓高 2.22 米，直径 1.40 米，系整张水牛皮蒙制，其确切制作年代无据可考，但据推断此鼓在光绪年间（1875—1908）便已服役，距今起码也有一百二三十年的历史了，被定为我国珍贵文物中的三级文物。

北京钟鼓楼不但是京城众多名胜古迹之一，更是爱国主义教育基地，每年接待大量中小学生团体。而陈列于鼓楼二层的这面残破的古代报时主鼓，就起到了爱国主义教育的核心作用。作为历史文物，此鼓是外国列强入侵中华，践踏北京城的见证，历史不会忘记他们，中国人民不会忘记他们，任何借口都不可能消灭这历史的罪证。也正因如此，民国十三年（1924），时任京兆尹薛笃弼为使民众不忘 1900 年八国联军入侵北京的国耻，曾一度将鼓楼易名为"明耻楼"（后新任京兆尹李谦六认为古迹名称不宜擅改，恢复原称"齐政楼"）。此残鼓让人们不忘国耻、记住历史的同时，也让人们反思，落后就要挨打，不论思想上还是科技上，都要与时俱进，它激励着世人奋发图强，不让历

year was disgraceful. A.D. 1900 awaked all Chinese. Eight-Power Allied Forces invaded Beijing. The Empress Dowager Cixi took Emperor Guang Xu to Xi'an city. Beijing was occupied. The invaders burned down houses, killed people and looted wherever they went. Countless national treasures were plundered or destroyed. They robbed many historic sites, such as, the Imperial Palace, the imperial garden Zhong'Nan'Hai, the Summer Palace, Ancient Observatory and so on. The government offices were ransacked badly. Definitely, Beijing Bell and Drum Towers can't escape from the doom. The wall of Bell Tower was engraved some foreign letters with bayonets. The Drum Tower suffered great losses. All of 24 mass drums were destroyed. Only the main drum survived. Unfortunately, it was also damaged that cuts can be found everywhere on the drum head. The height of the ancient main drum is 2.22 meters. Its diameter is 1.40 meters. It was made of a whole piece of buffalo's hide. Now we can't find any historical records about when it was made. But we can deduce that it has served as the watchmen's drum since the reign of Emperor Guang Xu. It owns the history from 120 years to 130 years at least. The ancient main drum was ranked the 3rd level in precious cultural relics.

The cultural relic preservation center of Beijing Bell and Drum Towers is not only one of the historic sites in Beijing but also the patriotic education base. It receives many student communities every year. The broken drum on the Drum Tower is the key point of the patriotic education. As

史的悲剧重演。作为文物，这面报时主鼓虽已有所残损，但时代赋予了它特殊的意义。而它本身就像一部纪录片，青少年们看着那刀痕累累的鼓面，仿佛重回历史，置身于那场浩劫，亲眼看到了那些狰狞、贪婪的侵略者。伟大的导师列宁曾教导我们，忘记过去，就意味着背叛。许多共青团日、少先队日活动在鼓楼开展，高校也时常组织学生前来学习、参观，其爱国主义教育的功能一直在延续。时至今日，此鼓以它特有的历史价值，不仅对本国的观众具有教育意义，就是对

the historical relic, it's the proof of Eight-Power Allied Forces' invasion. History will not forget it. Chinese nation won't forget it. Any excuse can't erase the evidence of the crime. As a result, 13th year of the Republic of China, the mayor of Beijing Xue Dubi altered the name as the Tower of Knowing the humiliation in order to make people remember the national disgrace well (Later, another mayor Li Qianliu thought that the name of historic site should not be changed arbitrarily. The original name Qi Zheng Tower was thus resumed). The broken drum makes us bear the history and humiliation in mind. Meanwhile, it helps us realize that a weak country is vulnerable to attack. We should keep pace with times on thoughts and science. The drum also encourages us to study and work harder to prevent the

国外观众也不失其教育作用，一些外国游人驻足于它面前，表情凝重，逐字逐句地阅读说明文字，仔细地观看这满身伤痕的主鼓，似乎看到了当时遍体鳞伤的旧中国，一些人怀有惋惜之情，一些人显出愧疚之意。

北京钟鼓楼与其文物，可谓历尽磨难，八国联军入侵、日伪政权统治、唐山大地震等，都对楼宇及个别文物造成了不同程度的损坏，楼体经历了几次大小规模的修缮，但本已残损的古代报时主鼓，却在"日渐衰老"（鼓为革木所制，本就不易保存，加之百年前被严重破坏，风化程度加快），鼓身已严重塌陷，由原本的圆形变成了椭圆形，鼓架也已变形，在北京市钟鼓楼文物保管所记录在案的文物检查中，发现该鼓鼓身仍在继续塌陷，随时有崩坏的危险。钟鼓楼文保所领导心系文物，保护文物刻不容缓。2015年末，钟鼓楼文保所计划对该古代报时主鼓进行修复，我们有幸联系到了北京市文物研究所相关专家，对该鼓的修复进行了研究、探讨，制定了修复方案。2015年12月10日至15日，专业文物修复工作者对鼓楼的古代报时主鼓进行了修复、加固，使其

tragedy of history from being repeated. As a cultural relic, the drum is broken, but the era endows its special meaning. The ancient drum is like a documentary. It seems that the adolescents return to 1900 and see the savage and greedy invaders with their own eyes when they stand in front of the broken drum. The great tutor Lenin taught us that forgetting past means betrayal. Many activities of Chinese Youth League Day and Young Pioneer day are organized in Drum Tower. The universities often organize its students to visit Drum Tower. The function of patriotic education goes on. At present, the broken drum with its particular historical value not only shows the educational significance to compatriots but also has the educational function on foreign tourists. Some of foreign tourists stand in front of it solemnly with their face stiffened. They read the information board word by word and look at the broken drum with many cuts carefully as if they can see the old China covered all over with cuts and bruises. Some of them feel regret or guilty.

Beijing Bell and Drum Towers and their cultural relics suffered all kinds of trials and tribulations. The invasion of Eight-Power Allied Forces, the reign of puppet regime of Japan and the Tangshan Earthquake damaged the two towers to different extent. The bodies of the buildings were renovated for several times with large or small scales. However, our ancient main drum which is broken is ageing day by day (The drum is different to be preserved well due to it was made of wood and animals' hide. It accelerated weathering that the

"大病痊愈"。考虑到该报时主鼓饱经风霜，且已残损，为了减少自然风化对其带来的损害以及游客对它的触摸，钟鼓楼文保所考虑为其制作保护罩。2016年3月末，更鼓保护罩工程开始，6月中旬完工。完工后的保护罩形制及颜色与鼓楼主体建筑一致，保护文物的同时也使后添设施与古建天然地融为一体。

对于文物，文物工作者最基本的工作是对其维护、保护，但是与其同等重要的还有对文物的研究、发现——研究文物的时代背景、与其相关联的所有历史事件及人，新发现也就随之

drum was damage badly more than 100 years ago). The body of drum is cracked. What's more, it's out of shape from a circle to an oval. Besides, its frame becomes deformed too. In the records of the cultural relic inspection, the main drum has been deformed with each passing day. It will collapse at any time. The directors of the cultural relic preservation center of Beijing Bell and Drum Towers care for cultural relic and worry about its condition. It's of great urgency to restore it. At the end of 2015, we planned to restore the ancient drum. Fortunately enough, we found a professor of Beijing Cultural Relics Research Institute. After discussion and research, we drew up the restoration plan. The professional workers from Beijing ancient cultural relic building company restored and consolidated the ancient watchmen's drum from 10th December to

而来了，这样，文物才会发挥真正作用，体现其价值。鼓楼的古代报时更鼓虽已残破，但它就像鼓楼近现代的守望者一样，见证着发生在鼓楼乃至北京的形形色色的事件，用无声的语言默默地向我们诉说着这座古建、这座古城一个多世纪的沧桑。

冯磊

北京市钟鼓楼文物保管所

15th December 2015. In consideration of its sufferings, the weathering and broken conditions, we decided to make a protective cover for it in order to prevent tourists from touching it. Besides, it can help to alleviate the weathering to the drum. The project of drum's protective cover began at the end of March. In middle ten days of June, it's finished. The color and structure of the protective cover is harmonious with Drum Tower. On one hand, it protects the ancient drum. On the other hand, the facility which we made integrates the ancient building perfectly.

With regard to cultural relics, maintaining and protecting them is the fundamental work of us (staff members of cultural relic preservation center). Moreover, studying and researching the cultural relics is as important as maintaining and protecting them. New discoveries will be made by studying the historical background and all of relevant people and historical events of the relics. In this way, the cultural relics can play their real roles. The genuine value of them will be reflected. Although the ancient watchmen's main drum is broken, it's like a watcher of Drum Tower in modern times who witnessed various events happened in Drum Tower or even in Beijing City. The ancient drum tells us the vicissitudes more than a century of Drum Tower and the ancient city with its silent language.

Feng Lei, Cultural Relics Management for Bell and Drum Towers in Beijing

熊猫牌 1502 型收音机
——特级收音机的传奇

Type 1502 Panda Radio
— Legend on the Super Radio

　　稍上点年纪的人们都知道，在20世纪五六十年代，姑娘们结婚是要求对方家里出"三转一响"的，所谓"三转"，指的是手表、自行车和缝纫机，一响，指的是收音机。在那个物资匮乏的年代，"三转"可以带给人们生活的便捷，而收音机，则是人们了解外部世界的重要渠道。国家的大政方针、公社集体的活动公告，都是通过小小的收音机被传递到千家万户的。我们平时见到的收音机，大多是摆在家里桌上的那种四四方方的电子管收音机，或者是小巧的可以装在口袋或持在手里的晶体管收音机，但是今天我们带大家见识一台足有钢琴大小的国产特级收音机——熊猫牌 1502 型收音机。

　　说起收音机，我们就不得不简单回顾一下广播的历史。广播是基于无线电发射和接收而形成的即时性、远

Many middle-aged people would be familiar with "Three Spinning objects", referring to watch, bicycles and sewing machine, and "One ringing object" referring to the radio. In the 1950s and 1960s, if you wanted to marry a girl, you need to have these furnitures. In the times lacking in materials, the "three spinning objects" could bring us convenience, while radio would provide us a window for us to see the outside world. The major policies of the state, the announcement of activities of those collective communes were all passed on to thousands of homes through small radios. The radio we commonly see are mostly square tube radio on the desk, or the transistor radio which could fit in a pocket or be held in hand. But today we are going to introduce you a radio as big as a piano. It is the

熊猫 1502 型收音机
type-1502 Panda radio

Type-1502 Panda radio.

Speaking of the radio, we are going to have a simple review of the history of the broadcasting in China. Broadcasting is a means of instant, distant and mass communication with broad coverage based on the transmitting and receiving of radio signals. It is commonly believed both in and abroad that broadcasting was born in 1906 when Fessenden, a Canadian, successfully broadcast a few Christmas songs and Bible chapters using radio waves. Since then, the radio as a way of mass communication has seen rapid development. Driven by the WWII in 1930s and 1940s, broadcasting has embraced its golden age. Emperor Hirohito Wars played an important role in stimulating the popularisation of radio. The broadcast technology saw rapid rise out of the need of wars. And leaders of nations found that radio could be used as an effective means of publicity to pass the state information fast and conveniently to the people. For example, speeches made by Roosevelt, Churchill and the ceasefire

距离、广覆盖的大众传播手段，国内外一般认为，现代广播诞生的标志是 1906 年加拿大人费森登在圣诞节期间利用无线电波成功播送了几首圣诞歌曲和《圣经》篇章，此后，广播这种以无线电信号为介质的大众传播手段便迅速发展，20 世纪三四十年代，在"二战"的推动下，广播迎来了自己的黄金时代。战争对广播的刺激作用非常明显，一是出于战时科研需求，广播技术快速提升；二是领导人发现广播可以作为有效的舆论宣传手段，将国家信息快速便捷地传递给百姓，如被人们所熟知的丘吉尔的演讲、罗斯福的炉边谈话，日本裕仁天皇的停战诏书，都是通过广播这种形式传递出去的。广播的极大发展自然也带动了收音机的普及，毕竟无线电信号从发射端发射出去后，需要以收音机为

载体的接收端接收以实现信息的传播。不过，在整个民国时期，在中国能收听得起广播的都是有钱人，因为那时中国市场的收音机 90% 以上是舶来品，进口自美国、英国、俄罗斯或者日本，仅有少数是国内民族资本家用进口的元器件，利用本国劳工和外壳组装的国产收音机。这些机器在当时都售价不菲，普通百姓是难以企及的。

1949 年新中国成立后，党和国家领导人充分认识到在一个文盲占多数人口的国度里发展广播事业的重要性，所以建国伊始，我们就成立了广播事业管理局，大力发展农村有线广播以及城市无线电厂，先后成立了生产红星和熊猫收音机的南京无线电厂，生产牡丹牌收音机的北京无线电厂，生产上海牌收音机的上海广播器材厂，生产东方红收音机的汉口无线电厂，俗称收音机生产的"国营四大厂"。今天我们故事的主角就是排行第一的国营四大厂大哥——南京无线电厂。南京无线电厂的前身是民国时期的中央无线电器材厂，1949 年 12 月定名为国营南京无线电厂，是现在的熊猫集团的前身。早在民国三十七年（1948），中央无线电厂曾以进口

imperial edict made by Emperor Hirohito, were all broadcast to the public. The great development of broadcast also led to the popularity of radio, which is the receiptor of the signal. However, in the Republic of China (1912 - 1949), those who could listen to the radio in China were generally rich. During that period of time, more than 90% of the radios in China were imported from Russia, the United States, Britain, or Japan. Only a few of them were assembled with imported components in our own country by those national capitalists. While those gadgets were all very expensive, at that time, thus making them definitely beyond the reach of ordinary people.

In 1949, when the People's Republic of China was established, Chinese party and state leaders had fully realized the importance of developing broadcasting industry in a country where most of its citizens were illiterates. In early days in new China, we established Broadcast Industry Administrative Bureau to develop wire-broadcasting in rural villages and

整套散件的方式组装生产过美国飞歌牌 806 型五等收音机，其设计、组装和生产工艺在当时的中国是处于前列的，所以中华人民共和国成立后党和国家领导人也非常重视南京无线电厂。1956 年 1 月 11 日，毛泽东主席视察南京无线电厂，参观了收音机生产线，看到国产收音机十分高兴，并鼓励再攀技术高峰。

1959 年是国庆 10 周年，各行业都加大干劲力争上游，为 10 周年国庆献上来自行业内部"赶英超美"的礼物。熊猫牌 1502 收音机就是在这个大背景下生产的。当时，主管工业生产的一机部十局向南京无线电厂下达任务，由其研制一款体现 10 年发展新水平的高级电子音响产品，产品外观要体现民族性，性能则要争取优于同类国外产品。当时主持这项工作的总设计师是龚剑泉，外形设计师是哈崇南，两人当时都 30 多岁，拥有多年工作经验，龚剑泉还曾于 1953 年主持参与了红星牌 502 收音机——新中国第一台全国产化收音机的设计生产过程，但是在接到这项政治任务时他表示压力很大。主要当时是 1959 年，新中国的收音机生产还不到 10 年，而国外同时

urban radio stations. Many radio factories were built at that time, including Nanjing Radio Factory producing Hongxing radio and Panda rad; Beijing Radio Factory producing peony radio; Shanghai Broadcast Equipment Factory producing shanghai radio as well as Hankou Radio Factory producing Dongfanghong radio. Four of them were so-called stated-operated big four radio factories. Our story today is about the NO.1 factory of the "Big Four"-- Nanjing Radio Factory. Nanjing Radio Factory, formerly the Central Radio Equipment Factory in the Republic of China (1912 - 1949), was named as State-operated Nanjing Radio Factory in December, 1949. It is also the predecessor of PANDA Electronics Group. In 37 years (1948), Central Radio Equipment Factory imported knocked-down kits and then assembled Type-806 Philco Radio. The designing, assembling and manufacturing technology were among China's best-performing. Since the founding of PRC, both our Party and state leaders paid great attention to Nanjing Radio Factory.

期如德国的德律风根，美国的 RCA 等老牌收音机生产厂商，都已经积累了四五十年的经验。收音机的生产涉及模具开发、元器件的生产等多种工序的合作，并非能一蹴而就的。但是在为祖国母亲献礼的感召下，南京无线电厂的员工们克服重重困难，想办法，深加工，在一年的时间内设计生产出了熊猫 1501 型特级收音机。

南京无线电厂对收音机的命名有自己的一套规律，首先品牌上有红星和熊猫两种品牌，前者是建国初期使用的，后者本来是与红星一起配套给出口机专用的品牌，后来因为市场反

应

1501 型收音机的宫灯造型猫眼
lantern-style peephole on the type-1501 radio

1959 marks the 10th anniversary of the founding of the PRC. All industries were sparing no efforts to racing to the top, presenting a gift of "surpassing Britain and the United States" for the birthday of our country. And Type-1502 Panda Radio was born against this backdrop. At that time, the Tenth Bureau of the First Machinery Industry Department asked Nanjing Radio Factory to invent a new and advanced electronic audio products reflecting our national characters, and the performance should be better than similar foreign products. Back then, Gong Jianquan, the general designer, presided over the mission. Ha Chongnan was responsible for the design of the shape. Both of the designers were at their 30s with rich experience. In 1953, Gong Jianquan had once hosted the design and production of the Type-502 Hongxing Radio, the first localized radio in our country. He said he was faced with a lot of pressure when he was handed the political task. The new china had only been established for ten years, which means Chinese radios had been developing

良好，所以国内的机型也开始用"熊猫"这个品牌，而 1501 这个型号的意思是该收音机有 15 根电子管的第一批机型，1502 则是指第二批机型。所以如果您看到熊猫 601 收音机，应该能马上明白，这是南京无线电厂生产的 6 电子管收音机的第一批机型。我馆收藏的是熊猫牌 1502 收音机，这款收音机和 1501 一样，都是特级收音机，是献礼机的第二批机型，与 1501 最大的差别是缺少录音功能，其他收音、录音和造型与第一批机型都是一样的。下面我们以 1501 为主介绍一下这两款特级收音机。

当时设计生产熊猫 1501 收音机的主要目的有 4 个：一个是用来装备人民大会堂、劳动人民文化宫等公共场所；二是放置在中国驻外国的大使馆处，如中国驻苏联大使馆等使馆内；三是给领导人专用；四是作为国家礼物送给来访的亚非国家领导人，如 1501 曾作为国礼送给加纳总统杜尔。在这种大背景下，从一开始就给 1501 定下了特级收音机的标准。在中国的收音机定级评比中，一共分为 5 个级别，即特级、一级、二级、三级、四级收音机，在 20 世纪五六十年代的中国，大

for less than ten years. However, the international counterparts such as Germany's Telefunken and America's RCA had rich experience for forty to fifty years. The radios' manufacture required various cooperation including designing molds and manufacturing components, which would not accomplish at one stroke. Staffs in Nanjing Radio Factory, with the great enthusiasm for offering motherland a gift, had overcome all the difficulties. By further processing, they designed and produced successfully Type-1501 Panda Radio.

Nanjing Radio Factory had its own rule of naming its products. In terms of brand, there were Hongxing and Panda radio. The former was made for domestic market in early days in new China and the latter was supposed to be exported to foreign countries together with Hongxing. But it turned out to be popular in the domestic market so Panda began to be sold in China too. Type-1501 means that it's the first version of radio with 15 radio tubes so Type-1502 means the second

家日常所能见到的收音机，大多是四级收音机或者没有级别的桌式收音机，特级收音机一般而言都是大型的落地式收音机。1501 和 1502 收音机的造型一致，都是长 1.42 米，宽 0.42 米，高 0.8 米，大小跟一台中等钢琴差不多。熊猫 1501 收音机采用上等优质木材制成，外形一边是方形，一边是圆形，体现中国传统的天圆地方思想，机身左侧上方打开后是双轨式录音机，下方是自动电唱机，右侧采用推拉式设计，推开后可以看到收音机的猫眼、

1501 型收音机的蝙蝠纹和福寿设计
bat-pattern and character-pattern of "Fu and Shou (happiness and longevity)" on the type-1501 radio

version. In the same way, Type-601 Panda Radio means it was the first version of the radio with 6 radio tubes produced by Nanjing Radio Factory. Type-1502 Panda Radio was collected here. Like the Type-1501, this one was a super radio and the second version of gift radio. Except for recording function, Type-1502 was similar to Type-1501 in terms of radio function and the shapes. Now, let's elaborate on the two super radios, and our focus lies on Type-1501.

The Type-1501 Panda Radio was made for four main functions. First, for public places such as the Great Hall of the People and the Working People's Cultural Palace; second, for China's embassies in foreign countries; third, for leaders; fourth, as a national gift for national leaders in Asian and African countries during their visits in China. For example, Type-1501 was a national gift for Ghanaian President Touré. Against this backdrop, Type-1501 was supposed to be the super radio in the first place. In China, radios have five levels, super radio, the

文物背后的故事
stories behind cultural relics

旋钮、琴键开关等，右侧下方是喇叭装置。为了凸显民族特色，造型设计师哈崇南费了不少心思。比如熊猫1501收音机的猫眼，采用的就是中国传统的宫灯造型。左侧电唱机开合面板的装饰上，四周装饰有四个蝙蝠样式的纹饰，中间把手处一个寿字纹，象征福寿满堂。在关乎收音机性能的指标上，1501和1502更是达到了世界先进水平。该机可用当时世界各国8种不同等级的市电电压，如245伏、220伏、145伏、110伏、90伏等，收音、录音、电唱三用时最大功率消耗小于200伏安。收音部分共有15只电子管，分6个波段，中波段520~1600千周，短波又分为4个波段1.6~26兆周，超短波段65.5~73兆周，采用9档按键式换波开关。中波段有机内可旋转的磁性天线，短波段除设有机内天线外，并有波段展阔装置。中、短波段有一级高放、二级中放，以三连电容器进行调谐。超短波段采用双桥双平衡线路，以变电感的方法进行调谐，有一级高放、三级中放。调频与调幅部分的中周线圈合装在一个罩壳内，调频部分第一中放利用调谐部分的变频管，第二、三级中放与调幅部分合

first level, the second level, the third level and the fourth level. During the 1950s and 1960s in China, most of the radios that people could use were the fourth level or even without any degrees. Super radios, in general, were console radios. Type-1501 and 1502 shared almost the same shape scale of around 1.42*0.42*0.8 meters, and they were as big as a middle-sized piano. Type-1501 Panda Radio was made of high-quality wood. With the shape of square on the one side and circular on the other side, it represented an ancient Chinese philosophy of round heaven and square earth. The left side of the radio had double-tracks radio on the top and a juke box on the bottom. The right side had the push-pull installation. The peephole, knob and switch could be seen when it's been pushed and there was a speaker at the bottom. Ha Chong, the graphic designer had made great effects to carry forward national characteristics. Take the peephole of Type-1501 Panda Radio as an example, the traditional Chinese lantern-style design was adopted. The record player on the left side was decorated with four

用，鉴频与检波部分分别进行。在输出功率为 50 毫瓦时，中、短波段灵敏度小于 50 微伏，超短波段小于 10 微伏，用机内磁性天线时也不大于 5 毫伏，调幅收音的中频为 465 千周，中频通带宽度可在 4~13 千周范围内平滑调节，共邻近波段的选择性在偏调 ±10 千周时大于 60 分贝，调频部分的中频为 8.4 兆周，中频通带宽度大于 180 千周，在失调 ±250 千周时的邻近波段选择性大于 30 分贝。该机的额定输出功率为 6 伏安，用 4 只扬声器组成立体声响系统，在额定输出功率时全机的非线性失真系数 200~400 周频率范围内不大于 7%，400 周以上不大于 5%。全机的频率特性在调幅广播时为 60~6500 周，调频广播时为 60~12000 周，高低音调分为连续调节，调节范围大于 15 分贝。调节音量时有音调补偿作用，外接拾音器插孔的灵敏度小于 250 毫伏。电唱机可自动启、停，自动落片，一次可叠放唱片 10 张，具有 78、45、33、16 转/分 4 种转速，能放送 12 寸、10 寸、7 寸 3 种大小不同或大小孔不同的唱片。唱机采用动圈式宽频带唱头、粗细纹两种长命唱针。录音机是双轨，9.75、19.5 厘米/

Bat-shaped Ornamentations around and a handle with a Chinese character "Chou" in the center, representing longevity and luck. Type 1501 and 1502 had reached the world top level in respect of radios' performance index. They were adaptable with 8 different international voltages, including 245V, 220V, 145V, 110V, 90V, and etc. The maximum power was less than 200 Volt-ampere even when radioing, recording and record playing were working at the same time. The radio part had 15 radio tubes with 6 wave bands. The mid band had a frequency of 520-1600 kilocycles. The short-wave band could be divided into another wave bands with 1.6-26 megacycle and the super short wave band had 65.5-73 megacycle. It had 9 different gears to switch bands. There was a build-in rotatable magnetic antenna in the mid band. The short-wave band had build-in antenna as well as wave band amplifier equipment. The mid and short wave bands have the first gear and the second gear, adjusted by a three-gang condenser. The rated output power is 6VA. Four speakers make a stereo system.

秒两种带速，是按键开关控制的磁带录音机。熊猫牌1502收音机和1501收音机唯一的区别就是前者没有装配双轨式录音机，其他性能指标工艺则一模一样。根据南京无线电厂的哈崇南先生回忆，当时国庆献礼机出来后，有一名德国的收音机制造业同行过来参观，得知1501是南京无线电厂基于10年的积累、一年内生产出来的后，表示极为震惊，因为其工艺水平对比同时期的德律风根，有过之而无不及。

该收音机于1959年元旦试制成功，于1959年国庆献礼前正式命名为熊猫牌1501型收音、电唱、录音三用落地式收音机，在当年全国工业品展示会上被定位为特级收音机。该机型计划生产350台，实际生产328台，当时每台售价高达580元，要知道在20世纪五六十年代，一位高级工程师的工资也不过一个月五六十元而已。而且即使有钱，1501收音机在当时也是买不到的。1501型连同1502型收音机在1960年就停止生产了，根据设计师的回忆，二者总共生产了400多台，很多还被送到了国外的驻华使馆，所以现在市面上很难看到完整的熊猫牌1501或1502型收音机。中国传媒大

Under the rated output power, the range of factor of nonlinear distortion is no more than 7% within the range of 200-400Hz, or 5% if it's higher than 400Hz. The AM frequency is about 60-6500Hz and the FM frequency is about 60-12000Hz. The tone control range is more than 15db. It has the tone-compensated volume control function. The sensitivity of the external pickup's jack is less than 250 millivolts. The record player could start, stop playing automatically. 10 records can be put inside at the same time. It has four kinds of speed, 78rpm, 45rpm, 33rpm and 16rpm. 12", 10", and 7" records can be played. The record player has a moving coil wideband playback head, thick and thin stylus. It is the double-tracks sound record with two kinds of speed, 9.75 cm/s and 19.5 cm/s. It is a tape recorder controlled by key switches. The only thing that Type-1502 Panda Radio differs from Type-1501 is that it has no double-tracks radio. Others like perchance index and technology are the same. According to Mr. Ha Chongnan from Nanjing Radio Factory, a German counterpart paid a visit when Type-1501

1501 型收音机左侧方形部分（录音机和电唱机）

the square part on the left of the type-1501 radio (recorder and record player)

学传媒博物馆收藏的这台是由东莞德生通用电器总裁梁伟先生捐赠的，据捐赠人讲述，这台 1502 是当时负责运输配送收音机的司机拿下指标私藏的一台。

时光荏苒，岁月变迁，科技的进步使得收音机已逐渐退出我们的生活，但新中国的无线电技术发展历程不应该被忘记。作为"赶英超美"的时代

was produced and was amazed at the fact that it only took one year for Chinese people to make that. The technological skills were even better than Telefunken.

The radio was assembled successfully in January, 1959 and served as the national gift for National Holiday in 1959. It was named as Type-1501 Panda Console Radio with three functions of radioing, record playing and recording. It was set as super radio at the National Industrial Products in the same year. 350 radios had been planned to be produced but the actual production was 328. The price was up to 580 yuan per set. In 1950s and 1960s, the salary of a senior engineer was only fifty to sixty yuan per month. And you probably won't be able to buy Type-1501 even if you had enough money. Because Type-501 and-1502 had been halted to be procured in 1960s. According to some designers, 400 was produced of which had been seen to foreign embassies. The complete sets of Type-1501/1502 Panda Radio are rare to see in the market these days. This one collected in our

1501 型收音机右侧圆弧形推拉设计

the circular-arc sliding design on the right of the type 1501 radio

产物和新中国电子音响产品的代表，熊猫牌 1501 和 1502 型收音机书写了国产特级收音机的传奇。

张涵烁

中国传媒大学传媒博物馆

museum was donated by Mr. Liangwei, CEO of TECSUN Co. Ltd. According to him, a driver who was transporting Panda radios gained one radio discreetly by his personal relationship.

Time flies. Radio has been fading out of our modern lives due to the technology development. But the history of radio development in new China won't be forgotten. As the products of the period of "Catch up with the United Kingdom than the United States" and the representatives of electrical equipments in new China, Type-1501 and 1502 Panda Radio had witnessed the legendary development of Chinese super radio.

Zhang Hanshuo, Media Museum of Communication University of China

文物普查中的故事

——记国家博物馆藏品保管一部第一次可移动文物普查

Stories in the National Census of on Cultural Relics

—on the First National Census on Movable Cultural Relics in the 1st Collection Storage Department of National Museum

根据全国可移动文物普查工作的部署，自 2014 年 3 月 1 日开始，国家博物馆藏品保管一部正式启动了馆藏可移动文物的普查工作。

藏品保管一部是国家博物馆的重要业务部门，收藏保管着国家博物馆 83 万余件的古代文物，因此物多、人少、时间紧这些问题都是摆在文物普查工作前的难题。在普查工作任务最为艰巨的时刻，共从 7 个部门抽调了 40 名工作人员予以支援，及时地解决了普查工作的人员吃紧问题，使普查工作得以顺利推进。

此次文物普查本着摸清"家底"，

Following the order of the National General Survey of Movable Artifacts, on March 1st, 2014, the 1st Collection Storage Department of National Museum officially started the general survey works on the museum collected movable artifacts.

The 1st Collection Storage Department is a very important division in the National Museum. It safely keeps more than 830 thousands of antique artifacts in the National Museum. During the national census, we faced many problems. For example, we had too many work to do but our personnel and time were quite limited. At the most difficult moment, 40 staffs from seven other departments were redeployed here to assist wiht the census, successfully

账、物一致的原则，补充了各类文物信息缺项，推进了藏品数字化建设，此外还解决了建馆百年来从未解决的历史遗留问题，如书画类库房清查了许多当年未曾清点的落选品，重新建账。国家博物馆馆藏钱币类文物数量大，精品多，此次文物普查，钱币库将原有按称重计算数量的参考品由专人负责清点、分类、整理，此项工作目前已经结束，共清点出此类钱币188550件。此项工作解决了国家博物馆保管部几代人未曾解决的老大难问题，对重新核算国家博物馆钱币收藏数量及丰富藏品内容有着重大意义。

钱币普查工作真正做到了"数钱数到手抽筋"，数钱既累又开心，同志们说从来没数过这么多钱，在工作中干劲特别足，数到手抽筋都不怕，在数钱的过程中认识了各个时代的钱

addressing the staff shortage in time, hence the smooth work.

In accordance with the principle of making the storage information clear and collating the registries and items accordingly, this round of census filled up various missing information of artifacts, and facilitated the digitalization of collection information. In addition, many unresolved historical problems during the past century were eventually solved. For example, many uncounted items in the calligraphy and painting storage were then counted with registries. There are a large number of currencies and coins collected in the National Museum, with many precious items within them. Through this census, specially-assigned staffs counted, categorized, and reorganized these coins which used to be counted by weighing in piles. This work has been completed and 188,550 pieces of coins were counted in total. The work resolved an old and difficult problem that haunted generations of staffs in the storage department of National Museum. It means great importance for the works of re-

币，以后再见着这种钱就大体知道是哪个时代的了。

文物普查又是互惠互利的，支援普查的同志分别来自展览一部、展览策划与美术工作部、文物科技保护部、经营开发部等7个部门。展陈部门通过文物普查更直观深入了解了库房馆藏文物，便利筹办展览。文物科技保护部通过文物普查，对哪些质地的文物需要保护有了直观的了解。普查后，更是进一步加强了部门之间的合作，共同来建立文物保护机制，使文物保护形成常态化。经营部门通过文物普查，有了更好的思路，便于开发文创产品。

在普查过程中，我们根据实物核对账目，对于账目中的缺项（尺寸、重量等）进行了补充，对实物与账目不符的情况（完残情况、质地等），以实物为准进行了登记。而且在工作中我们发现，由于此前建账时间较早，部分当时被划为参考品未受到重视的文物，如今已有资格进入基本藏品序列，这是文物普查的又一大收获。

这里特别值得一提的是我们对故

accounting the quantity of collected coins in the National Museum and enriching the content of collection.

The census on currencies and coins is really an exciting work "buried in the ocean of money". The staffs said they never counted so much coins. So they were highly motivated and never felt exhausted. They got to know the currencies of different ages through the work of counting, and if they would see those kinds of currencies in future, they would know which period the currency belongs to.

The census is a work of mutual exchanges and benefits. The staffs coming to help came from seven departments including the 1st Exhibition Department, the Exhibition Design and Artistic Work Department, the Artifact Scientific-preservation Department, and the Marketing and Development Department. Through the census, the Exhibitions Departments got to know the collected artifacts in the storage more directly, which helped them organize future exhibitions. Staffs from the Scientific-Preservation Department got a more direct understanding of which kind of artifacts need preservation. After the census, the cross-departmental cooperation were strengthened to establish the artifact preservation mechanism and regularize and normalize the artifact preservation. Through the census, the Marketing Department gained better ideas of developing cultural creative products.

宫西华门文物库房的文物普查工作。西华门库区位于故宫西华门，5层楼高，分别存放铜器库、瓷器库管理的大部分参考品和民族文物。因库房建设年代久远，房顶存在漏水现象，在普查之前需要进行一系列改造，如房顶重新铺设防水层，整楼水电及卫生间改造等，在这些工作做好之后，普查工作才可以开展。然而普查工作仍然面临一些困难，诸如故宫进出的问题、普查网络系统问题、故宫中午吃饭问题等，都需要及时解决以保证普查工作进度。各库房负责人带领普查小组克服库房简陋的条件——这里既没有安装空调、风扇等降温设备，也没有可供休息的办公区域，工作人员们在结束了上午的工作、吃完午饭后，便返回库房继续工作，不作休息。除

国家博物馆文物普查工作现场
the field scene of general survey work in
the National Museum

During the census, we collated the registry books with real objects and filled up the missing items (size, weight, etc.) in the registry books. For the discrepancies between real objects and registry records (completeness, material, etc.), we made new registries based on the real objects. Furthermore, during the work, we found some artifacts whose importance was at first overlooked and thus not entered in the early registries. Now they are justified qualified to be included into the basic collection lists. This is another achievement of the census.

What is particularly worth noting is our census in the Xihua Gate storage house of the Forbidden City. The Xihua Gate storage house is located in the Xihua Gate of the Forbidden City. It has five floors, separately storing most bronze and porcelain cultural relics along with some ethnographic objects. A series of reconstruction was needed because of the water leaks on the roofs due to the old age of the building. New waterproof layers were installed. The water pipes and restrooms in the whole building were rebuilt. After these works, the census could be conducted. Nonetheless there were still some difficulties to be addressed, such as the daily in-and-out and lunch problems in the Forbidden City, and many other problems about the census system, thus to keep up with the schedule of the census. The directors of those storages led the census team to overcome the simple and crude conditions in the storage house. There was no cooling equipment like air

了进行文物拍照、登编记录之外，库房保管员还对这些长期未经保养的文物进行了除尘清洁及申报修复等工作，不仅顺利完成了该部分文物的指定普查任务，还对文物做了简单的清洁养护。

文物信息咨询中心曾划拨国家博物馆27万余件瓷器，其中包含了大量的无号文物。为完成此次文留瓷器的普查工作，藏品保管一部集中10多名骨干力量，将所有纸箱中的瓷器，逐一取出进行照相、登记，严格分类后装箱，并分批运往库房存放。在多方人员的共同努力下，此次普查工作得以顺利展开，仅用近半年的时间就顺利完成。

由于普查是在冬季进行，库房内又常年不见阳光，温度很低。工作人员克服了很多困难，采取了多重保暖措施，以使自己的手部不被冻僵而保持灵敏，保证瓷器的安全。在库房工作的同志不知疲倦地投入工作，他们冒着严寒在户外进行点交，然后在空气质量严重不达标的库房里指挥工人将木箱按类码放好，匆匆吃过午饭，

conditioners or fans, and no office area for taking a break. After finishing the morning work and having lunch, the staffs needed to immediately return to work without a break. Besides taking photos and making registries for the artifacts, the storage housekeepers also did the cleaning for the artifacts that had not been taken good care of for a long time, and further applied for conservation works. They did not only successfully complete the designated census on this part of artifacts, but also performed basic cleaning and maintenance for these artifacts.

The Artifact Information Consulting Center once allotted more than 270 thousand pieces of porcelains to the National Museum, including many artifacts without registries. In order to complete the general survey work on this group of porcelains, the 1st collection storage department grouped more than 10 senior staffs for this work. They took the porcelains out from carton boxes for photo taking and registration. After strict categorization, the artifacts were put into boxes and transported to the storage houses. By the common efforts of staffs from various departments, this general survey work was carried out smoothly and was successfully completed in around six months.

Since the census was performed in winter and there was no sunlight in the storage house, it was really cold there. The staffs overcame many difficulties

来不及休息就又投入到工作中。

与此同时进行的还有大型石刻文物的普查工作。石刻文物体型庞大，无法随意移动，加大了普查工作的难度。由于工作人员难以在狭小的库房内对文物进行拍照，库房管理人员想尽一切办法，群策群力，克服了重重困难，终于在规定时间内圆满完成了任务。

在馆领导的高度重视下，在藏品保管一部各位同志的共同努力下，在不足两年的时间内，按照计划要求，国家博物馆已基本完成了馆藏文物的普查工作，对馆藏文物的数量和现状进行了详细的调查、认定和登记，进一步审核并掌握了每件文物的基本信息，并进行了全面的梳理和统计。通过这次大规模的普查工作，不仅全面

and used multiple methods to keep warm, preventing their hands from being numb, in order to maintain the dexterity to safely handle the porcelains. The staffs working in the storage house worked tirelessly. They lit fire outdoor to fight against the coldness, and they directed workers to put the wooden boxes in designated places following the category numbers. After a short lunch time, they waded into work again without taking a rest.

The census on the large stone sculpture artifacts was implemented at the same time. The stone sculptures have large sizes and cannot be moved easily. It made the census even more difficult. It is also not easy to take photos for these large relics in a small storage room. The storage management staffs tried every possible method and overcame difficulties after difficulties with their collective wisdom and strength, and at last successfully completed the work as scheduled.

Under the rigorous supervision of museum directors and the joint efforts of staffs in the 1st Collection Storage Department, the National Museum has fundamentally completed the national census on the museum-collected artifacts in less than two years as required. Detailed survey, recognition, and registration were performed on the quantities and current conditions of the museum-collected artifacts. Through this large-scale census, as the guardians and inheritors of the

摸清了国家博物馆文物家底，同时作为历史文化遗产的守护者、传承者，也向国家和社会提供了一份详细明了的文物账册。

于璐、姜玉涛、陈畅

中国国家博物馆

historical culture heritages, we did not only comprehensively understand the detailed information of the relics, but also offered clear list of artifacts in our museum to our country and society.

Yu Lu, Jiang Yutao, Chen Chang,
National Museum of China

文物背后的故事
——中国社会科学院法学研究所可移动文物普查记

The story behind the Cultural Relics
— the National Census on Movable Relics in the Institute of Law of Chinese Academy of Social Sciences

2015 年，作为中国文物信息咨询中心的员工，我有幸参与了全国可移动文物普查。9 月初，我被安排负责中国社会科学院法学研究所（以下简称法学所）可移动文物普查的协调、监督工作。法学所的普查对象是所内图书馆收藏的 1949 年前出版的古籍图书。

图书馆的老师们告诉我们，他们早在 2014 年末就开始按照国家文物局普查办的相关要求开展了普查工作，已经拍摄和登记了一部分古籍图书的信息，但图书总量较大，单靠他们自身的人力和物力，短期内完成有困难，我们的加盟，他们是极其欢迎的，还

In 2015, as a staff in the China Cultural Heritage Information Consultation Center (CCHICC), I had the privilege to participate in the national census on movable cultural relics. In the early September, I was arranged to take charge of the coordination and supervision of this census work in the Institute of Law of Chinese Academy of Social Sciences (hereinafter referred to as the Institute of Law). We are responsible to census ancient books published before 1949 within our library collection.

Librarians told us that they had started the census work as early as at the end of 2014 in accordance with the relevant requirements posed by the State Administration of Cultural Heritage and they had already taken photos of some books and registered them. However, the collection was too large. It was hard for them to conduct the whole census all by

有近 2 万册古籍图书需要我们拍摄和登记基本信息。

法学所图书馆中 1949 年前出版的藏书包括中文、英文、法文、德文、俄文和日文图书，很大比例上是法律方面的藏书。这些书主要是 20 世纪 50 年代末期，收藏自清华大学（1958 年接收）、北京交通大学（原北京铁道学院，1959 年接收）、中央人民政府法制工作委员会、国务院法制局和法律出版社（1959 年撤销）等机构。

法学所图书馆的老师告诉我们，这些书籍，能被收藏到法学所并妥善保存到现在，极其艰难，而居功至伟的一个人，就是法学所前院长张友渔先生。在 20 世纪 50 年代的各校合并大潮中，张友渔先生积极联系各校，主动收藏当时不被重视的古今中外法学书籍。当时保存下来的藏书不但珍贵，而且数量庞大，仅 1949 年前出版的就超过 3 万册，如果包括 1949 年以后出版的，据说有 30 万册。经过张先生的努力，在短短的两三年工夫里（1958—1960），法学研究所的资料文献从一穷二白，迅速提升到国内领

themselves in a short period. So they greatly appreciated our participation. There were still nearly 20,000 volumes of ancient books waiting for us to photograph and register the basic information.

In the Institute of Law, books published before 1949 were written in various languages including Chinese, English, French, Germany, Russian and Japanese, among which law books accounted for a large portion. And these books were mainly collected at the end of 1950s from Tsinghua University (1958), Beijing Jiaotong University (the former Beijing College of Railway, 1959), the Legal Work Committee of the Central Government, Bureau of Legislative Affairs under the State Council and the Law Press (before 1959), etc.

And we were also told that it was very hard to collect and keep all these books in the institute till today. And the greatest contributor is the former President of the Institute of Law, Mr. Zhang Youyu. In the 1950s when many schools merged, Mr. Zhang Youyu actively contacted the schools and collected law books, both ancient and modern, Chinese and foreign, which were ignored at that time. It is said that during the Cultural Revolution, red guards wantonly destroyed and burned books. Mr. Zhang had to label red quotations from Chairman Mao on every bookshelf

文物背后的 **故事**
stories behind cultural relics

先的水平，而由此开展的相关法学研究和成果，奠定了法学研究所在国内法学界的重要地位。

我们的普查工作主要分两部分，一是对古籍图书的封面、版权页、财产登记号等进行拍摄；二是把书籍的主要信息，包括财产登记号、索书号、书名、作者、出版年月、收藏单位、重量等，录入指定的 EXCEL 表格。

出于职业性的严谨、敏感，也是为了保障文物本体和文物数据的安全，法学所采取了一些严格的措施，包括自己配置电脑，在采集现场安装监控设施，采集数据期间断网，仔细修改和补充由我们提供的信息采集合同条款，索要数据采集保密协议复印件等。对于普查工作的开展，我们怀着激动的心情，迫切地等待，再等待。

终于，9 月 25 日，一个秋日暖阳的星期五，我们 5 个人——负责安装拍摄硬件、软件并传授用法的袁老师，运载拍摄设备的小孔，拍摄员小臧、小袁，还有我，兵分五路赶到了法学研究所。图书馆专门腾出一间约 20 平方米的办公室作为工作室。头一天，

to protect these books and succeeded. Those books are not only precious, but also preserved in a large number. More than 30,000 copies were published before 1949. If you include those published after 1949, it is said that there are 30,0000 copies in total. Thanks to Mr. Zhang's efforts, in as short as one or two years (1958-1960), the literature collection in the Institute of Law of information rapidly jumped out and ranked among the top in our country. And the relevant research and results consolidated the important academic position of the Institute of Law in the law academia in China.

Our census work was mainly divided into two parts. On one hand, we needed to photograph the cover, copyright page and property registration number of the ancient books; On the other hand, we needed to put all main information of books into EXCEL, including property registration number, call number, title, author, publishing time, collection place, weight, etc.

Out of professional rigorousness, sensitiveness, and past experience, in order to protect the cultural relics and archaeological data, some strict measures were taken, including the configuration of our own computers, the installation of monitoring facilities at the scene of the acquisition, collecting data with blocked network, carefully

在袁老师的指导下，我们七手八脚，安装拍摄软件，搭建拍摄平台，试拍了20多册图书。

此后的工作日，我们小组成员不断增加，除了之前的小袁、小臧，还有小张、小吴、小郝、小俞、小阳等陆续加入。图书馆的4位老师轮流给我们找书、运书、补码。图书馆的藏书，并没有按出版时间在1949年之前和之后进行区分保存，老师们要一本一本地过目、挑选，工作量很大。这样辛苦了一段时间后，老师们个个腰酸背痛，有的甚至感冒生病了。后来，所里调派了大李和小李两位年轻力壮的保安来帮忙，情形才有所改善。而我们在拍摄或登录的同时，也不断寻找最佳协作方式，很快，我们形成了3对比较稳定和理想的"拍摄"和"录入"搭配小组，进入稳定、顺畅的工作阶段。在每天工作结束以前，3对拍、录小组各自查漏补缺，核实数量，然后进行汇总，之后再统一核实，拷贝并存储数据。

普查工作繁琐、忙碌然而充实。当然，拍摄和录入工作并非一帆风顺，

revising and supplementing the information in the terms of the Contract on Information Acquisition provided by us, and asking for the copy of confidentiality agreement, etc. We waited for the day with a great deal of apprehension.

Finally, the day came. Our 5-member team went to Institute of Law on a warm Friday of the Sept. 25th. Our team included Mr. Yuan, who was in charge of the installation of photographing facilities and software, and he taught us how to use these facilities, Kong, who was in charge of transporting these facilities, as well as Zang, Yuan and me, who were responsible for taking photos. The library set aside a 20-square-meter office as our studio. At the first day, with the guidance of Mr. Yuan, we successfully installed the photographing facilities and established the photo table, and then we experimented to photograph some 20 books.

Later on, the members in our team increased. Zhang, Wu, Hao, Yu, Yang, etc. also joined us. Mr./Ms. Jiang, Jin, Zhang and Fan, four librarians took turns to help us find books, transport books and complete the information of these books. The collection in the library was not arranged according to the chronological order with 1949 as a distinguishing year. Therefore, librarians had to pick up books one by one. The working burden was large. After some time, librarians

文物背后的故事
stories behind cultural relics

中间也出现过不少问题。比如，有些电脑因不明原因无法安装拍摄软件，拍摄和录入模式前后不一样（开始只拍不录，后来拍录同步但速度不一致，直接影响工作效率），图书馆要求录入的信息项比普查工作要求录入的多，数据采集出错或者核对不上，老师们加班时间无法统一等。初时，大家欠缺经验，手忙脚乱，出现了一些乌龙事件，比如拍摄和录入的册数不一致，导致重复拍摄和录入等。随着时间的流逝，大家献计献策，各展所长，分工明确，问题一一解决，乌龙事件不再发生。拍、录工作紧张、忙碌的同时，大家相谈甚欢，工作中不乏幽默

部分普查队员照片

picture of some team members

were weary and got sick. Therefore, Li Senior and Li Junior, two strong security men, were dispatched to help us. And things became better. And we were also constantly looking for the best cooperation method when photographing. Soon, we formed the three groups of relatively stable and ideal matches of "photographing" and "inputting" group, entering into a smooth working stage. Before the end of the work every day, three groups would check each other's work carefully and then integrate, verify, copy and finally store the information and data.

The census work was trivial, busy but substantial. Of course, there had been some problems during the process. For example, software could not be installed in some computers for unknown reasons, photographing and inputting mode didn't match (at first we only photographed but not input; then we started to do both but the tempos were different, directly affecting the work efficiency), the library requires more inputting information items than the census, data acquisition error or incompatibility and the schedules of librarians could not be unified, etc. At the beginning, we lacked experience, and made some mistakes in a hurry-scurry, for example, there had been some mismatches between photographs and the information input, as well as some repeated photos and input. Generally, we came up with new ideas, tapped into everyone's advantages, and clearly

诙谐、欢声笑语。

有一天早晨，大约开始工作一个多小时之后，大家正在忙碌时，突然一声巨响，把大家吓了一跳。照明灯和摄影灯都灭了，电脑也停工了，经过问询和打探之后才知道，法学所门口的变压器爆炸了。也许，我们火力太猛了吧，大家开玩笑地说。维修人员很快到达，但什么时候能修好却是未知数。大家没有放弃，一边休息，一边等待。下午1点多，故障排除，来电了，大家马上开始投入工作，紧赶慢赶，把耽误的时间都补了回来。

作为中国文物信息咨询中心的"特派"协调、监督员，我的日常工作是这样的：图书馆老师们把古籍图书从书架或仓库里运过来后，我拍照书籍的书架号或者包装箱号，核实数量，分给各组进行拍摄和录入并一一登记在册，实时核实各组拍录的数量，最后进行汇总；在书籍缺失相关信息的情况下，找老师们查找和补充；负责普查涉及的三方单位的信息来往、通报、沟通；帮助安装拍摄和录入硬件、软件；拷贝和报送数据；做些后勤保

divided our responsibilities to avoid the above mistakes. Though we were busy, we would talk to each other happily and laughed during working.

One morning, everyone was busy working. After about an hour, a sudden thud frightened all of us. Then all the lights shut down and so did the computer. It turned out that the transformer at the gate of the institute blew up. We joked that maybe it was because we had been working too hard. Maintenance personnel arrived quickly, but we did not know when the maintenance would be done. We did not give up. Instead, we took a rest and waited. After 1:00 pm, electricity supply was restored. Then we went back working immediately and got the due work done by the day.

As the "Special" coordinator and dispatcher of the China Cultural Heritage Information Consultation Center, my daily work is as follows: Librarians transported the ancient books from the library bookshelves or warehouse and I would take the photo of bookshelf number or packing case number, check the volume, and dispatch these books to different groups for them to photograph and input the information of these books. I would also in real time verify the work done by each groups and finally integrate all the data. When we found some books lacking information, I would ask librarians to help check that out and

障工作，例如打开水、扫地、浇花等。

在这次古籍普查中，法学所的所长、图书馆的正、副馆长以及4位老师，全力支持我们的工作。尤其是图书馆的4位老师，除了图书馆日常的管理和运行工作外，还要付出额外的辛苦，陪着我们日复一日地进行普查，加班加点，不厌其烦地给我们解决各种各样工作的难题，关心我们的头疼脑热，让我们很感动。7个年轻的普查队员，个个朝气蓬勃，勤奋睿智，和他们在一起，让老师们和我都感觉自己也变年轻了。可以说，我们一起度过了有意义、有作为的3个月。12月底，在结束了全部工作之后，闲暇时，我诌了一首诗：

法学所文物普查总结

秋雨伴驻法学所，数十日月忙穿梭。

中外古籍两万册，出入拍录均安妥。

文物普查为谁做？利国利民好处多。

深情厚谊聚又散，心有戚戚不忍说。

书籍是人类进步的阶梯，这次对古籍图书的普查，虽然还未能将书籍

complete the information. I was responsible for reviewing the information exchange, reporting and communication among the three parties involved in the census. I helped to install the photographing facilities and the inputting hardware and software; I helped copy and transmit the information and data. I would also do some logistics work including boiling water, sweeping floor and watering flowers, etc.

During the census work, the President of the Institute, Curator and Vice Curator of the library, as well as four librarians fully supported our work. I would express my sincere appreciation and gratitude especially to the four librarians for their great endeavor to help us do the census work after finishing their own daily job of operating and managing the library. Besides, they also helped us solve lots of problems and cared about out health condition which touched us a lot. And the seven members in my team are also energetic, vital, clever and diligent. Working with them made us feel much younger. We've been through three months of great significance. At the end of December when we had done all of our work, I wrote a poem to summarize our work.

We went to the Institute of Law and worked there for a long time.

We successfully photographed and input the

本身的内容进行数字化和共享，但我们已经迈出了第一步，展望未来，让人向往。我们这次普查工作，是一项"功在当代，利在千秋"的工作，我坚信，我自豪！

刘　红

中国文物信息咨询中心

information of 20,000 volumes of ancient Chinese and foreign books.

Why did we do all this? For people's sake, for our country's sake.

During working, we have forged great friendship and when it was about the time to say goodbye, we felt sad.

Books are the stepping stones to human progress. Although the census has yet to enable the online accessibility of all the book, we have made our first step toward the digitalization of books. We are looking for the future. I believe that our work will have far-reaching impact on the society and benefit a lot of people.

Liu Hong, China Cultural Heritage
Information Consultation Center